Kaisha, The Japanese Corporation

KAISHA, THE JAPANESE CORPORATION

JAMES C. ABEGGLEN

GEORGE STALK, Jr.

Basic Books, Inc., Publishers / New York

To Hiroko and to Henri

Our Partners in the Venture

CONTENTS

PREFACE

THIS BOOK is about the business corporations of Japan—the *kaisha*—which now play key roles in the world business arena. We have sought to describe and explain the competitive behavior of Japan's companies to those Western businessmen whose own competitive decisions and actions require a more complete understanding of the kaisha.

This book is not another explanation of Japan's economic success. It does not deal with miracles, nor with conspiracies. It is the authors' hope that a more analytic and less emotional discussion of competing with Japan's companies will be of interest and value to the Western business community.

The analyses and conclusions are the results of our combined management consulting experience of nearly forty years. About half of that consulting experience has been as residents of Japan. We have worked on client assignments not only in Japan but also throughout the countries of Western Europe, in East, Southeast, and South Asia, in Australia and Africa, as well as in North America. Our clients have included American, Japanese, British, French, German, Dutch, Spanish, Swiss, and Swedish companies.

Our client work has involved us deeply in a number of industries, including food, personal products, pharmaceuticals, chemicals, autos and trucks, electrical and electronics equipment, general machinery, as well as banking, distribution, and services. Most of our consulting work has been with manufacturing companies, those companies most directly involved in international trade competition.

We are deeply indebted to the executives and staff of our client organizations. It is their willingness to entrust us with difficult and complex management problems, to share views and data, and to support our research and analysis that has made possible the preparation of this book. We thank them, and regret that the need to respect client confidentiality prevents more specific acknowledgement of our obligations.

We would like also to thank the past and present staff of The Boston Consulting Group for their support in much of our consulting work. We are especially obliged to Bruce D. Henderson, founder of BCG, as leader and teacher.

—JAMES C. ABEGGLEN
—GEORGE STALK, JR.
Tokyo

Kaisha, The Japanese Corporation

1

THE PACE SETTERS:

JAPAN'S COMPANIES

AS COMPETITORS

THE dominant competition for a great many of the companies of the world today is from the Japanese, who are increasingly setting the pace of competition throughout the markets of the free world. The rapid development of Japan's companies, or *kaisha*,[1] is startling. They have grown from the debris of a lost war to take world leadership positions in a surprising number of industries. Their size is formidable: in a *Forbes* listing of the largest 200 non-U.S. companies, 61 were Japanese; in a *Fortune* listing of the largest 500 non-U.S. industrial corporations, 146 were Japanese, while 28 of the 100 largest commercial banking companies outside the United States were Japanese, including the top four.[2]

The kaisha now hold important positions in most of the world's major business sectors. Their positions are strengthening as the kaisha are growing at rates substantially higher than those of their Western competitors. Toyota Motor Company

---

1. Elsewhere in this book, Japanese words and names have been set in roman type, omitting macrons to connote long vowels. Japanese names are presented in the Western manner, with surname following given name or initial.

2. *Forbes*, 2 July, 1984, pp. 134–40; *Fortune*, 20 August, 1984, pp. 176–95.

and Nissan Limited are the world's third and fourth largest automobile companies after General Motors and Ford. In the steel industry, Nippon Steel is larger than U.S. Steel. Hitachi and Matsushita Electric are second and third in size to General Electric and are larger than Philips and Siemens. Caterpillar's principal competitor is now Komatsu. Eastman Kodak's main competitive threat is Fuji Film; NEC is now second to Texas Instruments in world semiconductor production and is moving to the leading position. IBM's only serious rivals in the mainframe computer industry are Fujitsu and Hitachi.

Japanese companies are also taking leadership positions in businesses other than manufacturing. Depending on the measure chosen, Dai-Ichi Kangyo Bank is first or second in size in banking with Citicorp and BankAmerica. Japan Airlines is first or second with United Airlines in commercial aviation. Some of the world's largest insurance companies are Japanese.

Much has been written about the success of Japan's kaisha by both Westerners and Japanese. Most of the explanations come from one of two basic theories. One that became popular in the late 1970s and early 1980s is that the success of the Japanese is the result of a benign conspiracy. Japanese society is believed to have traits that give its members inherent advantages when competing with Westerners. Key traits include the homogeneity of the society, a nonconfrontational mode of discussion and decision making, and a national sense of purpose. These traits are believed to generate helpful government bureaucracies and paternalistic corporate cultures. Compared to their Western counterparts, the Japanese employees of these organizations have a greater commitment to their jobs and, therefore, a dramatically higher productivity. Supporters of the benign conspiracy perspective maintain that until labor, management, and government in the West can learn similar techniques, they can expect the continued loss of markets to Japanese corporations.[3]

At the opposite pole, a view that is currently increasing in popularity, is the theory that the success of Japanese corporations is the result of a sinister conspiracy. Advocates of this

---

3. Books representative of this position are: William Ouchi, *Theory Z* (Reading, Mass.: Addison-Wesley, 1982); Ezra F. Vogel, *Japan as Number One* (Cambridge: Harvard University Press, 1979); Richard Pascale and Anthony Athos, *The Art of Japanese Management* (New York: Warner Books, 1981); Frank Gibney, *Miracle by Design* (New York: Times Books, 1982).

4

attitude argue that the Japanese government, corporations, and groups cooperate closely to further their shared interests. In this view, these shared interests are conspiring to achieve worldwide dominance of industry. The participants, managed by the Ministry of International Trade and Industry (MITI), target segments of industry and subsidize the efforts of companies with grants, tax relief, tariff protection, and market sharing agreements, then press forward into Western markets until all effective opposition has been destroyed. Today, according to this theory, the Japanese are believed to be targeting fifth-generation computers, aerospace, and pharmaceuticals as among the next sectors to receive their attentions. Supporters of the sinister conspiracy view are calling for increased and visible government participation in managing the evolution of U.S. and European industry as the only way to check the advances of the Japanese. So strongly has the sinister conspiracy theory been argued that first time visitors to Japan will often ask some long time resident where his product (ranging from plastic pipes, to valves, to jet engines) fits into MITI's plans.[4]

The need for an explanation of the success of the Japanese is not satisfied by either the benign or the conspiracy theory. These simply do not address the realities of international business: companies, not societies, compete for markets; companies, not governments, trade; and in the end it is companies that prosper or stagnate—in Japan, as well as in the United States and in Europe.

The Japanese companies that succeed do so principally because of their choice of competitive fundamentals, of which many can be readily adopted by determined Western competitors. The competitive fundamentals chosen by the successful kaisha include:

- A growth bias
- A preoccupation with actions of competitors
- The creation and ruthless exploitation of competitive advantage
- The choice of corporate financial and personnel policies that are economically consistent with all of the preceding.

4. Books representative of this position are: Marvin Wolf, *The Japanese Conspiracy* (New York: Empire Books, 1983); Jared Taylor, *Shadows of the Rising Sun* (New York: William Morrow and Co., 1983); Russell Branddon, *The Other Hundred Years War* (London: Collins, 1983).

The strong bias toward growth of successful kaisha is closely linked to their desire to survive. These kaisha have been built in a very rapid growth economy. They have been witnesses to the fate of companies that failed to grow faster than their competitors. For example, in the late 1950s Honda increased its production 50 percent faster than demand called for to displace Tohatsu in less than five years as Japan's leading motorcycle manufacturer. Tohatsu went bankrupt and forty-five other Japanese producers eventually withdrew from the manufacture of motorcycles.

The desire to survive by growing is heightened by the standards of the Japanese society. Wholesale layoffs by a company in response to a weakening demand for a product are unheard of in postwar Japan. It is considered to be the task of management to increase demand or to find another product in which the capacity of the industrial organization can be utilized. Canon, originally a camera company, has responded to the pressures placed on its organization by the falling demand for cameras by diversifying into printers, computers, word processors, facsimile machines, copiers, and semiconductor manufacturing equipment. Today cameras represent less than a third of Canon's sales. In contrast, Western companies often delay making fundamental changes in their strategies when their market or competitive environments change and instead lay off employees and cut back their operations. Often, when the changes are finally evaluated, there are no viable options left for the company. It is, for instance, difficult to name a healthy Western camera company. Almost all of the great German and American camera manufacturers have sharply scaled back or closed their operations.

Managements with a bias toward growth have distinct mindsets which include the expectation of continued growth, decisions and plans formulated to produce growth, and the unfaltering pursuit of growth unless the very life of the organization is threatened. Companies with a bias toward growth add physical and human capacity ahead of demand. Prices are set not at the level that the market will bear, but as low as necessary to expand the market to fit the available capacity. Costs are programmed to come down to support the pricing policies and investments are made in anticipation of increased demand.

The Japanese manufacturing plunge into the field of video cassette recorders (VCR) and compact audio discs (CD) exemplifies the extent of their bias toward growth. The first production models of these devices in the West were priced well over a thousand dollars. These prices placed the devices out of the reach for most consumers except the wealthy high-tech afficionados. In the United States RCA and in Europe Philips chose to wait and see how demand would develop, while in Japan Sony and Matsushita, along with other kaisha created demand by continuously slashing prices as the volume of production increased and costs declined. The Japanese found themselves in a business that doubled in volume every year. The kaisha now totally dominate the production of VCRs and CDs and the Western companies have been forced to buy from the source or obtain a license for domestic manufacture from the Japanese.

When demand is strong, the kaisha tend toward "doubling strategies," by which within a short planning period of two to four years capacity and output are doubled. These strategies can result in growth rates of 50 percent per year and sometimes 100 percent and more per year. Today these "growth biases" can be observed in the Japanese producers of video cassette recorders, compact discs, personal computers, magnetic tape and discs, personal radios, robots, facsimiles, and word processors. Japanese companies in other businesses also pursue doubling strategies when the opportunity exists. This has happened with convenience stores and, more recently, fast-food restaurants.

The growth bias is not limited to companies in fast-growing industries like electronics. In recent years, when the Japanese domestic automobile market stagnated (domestic demand reached a saturation point in 1979), the response of Toyota and Nissan was to more than double their rate of new product introductions and full model changes, and to increase advertising and expand their number of distribution outlets by 15 percent. Each company is struggling to take whatever growth there is in the market.

Rather than cutting back when demand is weak, kaisha with a growth bias typically step up their levels of investment. Product variety is increased, prices are cut, and distribution is expanded. In the face of stagnant or falling demand the Japanese

7

manufacturers of trucks, refrigerators, audio equipment, and airconditioning equipment have all dramatically increased their product variety and expanded distribution.

Some Western companies also have a growth bias similar to the successful kaisha. Apple Computer and IBM are among the best known examples in the United States. American semiconductor companies have also demonstrated a bias for growth. In 1976, however, this industry cut back its investment when semiconductor demand weakened while the Japanese pressed on, taking the lead in production of 16 K RAMs (Random Access Memories) and then 64 K RAMs. Cutting back was a mistake that American producers are still working to overcome.

In the West, it is generally small companies that have growth biases as strong as those of the leading kaisha. There are very few large companies in the United States or Europe whose managers are trying to expand sales at the rate of 50 to 100 percent per year or that receive continued high investment in the face of weak demand. The reasons are understandable—a strong growth bias can be risky. Markets may not expand enough to absorb the added capacity, and falling demand can mean continued investment will not be recoverable; profits would suffer.

The Japanese face the same risks. Yet the risk of falling behind a competitor is regarded by most kaisha as a far greater risk than the risk that profits will be depressed. To fall behind one's competitor can mean that profits will never materialize. To minimize the risk of falling behind, the kaisha are preoccupied with the activities of their competitors to a degree that is unusual by Western standards. This preoccupation is the second competitive fundamental of the kaisha. It has two objectives:

· Be better, not behind.
· If not better, be different.

Being better means having better—or at least equivalent—products. Being different means finding a niche that is out of the main stream of competition.

Matsushita and Sony, two of Japan's largest producers of

consumer appliances and electronics are good examples of kaisha that seek to be better or different. Matsushita generally allows its competitors to experiment with new product concepts. When potential is demonstrated, Matsushita enters the market with a state-of-the-art product backed by large investments and sales targets geared to make the company the volume leader in two to three years. Sony, which seldom seems willing to play for stakes as large as Matsushita does, tries to find a new product concept or a special variation of the old concept. So as Matsushita was establishing itself as the dominant producer of video cassette recorders, with brand names such as National, Panasonic, and JVC, Sony, which had initially commercialized the VCR, had moved on to other products, such as high quality component television and the Watchman.

The typical response of the *kaisha* to a competitor's initiative fall between the characteristic responses of Matsushita and Sony. Some kaisha drive for volume but do not always achieve total market dominance as does Matsushita, others attempt to differentiate themselves but still are sure that each competitor's product offering is matched, and, occasionally, a kaisha withdraws. The point is that kaisha *respond* and rarely leave an initiative by a competitor unmet. The response is often very fast and, in the case of manufactured products, is offered with a flurry of new product introductions.

Although there are exceptions, Western management generally prefers a more carefully considered process of responding to competitors' initiatives. Some initiatives are met and others are rationalized away. Typical rationalizations include the arguments that the new products are not significant improvements, or that the market does not really want the product, or that the innovation is not economically justified. This process is naturally a drag on the pace of technology and product evolution, but it is done to minimize the financial consequences of a mistake. The kaisha have a greater fear of the loss of competitive position.

The effects of these very different responses to competitive initiatives are beginning to show. For example, Japanese automobile manufacturers are selling cars with four-valve engines, electronically controlled suspensions, ceramic engine components, turbochargers with intercoolers, lightweight nonmetallic body panels, synthesized-voice hazard and diagnostic warnings and more. Most of these innovations are unavailable in Western automobiles except, occasionally, in the highest premium optional offerings. Similar product innovation gaps are observable in Japanese airconditioning equipment, machine tools, robotics, vending machines, and parking meters, to name just a few.

The common Western response to emerging innovation gaps appears dangerously naive. The line of reasoning goes something like this: "The Japanese competitors are not using any technology or innovation we are not already aware of. We could do the same if we wanted to. Anyway, it does not do us much good to copy them—our challenge is to 'leap frog' them." While the Western competitors consider the virtues of an appropriate response to Japanese innovation, the gap that has to be leaped continues to widen, and the probability of a successful leap continues to fall.

The third fundamental of competition chosen by the successful kaisha is the creation and ruthless exploitation of competitive advantage. The leading exporters of Japan, of course, have been and are the manufacturing kaisha. These companies typically utilize some advantage inherent in their manufacturing process as the underpinnings of their export strategy. Historically this was most apparent in the use of a low-cost manufacturing advantage as a competitive weapon. Based on low wages, the Japanese built major export businesses in textiles and shipbuilding. Today wage rates are, on average, comparable to those in other developed countries, and the Japanese companies whose competitive advantages were based on low-wage rates have faded in importance. More recently, the Japanese have been focusing their attentions on their ability to create competitive advantage through product line variety, high quality, and technological innovation. These advantages are used in combination with market selection and product choice to carve out a position in foreign markets.

The industries that are today's leading exporters in Japan have created manufacturing processes and products that make maximum use of the Japanese worker. This was first accomplished through heavy investments in facilities whose scale was the largest in the world. Such investments carried the kaisha of the Japanese steel and shipbuilding industries beyond the point where increasing wage levels would have diminished their competitiveness, and companies in these industries have been able to maintain their international leadership positions. They are just beginning to be pressured by the Taiwanese and South Koreans who have made similar investments and have much lower wage rates.

Japanese companies began to develop major positions in the world market in the 1960s and 1970s with engineered products like ball bearings, forklifts, and machine tools that were long regarded as the province of the Americans and Europeans. The Japanese offered low-cost but high-quality products. The low cost of these products was not achieved with cheap labor. Instead, the Japanese produced a narrow line of product in very focused factories. Properly focused, a smaller factory producing a narrow line of product can have much lower costs than a larger factory producing a wide line of product. The Japanese utilized their low costs to make deep penetrations into the hearts of many Western markets. Many Western companies failed to respond to the Japanese. Those that did chose either to escape the Japanese price competition by adding specialty products or by reducing their product offerings so that they could lower costs by focusing their factories on a narrower line of product.

But recently, many Western competitors have been surprised to learn that their Japanese competitors are producing a wider line of product more efficiently and at lower costs than they ever had. Further, instead of paring their product lines and focusing their factories like many of their Western counterparts had been doing, the kaisha are now increasing the variety of their product offerings and fragmenting their production volumes. So that they can continue to grow, the Japanese are increasing variety to meet the specific needs of their customers.

The kaisha can increase variety without being crippled by increased costs because over the last decade they have increased the flexibility of their factories. The time required to change from the manufacture of one product to another has been dramatically reduced. Production batch sizes, or run lengths, have been decreased and inventories have been reduced. Production lead times (or time required to manufacture a product) have fallen significantly and quality has improved. The investments required to do this are simple in concept and are not capital intensive. However, the reasons for making these investments are not intuitive, but are well worth understanding. An attempt by a Western company to match a kaisha's expansion of variety will be disastrous unless the Western company has also modified its factories as the Japanese have.

The attentions of the kaisha are broadening from creating and exploiting competitive manufacturing advantages to creating technology-based advantages. An oft-cited weakness of the Japanese is that they are not creators of innovations but skilled adapters of the inventions of others. Certainly, the history of the development of the Japanese economy supports this point of view. In today's world, however, the kaisha are increasingly tipping the balance from being copiers to becoming adaptive creators.

The Japanese have embraced research. The kaisha's investment in the research and development (R&D) of key technologies has heavily increased in the last five years. As a percent of sales, the largest kaisha in Japan are spending about 40 percent more of their revenues on R&D than the largest U.S. companies are. Although the average R&D budgets of the largest kaisha are only about half those of the largest U.S. companies, the kaisha's expenditures are growing in real terms while the R&D budgets of the average large U.S. companies are declining. Reasonable projections are that the R&D expenditures of the twenty largest kaisha could very well exceed those of the twenty largest U.S. companies in the next decade.

Of course the linkages between expenditures on R&D and creative output are difficult to establish. But the Japanese attempt to assess their relative global position in key advanced technologies. This is the kind of assessment that generates intense interest in Japan because, whatever the answer, it will strike a resonant chord in the minds of the Japanese. If the assessment is negative then it will serve as a rallying cry for increased devotion to the task of improving the technological base. If the answer is positive it serves as a source of pride and of continued effort to maintain position.

One assessment of Japan's research status by a respected Japanese study group concluded that for semiconductors, office automation, computer hardware, robots and unmanned production systems, optics, and new materials, such as ceramics and composites, the level of technological development of the kaisha was equal to or greater than the level in the United States. In aerospace, computer software, data communications, and space hardware the kaisha definitely lag behind the United States. In biotechnology, the kaisha are quickly catching up to it.

If one accepts the accuracy of the Japanese self-assessment, it is surprising how broad based the Japanese technological capability is. Given that the U.S. lead in aerospace, data communications, and space hardware is probably due to the needs of U.S. defense policy, the Japanese have done quite well for themselves in closing the supposed "creativity gap."

The combination of the kaisha's improvements in the competitiveness of their manufacturing processes and their continuing investments in technology are beginning to yield entire product and industrial sectors for the Japanese in which there is little competition from Western companies. In late 1984, for example, Sony and Hitachi independently developed and simultaneously announced production prototypes of erasable, optical disc mass data storage systems. These systems are expected to replace tape drives, many disc drives, most high volume videotape systems, and possibly microfilm systems. Toshiba, Sharp, and Matsushita quickly announced that their versions of the same system would be ready in a year or two. Fuji and TDK, companies with heavy investments in magnetic tape manufacturing facilities, instead of rationalizing away the threat these discs posed to their businesses, announced they intended to be among the front runners as suppliers of the discs when demand takes off. This is for a market that is conservatively estimated to become as large as $10 billion per year. Because Japanese companies are the highest-volume producers of virtually all the non-erasable optical disc machines in use today, industry specialists and company analysts were not expecting much of a fight from U.S. and European manufacturers. This could very well become a replay of the development of the international competitive structures of the small copier, facsimile, and VCR industries where there are no serious competitors who are not Japanese.

The fourth competitive fundamental of the leading kaisha is the use of corporate financial and personnel policies that are economically consistent with a bias toward growth, a preoccupation with competitors, and the creation and exploitation of competitive advantage. Growth orientations and investments, made not only to remain competitive but to engineer competitive advantage, require money. Like most companies, the kaisha generate cash for some of their needs and borrow the rest. Where the growing kaisha tend to differ from their Western counterparts is in the amount of money they borrow and in their attitudes toward dividends and profits.

The kaisha rely much more on debt financing than do their Western counterparts. Although this exposes them to greater financial risks, their all important competitive risks are reduced. If the competitive fundamentals are correctly chosen, a highly leveraged company can aggressively use debt to fund growth at significantly higher rates, even with lower profitability, than can a more conservatively financed company with higher profits. This means that the more aggressive company can "spend" profits by shaving prices, accepting higher manufacturing costs, or investing more heavily in expense items such as R&D and market development and still grow faster than a conservatively financed counterpart. Of course, a company with large debts assumes higher financial risks and cannot waste cash on dividends. Further, the company must expect that its financial institutions are going to want to be very well informed about the plans of and progress of the company.

The participants of the U.S. semiconductor industry are very aware of the effect of the kaisha's different financial policies on their ability to compete. The kaisha typically earn less as a percent of revenues, pay less in dividends, borrow more, spend more, and grow faster than their U.S. competitors. And yet, while U.S. industry is deeply concerned, few if any companies have taken steps to match the financial policies of the Japanese. Traditional financial institutions in the United States are uncomfortable with the aggressive financial policies of the Japanese; U.S. shareholders are assumed to want high profits and dividends.

14

The evidence in Japan shows that financial institutions are taking few risks. Until very recently, Japanese financial institutions only lent money against collateral. Many of the kaisha have assets serving as collateral whose values are very much understated on their balance sheets. These assets include land, marketable securities, and long-term receivables. The existence of these assets reduces the financial risks of many kaisha which aggressively use debt to fund their growth.

Japanese stockholders benefit more if their company grows than if it pays dividends. In Japan dividends are taxed as ordinary income, but no taxes are paid on capital gains. The Japanese shareholder is less interested in the profits of a company than its growth prospects. Indeed, when the returns to a typical stockholder in a leading Japanese company are compared to those of a typical stockholder in a leading U.S. company, the shareholder in the Japanese company almost always does better and does so because of greater capital gains.

The financial policies of the Japanese semiconductor industry are consistent with their orientation toward growth and increased competitiveness while the policies of the participants in the U.S. industry with orientations similar to the Japanese are not. The high profit, low debt, and continued dividend payment policies by U.S. companies increase their difficulties in financing growth that will rival the speed of Japanese growth. American semiconductor companies are risking their future while pursuing "safe" (conservative) financial policies.

The leading kaisha also have personnel policies consistent with their orientation toward growth and enhanced competitiveness. These policies include a real effort to avoid surges in hirings and firings, to build strong and cooperative enterprise unions, cross-functional training, compensations with large variable components, proportional bonus plans, and recognition that senior management will pay as great a penalty for the failing fortunes of the kaisha as the worker. Employees who improve productivity and reduce costs need not fear the loss of their jobs if they have been cross-trained in other activities. The large variable component in the compensations of Japanese workers enables the reduction of labor costs in a recession by 20 to 30 percent without layoffs. Management must find markets where the energies of their organizations can be focused or face the same pay cuts or layoffs that threaten the workers. These policies combine in interesting ways to support the growth bias and the creation of competitive advantage.

The competitive fundamentals chosen by Japan's leading kaisha are not uniquely Japanese. When each competitive attitude and policy is examined—in isolation and in combination—one is left with the impression that much of what has made many kaisha successful is transferable to Western companies. The more Western executives are able to understand their Japanese competitors, the greater their opportunity to select and adopt the most attractive characteristics of the Japanese approaches to competition and build upon them.

2

THE DYNAMIC

ECONOMY

ALTHOUGH Japan's kaisha have become the main competitors of a great many Western companies they are not well understood. Relatively new to the world market, the kaisha were for a long time underestimated, their successes explained away in terms of the stereotypes of cheap labor, copying, reckless price cutting (dumping), or government subsidy. More recently, with continued and increased competitive success, the balance of opinion regarding the kaisha has tended to the opposite extreme. Japanese business methods are held out as models for Western competitors, and their personnel, manufacturing, and financial practices are the subjects of admiring study.

But now there is danger of the strengths of the kaisha being overestimated just as these companies were for so long underestimated. Some Japanese firms do well; others do badly. The strengths and tactics of the kaisha need not be surprising to those who analyze their behavior and who develop plans for effective competitive response.

KAISHA, THE JAPANESE CORPORATION

Economic Growth, Industry Restructuring,
and Corporate Response

The competitive behavior of the kaisha has been shaped by a key factor in the Japanese environment: the historically unprecedented rate of growth and change in the Japanese economy. The requirement to keep pace with change—in a context of intense domestic competition—has been the principal driving force behind corporate strategies. More than any other factor, this dynamism in the economy has shaped the policies and practices of Japan's companies.

Only a generation ago, in the mid-1950s, the Japanese economy comprised only 2 percent of the world economy. At the time, its output was a little less than that of Italy, while the U.S. economy alone made up more than 35 percent of the world's total. Japan's companies were hardly visible in international competition, except for the increasing nuisance they posed in the textile sector. That the trade and investment policies of Japan were totally protectionist simply did not matter, given the small size and remoteness of the economy. But in only thirty-five years, by 1980, the Japanese economy grew to make up 10 percent of world gross product, an economy as large as that of West Germany and Great Britain combined. As the Japanese economy became a tenth of the world economy, the position of the United States diminished from its earlier 35 to 40 percent to its current level of a little over 20 percent of the world economy. With three-tenths of a percent of world land area and approximately 3 percent of world population, the Japanese created the second largest market economy in the world.

The consequences of this enormous change are only beginning to be understood. With the success of the Japanese—and in good measure because of it—East and Southeast Asia have been the fastest growing region of the world economically for two decades. The center of world economic activity is moving from the North Atlantic to the Pacific, signaled perhaps by the fact that in the 1980s, for the first time in history, U.S. trade across the Pacific is greater than U.S. trade across the Atlantic.

Japan's companies are major factors in world competition in a whole range of industries. In high-technology trade, the

German government reports that Japan has overtaken West Germany as second in trading volume to the United States. Japanese trade and investment policies now matter very much indeed and are the source of continuing trade and political tensions as companies and governments of other nations struggle to adjust to the great changes in the world's trade and economic systems brought about by Japan's achievements.

A minor industry has grown up around the search for and weighing of the many sources and causes of Japan's economic success. The Japanese company represents that success, but more important, it has been basically shaped by the experience of very rapid economic change. For the kaisha, change has several components. The first is the swift and continuing shift in the composition of the Japanese economy, as rapid growth causes, and in fact requires, rapid restructuring of the economy. Management must either perceive and change with this restructuring or decline and slowly disappear.

The second component of rapid economic change for the company is the impact of fast growth on the company's competitive position within its industry. Like heat in a chemical reaction, fast growth accelerates competitive interaction: relative cost position can change quickly, market share is liable to sudden change, investment requirements become massive, and immediate organizational adaptation is essential. The kaisha are the product not only of change in industrial structure, but of the consequences of the rate of change itself.

Third, and lastly, the combination of rapid change in the industrial structure within which the company operates and rapid growth in the specific sector in which it competes impacts on the nature of the company itself in terms of corporate objectives and approach to competition. The kaisha that survive and prosper under these conditions of rapid change and fast growth acquire a different view of the world, and very different ways of creating and reacting to competitive pressure, than do companies that operate in more stable and predictable environments. Thus, the kaisha differ a good deal as a group from companies in most other economies, but have a considerable resemblance to U.S. and European companies who have had similar corporate experiences.

A sense of the speed of change in the structure of the

Japanese economy can be gained from again noting change over a generation. In 1955, 25 percent of Japan's economy was in the primary sector—that is, agriculture, forestry, and fisheries. It was essentially a rural economy compared with the United States and West Germany, where the primary sector made up only 5 to 8 percent of the economy. Yet by 1980, Japan's economy had become basically industrial, with the primary sector accounting for less than 10 percent of the total. This very rapid change in economic structure carried with it a host of basic social changes —migration to the cities, a shift from the extended to the nuclear family, an extraordinary increase in levels of formal education, large-scale retraining of the rural work force, and a shift to Western urban life-styles. It is a profound tribute to the strength and integrity of Japanese society that these sweeping social changes were accomplished while remaining notably free of the symptoms of social disease—crime, political instability, disaffection, discontent, or alienation.

The shift out of the primary sector is only one of the many changes that continue to take place in the economy of Japan. In terms of the Japanese company, it is the transformations in the industrial sector that have been critical and formative. Japan's economic growth over the past three decades is a record of a steady shift forward from labor-intensive, low-growth, low value-added sectors to an ever higher level of technology-intensive, capital-intensive, and higher-growth sectors. This is, in fact, what economic growth means. Real incomes can increase only if productivity increases. Productivity increases as there is a rise in the value of output of each input of labor or capital. The case of the Japanese textile industry dramatically illustrates this progression and its consequences.

As recently as 1960, 30 percent of the exports from Japan were textiles. On the whole, the textile industry is characterized by labor intensity, low value added, low technology, and relatively slow growth of demand. It is the prototype of an industry suitable for a developing country with low wage rates, limited capital, and limited labor skills. It is the sort of industry highly appropriate for the economy of the Japan of several decades ago, but quite unsuitable for an economy that intends to raise real wages and real standards of living.

Today, textiles comprise less than 5 percent of Japan's exports. Rising wage levels, higher skill levels, competition from less developed economies, and the drive to higher technologies have all worked to diminish dramatically the importance of the industry in Japan. Economic growth accomplished what no amount of trade barriers could bring about, and Japan now has the lowest level of textile tariffs in the world and is the world's second largest textile importer.

Cotton textile manufacturers Kanebo and Toyobo were for a long time the largest companies in Japan, but since the mid-1950s they have lost their position to steel, auto, and electronics companies. In 1955, Toyobo led all manufacturing companies in total sales. Ten years later, in 1965, Japan's largest shipbuilder, Mitsubishi Heavy Industries, was the leader. It in turn was displaced in 1975 by Nippon Steel. The sales leader by 1983 was Toyota.

In retrospect, it is ironic that the intense trade conflict between Japan and the United States in the 1960s over textile exports took place at precisely the time that the competitiveness of Japan in textile exportation was diminishing. Employment in all types of textile production in Japan peaked in the early 1960s at about 1.2 million workers. By 1981 employment in the industry was halved to 655,000. The cost to political relations between the two countries caused by rancorous and extended tensions could have been avoided given an appreciation by the United States of the process of change then underway in Japan.

The first example in the postwar period of this phasing out of an industry in Japan occurred in the coal mining industry in the early 1950s. Coal is one of the few resources that Japan has in any abundance, but even this resource is deficient because the coal is of low quality and the coal seams difficult and costly to work. Coal mining was the first Japanese industry marked for decline after World War II by high costs, labor intensity, and effectively competing substitutes that had industry concurrence and government support for its decline. Employment in the coal industry fell from 407,000 workers in 1950 to 31,000 in 1981.

After coal and textiles, the next major industry to undergo this process was shipbuilding. This is an especially intriguing case because the industry was of major importance, with Japanese companies holding a 50 percent share of total world ship-building in the early 1970s, and because neither the Japanese government nor the leaders of Japanese industry predicted the crisis, which had resulted from the run-up in oil prices and the worldwide recession that followed. New orders for ships suddenly stopped, and the Japanese were left with a massive surplus of shipping capacity.

The shipbuilding crisis is of special note as a case in which reaction to economic need was rapid and sensible, with resources devoted to shrinking the industry rather than shoring it up in a costly and futile effort to protect production capacity or employment in an obsolete sector. The contrast with the reactions of Western governments and companies to the same crisis is dramatic and instructive.

The huge—40 percent—surplus capacity left by the 1974 collapse of the shipbuilding market was in an industry that should have been phasing out in Japan, at least in the lower end of the line of less complex and less specialized ships. For example, large tankers are essentially a combination of steel and labor with little special technology embodied in them. This is the kind of industry that will migrate to lower-wage-rate economies, especially when those economies develop cost-efficient steel sources. Not surprisingly, the big increases in shipbuilding capacity and output in the last ten years have been in South Korea, now probably the lowest cost steel producer, with labor rates a fraction of those in Japan.

Neither the Japanese government nor the companies in the shipbuilding industry showed any special foresight or planning ability in anticipation of this industry migration. In fact, Japanese shipbuilders were expanding capacity right up to the crisis in the market. But when the nature and extent of the problem became clear, their response was rapid and effective. The major shipbuilders agreed on capacity reductions—both in volume and type of capacity—and petitioned the government for assistance in carrying out a program to reduce production capacity. The government responded with financial support for the scrapping of facilities and with a temporary cartel law to put a floor under prices and allow allocation of new orders while the capacity reduction was being carried out. In two years, from 1976 to

1978, shipbuilding capacity in Japan was reduced by 40 percent. The remaining capacity is the most efficient and most suitable for the kind of shipbuilding market that was expected to emerge after the crisis.

Government money was not spent in supporting this "sunset" industry, as was the case in Western Europe during this period. Furthermore, antitrust law was not seen as a higher religious principle. In the Japanese view, monopolies and cartels are economically inefficient and need to be prohibited, but this is an economic judgment to be modified when economics dictate. The limited number of producers in the shipbuilding industry, with six firms accounting for more than a third of capacity, was one of the factors that made rapid government response possible. This was in contrast to textiles, where the very large number of small firms—and ease of entry and exit at the margins of the industry—made concerted action difficult and reduction of capacity a slow process.

"Creative Destruction" in Japan's Economy Today

The early shifts in industrial structure were caused mainly by increasingly higher wage levels, which in turn were caused by increasing levels of productivity. By the late 1960s, however, it became clear that still another level of restructuring would be necessary because continuing economic progress would reduce the effectiveness of a whole range of raw material-processing industries such as petrochemicals, non-ferrous metals, paper and pulp, chemical fertilizers, and petroleum refining.

These industries had grown the most rapidly in Japan in the 1950s and had consumed much of the country's total capital investment during that period. The almost total absence of raw material resources in Japan had led to a long period of focusing on importing basic materials and processing them in Japan. The economics of this emphasis on domestic processing of raw materials had once been appropriate but was becoming inappropriate under several pressures. First, for the most part, these industries were pollution-intensive, and the capital costs of complying with very stringent pollution control requirements in the 1970s reduced the competitiveness of on-shore processing. Second, because these industries were land-extensive, the soaring prices of Japanese land proved another economic handicap. Third, raw material-supplying nations were increasingly eager to add value to these materials by processing them before export to Japan. Off-shore processing, using Japanese capital and technology, not only would help ensure continued supply but would also increase the ability of the supplying economies to import more sophisticated products from Japan, to the advantage of both parties in the cycle.

The explosion of energy prices after 1973 made this not just an impending problem, but one of the utmost urgency. All of the processing industries are energy intensive as well as raw material intensive. Just as companies in Japan had enjoyed and taken full advantage of the very low energy prices of the postwar period in building these industries and the economy as a whole, so the abrupt increase in energy prices now worked to reduce the competitiveness of these industries. By great good fortune, this requirement to shift out of material-processing industries came about only after the Japanese economy had sufficient export earnings to fund off-shore investment and had developed enough technologically so that alternatives to these industries in terms of employment in other manufacturing areas were available and growing.

The aluminum industry is the prototypical example of the acute problems of material-processing industries in Japan. At its peak in 1974, the aluminum industry had bauxite smelting facilities for the production of over one million tons of aluminum ingots. Companies like Mitsubishi Chemical, Sumitomo Chemical, and Showa Denko were steadily adding capacity in modern smelting facilities right up until the crisis (another example of the need to be cautious in attributing special prescience to Japanese planning). The production of aluminum ingots is energy and capital intensive. Indeed, it is so energy intensive that aluminum has been called "canned electricity," and Japan is a poor place for this with electricity prices ten times higher than those of Canada, for example.

Under these cost pressures, the Japanese bauxite smelting industry has virtually collapsed. Output in 1984 was less than

300,000 tons of ingots. Japan's market has seen a real flood of ingot imports, the obverse of the export flooding of which Japanese industry is often accused. More than 1.6 million tons of aluminum ingots were imported to Japan in 1983, along with 300,000 tons of scrap aluminum.

Japan's aluminum ingot-producing industry will not disappear. A few domestic smelters have access to captive hydropower and will remain in production. There will be no capacity additions, however, and a great reduction in capacity is underway. A modern facility that was being constructed by Sumitomo Chemical as the crisis hit is said never to have gone into production. The aluminum producing units have been separated from their parent companies to isolate the problem and the losses, and their production facilities are being steadily reduced.

The aluminum industry is the extreme example of a problem that exists for most of Japan's material-processing industries. Ethylene capacity is being reduced by one-third. The electric furnace steel industry is virtually shutting down. Moreover, a whole range of large industries in Japan are now afflicted by high costs and are not competitive in world markets. These industries will not quickly disappear—the capital and labor resources they represent are too substantial for abrupt closure. Determined upgrading of facilities, as is now taking place in Japan's pulp and paper industry, can defer the day of final reckoning and extend the life of the best of the industry's plants. But Japan's capital and labor resources will no longer flow into these sectors; they have joined the ranks of Japan's sunset industries.

The full extent of continuing pressure on troubled industrial sectors in a growing economy can be appreciated by a review of Japan's steel industry. Long the country's premier industry, its wage settlements have determined the national pattern and its leaders have become Japan's industrial statesmen and spokesmen for the business community. The postwar growth of the industry was spectacular, jumping from 5 million tons of capacity in 1950 to nearly 150 million tons in 1980, and rivaling steel output in the United States. With rapid growth came extraordinary improvements in cost efficiency—world-scale facilities sited on deep water to take the world's lowest-cost ore and coal; the most modern technology, from oxygen furnaces to continuous casting; and optimal computerization of all aspects of the business. Japan's steel industry is the standard for the world, helping the United States and other countries to modernize production, showing the Korean industry how to develop, and, as the low-cost producer, providing the basis for U.S. price controls regarding imports of steel to the United States.

The Japanese steel industry's response to the oil crisis was prompt and vigorous. Oil, previously a main source of energy in the industry, was taken out of the process. Massive capital investment resulted in a total switch to coal during 1974–1980. Energy and cost-saving continuous casting climbed to 80 percent of total casting capacity, against 15 to 20 percent for the United States. Despite the shift to coal, the industry held its level of coal-per-ton-produced to a level far below that of the Western industries.

Yet, for all of its achievement and strenuous and costly pursuit of increased cost effectiveness, Japan's steel industry is now in trouble. World steel demand is down, and given the changes in the economy, it is down permanently in Japan. The developing economies—notably South Korea, Brazil, Taiwan, and Venezuela—are becoming effective producers with new facilities and lower labor costs and are able to adapt all the methods Japan used earlier to build a competitive capability. Steel imports to Japan, especially from South Korea, still constitute only 5 percent of demand, but in the lower end of the line—carbon steel in standard shapes—are increasing rapidly, rather like Japanese steel exports to the United States in the late 1950s. All of Japan's steel producers reported substantial losses in 1983. Exports of steel as a percent of Japan's total exports peaked in the mid-1970s and despite increased sales to mainland China, will diminish steadily as a percent of total exports as the economy moves on to still higher value-added products.

Japan's steel industry leaders recognize publicly that change is taking place. The president of Nippon Steel said:

[The expansion of] research and development and commercialization of new materials, such as ceramics and non-ferrous metals, starting in the current fiscal year . . . is an indication of the steel industry's intention to develop itself into a comprehensive material industry from one exclusively depending on steel. The new policy is naturally based on the recognition that the industry cannot rely on steel alone.[1]

Yet, even these examples of structural change in industry understate the overall degree of change occurring in Japan to which the kaisha must constantly adjust. While the textile industry as a whole diminishes in importance, within the industry there is a steady shift to higher value added products taking their place, from cotton gray goods, to textiles more difficult and costly to produce, to synthetic fibers; from the dollar blouses of old to high fashion designers making Tokyo a style center for the world. In the same way, consumer electronics production shifts from the transistor radio (now made elsewhere in Asia), to monochrome television (also now made elsewhere in Asia), to color television, to the video cassette recorder, which with production at more than 20 million sets a year has created a Japanese monopoly in world production. While whole industries are moving from central to declining positions as labor costs change, technology advances, competitors strengthen, and material costs change, so within any industry in Japan's dynamic economy there is a steady shift from the less sophisticated to more sophisticated products.

This whole process is, of course, nothing more nor less than economic growth. It is the kind of change that must take place if a people are to increase their productivity and thus their standard of living. This process of change is not unique to the Japanese economy, but what is unique in Japan is the speed with which these changes take place, and the ability of the Japanese company to deal with them continously over a long period of time. This process of continual restructuring requires a continuing shift of the resources of the economy—capital and labor—out of relatively low-growth, low-technology, labor-intensive sectors, toward higher-value-added, higher-technology sectors. The economy has moved on this course very steadily and rapidly, the process both a result and a cause of its ability to out-

1. Mr. Y. Takeda, quoted in "Limit to Domestic Demand—Steel Industry Sees No Way Out of Lingering Recession," *Japan Economic Journal,* 20 September 1983, p. 7.

perform other economies in terms of real growth of output.

Not surprisingly given their experience, the general expectation of the Japanese is that this process will continue. Japan's Economic Planning Agency sponsored a 1982 study predicting developments in Japan's economy and society through the year 2000 (see table 2–1). The forecast of the study group was that Japan's real economic growth to the end of the century would be about 4.5 percent annually (somewhat faster than the growth of the United States and other economies of developed nations), with Japan's real output per capita per year reaching approximately $17,500, compared with approximately $15,000 for the United States. Essentially all of the increase in the labor force over the period is expected to be employed in the service sector of the economy. Employment in manufacturing is expected to increase very little, if at all. Such major sectors as metals and chemicals manufacturing are expected to show a steady decline in employment, with increases in employment expected only in Japan's fast-moving electronics and electrical machinery industry.

The study's projection describes the completion of a full turn of the economy. The growth sequence in Japan has been from labor-intensive activities, through raw-material and energy-intensive sectors, to the present concentration of competitiveness in the manufacture of intermediate technology and mass-production goods, such as autos, cameras, office equipment, and machine tools. The next stage, already underway, is moving from mass-produced goods into the leading technology sectors, especially electronics-driven and biology-related product areas as well as knowledge-intensive service sectors, like software and communications. As the next transition is completed, the Japanese economy will have the world's highest levels of output and income per capita, and become a major source of capital and technology to the world.

In only fifty years, Japan will have moved from poverty to the highest levels of income, from economic insignificance to leadership, from the import of technology and capital to being a major source of their export, from less developed status to the lead economic position. It is natural that there should be considerable discussion and controversy over how all of this has been

TABLE 2–1
Japan's Economy in the Year 2000

	Composition of Gross Domestic Product (%)		Structure of Employment (in thousands of persons)		Annual Change (%)
	1980	2000	1980	2000	
Primary Sector	3.7	4.2	5,770	3,080	−3.1
Secondary Sector	38.2	31.5	19,250	21,110	0.5
Manufacturing	29.3	21.6	13,770	14,200	0.2
Chemicals	5.4	1.5	1,750	1,450	−0.9
Primary Metals	3.6	0.8	670	540	−1.1
Machinery	11.9	15.7	5,380	8,930	2.6
Other	8.4	3.6	5,970	3,280	−3.0
Construction	8.9	10.0	5,480	6,900	1.2
Tertiary Sector	58.1	64.2	30,190	39,120	1.3
Utilities	3.0	1.5	300	330	0.4
Finance, Insurance, Real Estate	15.5	8.5	1,910	2,410	1.2
Transport and Communications	6.6	5.6	3,500	3,550	0.1
Service, etc.	33.0	48.6	24,480	32,830	1.5
Total	100.0	100.0	55,360	63,290	0.7

SOURCE: Adapted from Keizai Kikaku Hen (Economic Planning Agency), *2000 Nen No Nihon* (Japan in the Year 2000), (Tokyo: Okurasho, 1982), pp. 64–65, 72.

and is likely to be achieved, so a considerable effort is often made to draw lessons from the Japanese experience that can be applied to other countries.

Government as Help and Hindrance

This will not be another exercise in "explaining the Japanese miracle," but to understand the nature and role of the Japanese company some review of the relative roles of the government of Japan and of the companies in the private sector is needed to provide a context for an analysis of Japan's kaisha.

That the Japanese government has played an important role in the dynamic of the nation's change and growth is self-evident; certain critical elements in that process can only be managed by government. A major element is education, and as will be discussed, the increase in the educational level in Japan has more than kept pace with the economy's needs for a highly educated workforce. Equally important elements are savings and investment. Growth can only come about with investment, which in turn can only derive from savings and from a solid financial infrastructure to manage the flow of funds. The government of Japan has worked to maintain high savings rates rather than high consumption, as in the United States; this takes no special ingenuity, only commitment. One result is low interest rates, which support rapid and continuing investment.

In such an atmosphere of growth, it helps if the government is competently staffed, and, in fact, the best of Japan's best educated university graduates enter government service by preference. It is helpful too if government staffing is kept small; proportionally, Japan has fewer of its labor force in government service than any other major country. It helps too if government is stable, avoiding abrupt swings in economic policy, and that economic policy making is in the hands of a competent bureaucracy which can take a long view of economic policy issues, relatively free from short-term political pressure groups.

This is not to say that all Japanese government policies are economically sound, that all sectors are rationally managed, or that there is public concurrence with all policies and no pressure groups. Japanese agricultural policy is about as economically irrational as that of the other developed economies, and for much the same reasons. Political pressures have given rise to policies that protect small shopkeepers and block rationalization of the distribution sector. Extravagant spending programs are geared to keep rural districts safe constituencies. Bureaucratic bumbling and resistance frustrates or slows the execution of economically desirable policies. Business groups lobby; protest groups demonstrate; the press fulminates.

With government, however, as with business competitors, and as with baseball players, it is relative performance—relative competence, relative stability, and relative rationality of policy—that determines who does well compared to others. The Japanese government is far from being a perfect government, the Japanese body politic far from a creature of beauty, and the Japanese public by no means perfectly informed and altruistic. But in the economic area, especially with respect to manufacture and trade, the government of Japan performs relatively well.

Lastly, it is helpful for economic change and growth if the government helps do what no business firm can, which is to undertake a steady educational process regarding the prospects and direction for the economy. The study in table 2–1 regarding the year 2000 was exceptional only in that it was a one-time study. Japan's Ministry of International Trade and Industry provides business with a "vision" (note, not a "plan") of where the economy could best be directed in the national interest. The efforts of it and other agencies no doubt help explain the general acceptance by the Japanese public that as some industries grow and flourish others must in the nature of things languish and decline. There seems to be no other nation in the world where even relatively low-ranking bureaucrats can with impunity publicly list industries that will and must phase out of the economy.

With all of these strengths it is critical to the economic growth process that the government of Japan sees, as it does, the private company as the necessary, effective, and appropriate instrument for the nation's economic development. When this policy view by government is coupled with a perception by the business community of the government as generally competent and supporting, a degree of government-business dialogue and cooperation becomes possible that is rare in the West.

There are several things, however, that the government of Japan has not been able to do. It has not been able to manage its own businesses competently. Japan's National Railroad, with its huge debt and continuing losses, is one testimonial to this. The Sales Monopoly Corporation, with its high prices and closed market—especially for tobacco products—is another. The high prices and slow service of the national telephone corporation, a principal barrier to further computer development, another. Yet, in fairness to the government, it should be noted that these government-dominated corporations are scheduled for transfer to private or semi-private ownership.

Not only is the government of Japan demonstrably unable to manage a business, it has also shown no special foresight in recognizing the value of new technologies or the probable directions of change in its specific businesses. For all of its considerable value in planning at the broadest level of the economy, as several examples cited have shown, business planning has not been distinguished, nor has technological foresight been exceptional. Japan's list of technologies to be developed is much the same as that of all other governments—electronics, biotechnology, aerospace, and new materials like fine ceramics. Even in so seemingly obvious an area as robotics, it was only after a decade of robot experience by private companies (with more than one hundred companies already producing robots) that the first government developmental program in robotics was implemented.

With the managerial ability and foresight of the Japanese government open to question, its ability to command the private sector has limits. Long efforts to bring about consolidation of Japan's auto industry, beginning as early as the 1960s, still have not shown results; eight manufacturers are still in place. A similar situation exists with computers, where modest consolidation has been the result of competitive issues rather than pressures of MITI. The private sector simply does not follow business level guidance when it is not in its interest to do so. The Japanese government's role, while critical and brilliant in those sectors where government alone can achieve results, has been undistinguished and even counter-productive in those sectors where a firm alone can achieve results.

The role of the Japanese government in accelerating change in industry structure brings to mind the suggestion that it is in the power of governments to prevent great harm but not to do great good. In contrast to the governments of the Western economies, it is the Japanese government's policy toward declining industries that is most impressive. The government is capable of a real recognition of the need for and desirability of industrial structural change. Money is not spent in efforts to shore up declining industries—a parallel to Britain's shoveling money into its auto, steel, and coal mining industries simply cannot be found in Japan. Tariffs are not raised to defend declining industries. Instead, assistance is given to the prompt and effective closing down of capacity, as witness the shipbuilding case.

On the positive side in terms of industry restructuring, while the Japanese government has shown no particular technological foresight, it has shown a clear ability to identify emerging market forces and to work to ensure that those forces get full play. In robotics, once it was clear from the workings of the market that this was an important and perhaps even a strategic technology, the government of Japan provided accelerated depreciation schedules to support the purchase of robots, set up a financing company to allow small business to buy robots on favorable terms, and provided research seed money to encourage industry development.

In sum, the principal role of the government of Japan at the operating, business level of industrial change and growth has been to facilitate and accelerate the workings of the market, to speed the process of reduction of declining sectors, and to work to clear the way for market forces to have full play in emerging growth sectors. At the broader level of national policy, the government of Japan has been a critical force in providing the social infrastructure, in providing supportive fiscal and monetary policy, and in providing general directions for the business community.

The Competitive Impact of High-Growth Rates

Japan's kaisha are both the instruments and the products of the nation's extraordinary economic growth and change. Their view of how to compete in the world has been formed from their experience with rapid growth which collapses the time in which competitive interaction takes place. The kaisha share four key perceptions: (1) market share is the key index of performance in a high-growth market; (2) investment in facilities must at least keep pace with—and preferably exceed—the growth of the market, regardless of short-term impact on profits; (3) price is the principal competitive weapon to gain and hold market share; therefore, prices must decline steadily as costs decline; and (4) new products must be constantly introduced to continue the cycle of investment, cost reduction, price reduction, and market share gain.

These keys to competitive success apply at all times, in all markets. Their interactions, and the consequences of failure to follow these rules, are obscured if growth is slow, but the working out of the rules is dramatic when growth rates are high. Events take place three times as rapidly in a 9 percent growth economy as they do in a 3 percent growth economy. Inflation and other interferences obscure the results in the slower growth economy; but the effects are starkly apparent in a high growth economy.

The pocket calculator industry in Japan provides an example of the impact of growth. The industry has gone through a typical growth cycle, with extremely high growth for many years and rapid price reductions (see figure 2–1), followed by low growth as the market demand is satisfied. The initial pioneers of the product were quickly followed by a great number of new entrants who exited from the business as the industry matured. These included very substantial companies like Sony which could not or chose not to stay in the competitive race.

During 1967–1973, output in Japan of pocket calculators

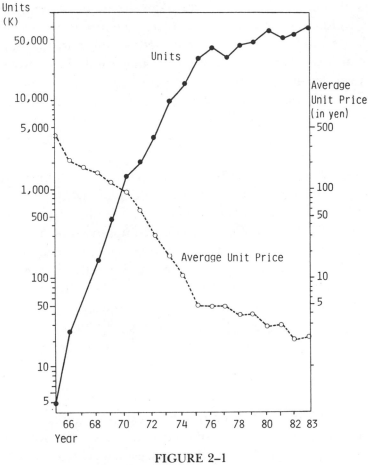

FIGURE 2-1
Production of Electronic Calculators
1965–1983

SOURCE: Adapted from Research and Statistics Department, Ministry of International Trade and Industry, *1983 Year Book of Machinery Statistics* (Tokyo: Tsusho Sangyo Chosakai, 1984), p. 132.

grew at an annual rate of 133 percent. The effects of this kind of growth on market share warrant mention. Let us assume that two companies share a market, and the market doubles each year for the next three years. If one of the two companies chooses not to grow with the market, either through failure to perceive the growth or from a reluctance to invest, while the other elects to take all of the growth of the market, in only three years the more aggressive company will have over a 90 percent share of a market eight times larger than three years before. The less aggressive company will now hold less than 10 percent of the market, even though its sales volume has not declined. In terms of sales power and product development capability, the game will be over for the less assertive competitor.

More fundamental to the competitive interaction, the less aggressive company has little if any opportunity to improve its cost position because its scale of production has not been increasing. The bolder company will be able to take full advantage of the generally observed effect of volume on cost, in which cost tends to decline about 20 to 25 percent with each doubling of output. In three years the bolder company's output will increase fourteen times, with its costs only a fraction of its competitor's. Without reducing profit margin the bolder company can reduce prices far below the competitor's cost position.

A small, Japanese family-owned company, now famous as Casio, did something like this in the pocket calculator market during the market's high-growth phase. While the market more than doubled each year, the Casio share increased from 12 to 36 percent. Casio needed to increase its output more than thirty-two times to keep pace with the growth of the market, and then to increase output more than ninety-six times to triple its market share.

The kind of investment commitment Casio made can not be dependent on approval from the chief financial officer, or based on discounted cash flow or other investment return analysis. Instead, the investment is justified on the basis of the long-term strategic interests of the firm. It requires that the kaisha be free of the tyranny of accountants. It also means that a failure by a competitor to keep pace with this rate of investment, and the implied rate of cost and price decline, will result in a total failure of that competitor's business.

The current data on semiconductor investment reveal a quite similar pattern. All nine of Japan's major semiconductor producers announced capital investment increases in 1984 of more than 53 percent over 1983. Several, including the giant Matsushita Electric, announced a 150 percent increase in semiconductor capital investment. Yet even Matsushita's total budget is only half of that announced by the two leaders in the field, Hitachi and NEC, each of which intended to invest $400 million dollars in the semiconductor area in 1984.

Semiconductors are a high-growth sector in which costs

decline predictably with increases in production volume. Loss of market share means a loss in relative cost position and therefore a loss of competitive position. For both Hitachi and NEC, leadership in semiconductors is seen as critical to long-term leadership in the electronics industry as a whole. They are prepared to pay what is necessary to maintain their market share and cost leadership position.

In this fierce, investment-driven, market share-obsessed competition there are winners and losers. Competitors in foreign markets do not meet the losers, but feel the full force of Japan's winners. Losing in Japan is painful; the kaisha have no quick escape from losing positions. First, the pressures on a Japanese company in trouble are severe. Not only do many companies (though by no means all) have the fixed costs that result from high levels of interest-bearing debt, but under Japanese conditions of employment, most of the labor cost of a large company is a fixed cost. Further, because in Japan it is still unusual that companies or even businesses of a company are bought or sold, there is no quick fix available to management through the divestiture of a troubled business or acquisition of a new business as a way toward renewed growth.

If the kaisha are to escape their troubles, they must grow out of them, and moreover, must bring about that growth through internal resources and internal development. The pressure is intense, and this fact alone helps intensify competitive interaction within the Japanese economy. The cost of failure is high, and therefore the drive to product and share leadership is commensurately high.

Thus, the intensity of competition among the kaisha in new product areas and in growth areas is especially intense. The propensity and ability of the Japanese company to bring out a copy of a new product is well known, a propensity not confined to nor especially aimed at a foreign company's products. In new product areas, the number of entrants in pursuit of sales growth has an avalanche effect. For example, at the beginning of 1983, the Japanese authorities released radio channels for a new and rather sophisticated product called a personal radio—a follow-up to the now outmoded citizen band radio. Within ten months of the product's authorization, twenty kaisha were in the market with competing products, and monthly production was growing at an annual rate of 100 percent.

The current high-growth sector of electronics is a maelstrom of competition. With VCRs, videotape, word processors, personal computers, semiconductors, office copiers, robots, and the whole range of household, office, and factory electronics and automation equipment, the pattern is the same: large numbers of entrants; rates of investment as rapid as market growth; little difference in investment rate or market share during the high-growth phase as each competitor drives for share; rapid price declines; and increasing quality and variety. For the Japanese economy as a whole, the pattern is a sound one: fierce competition for expanding, high-technology sectors with the outcome decided by very severe economic tests. For the consumer, the pattern is an ideal one: increasing quality and variety and falling prices. For the kaisha the pattern is a familiar one, a replay of the experiences and lessons of the postwar period.

The foregoing describes Japan and its kaisha at the cutting edge. To keep perspective, one needs to remember that a large part of the Japanese economy is not competitive. Companies in decline have the same tendencies toward legal and illegal anticompetitive arrangements that one finds with companies in declining sectors everywhere. One view of Japan, then, would be of fragmented industries, with most manufacturers below world-scale levels of production, operating at high cost, with little prospect of renewed vigor. An equally accurate view, however, is of fast-growing, fiercely competitive, and highly competent companies competing everywhere in the world without apparent disadvantage.

This is simply to say that the Japanese economy is now a very large one which can no longer be broadly characterized without severe risk of over-generalizing. Competitive advantage is shifting, as it has for so long, as the economy shifts forward into higher value-added sectors. It is the companies at the cutting edge, however, that present competitive threats. It is these companies that must be examined if strategies and tactics to deal with the kaisha as competitors are to be developed.

The Dynamic Economy

Two Scenarios For the Japanese Economy's Future

If, in fact, the competitive characteristics of Japanese companies are the results of the dynamism of the economy in which they have developed, then the question of the future of the Japanese economy becomes critical in predicting whether these companies will continue to operate in the future as they are doing now. Recent discussions of the prospects for the Japanese economy fall into two main categories, or scenarios, as outlined in table 2–2. The two possible scenarios outlined have equal credibility. One has the Japanese economy experiencing industrial decline: the country succumbs to affluence with deteriorating work habits and increased government programs to expand welfare and reduce savings and investment. It invests in an expanding and substantial military capability; it fails to make significant progress in industrial research and development; and it fails to deal with the political and fiscal issues that are already serious problems. This is an affluent, mature society and economy that has lost its dynamism but is comfortable with its level of achievement.

In the second scenario, Japan emerges as world leader. It

TABLE 2–2

Two Scenarios For Japan's Future

Maturity and Industrial Decline	Renewed Growth After a Readjustment Period
Aging population	Moderating welfare increases
Rising welfare costs	Reorganization of tax structure
Larger government budgets and tax levels	Political redistricting; lower land and agricultural prices and subsidies
Slowing savings and private investment	Reorganization of public corporations (Japan National Railroad; Nippon Telephone and Telegraph)
Basic industries losing competitiveness	
Inability to innovate and invest	
Closing export markets	Automation of conventional manufacture
Competition from NICs (newly industrialized countries)	Shift to higher technologies
Increased military spending	Heavy foreign investment
	Stimulus from Asian growth
	Moderate defense expenditure
Low growth and declining competitiveness; An affluent but static economy	Moderate growth in 1980s; Higher growth in 1990s; World economic leader

succeeds in restructuring its industry; it solves its fiscal crisis by revising tax policies, reorganizing government agencies, and capping its welfare programs; it establishes an independent and substantial R&D capability; and it emerges by the end of the 1980s into another period of high growth driven by major positions in the cutting-edge industries of the world's economy.

Japan is now in transition, as indeed it has been for the extent of its modern history. Each of Japan's many transitions has been marked by special characteristics. The current transition has three main themes. The first of these is the transition from an extended period of high rates of economic growth to moderate rates; that is, from 8 and 9 percent annual real growth rates in the 1960s and early 1970s to the 4 and 5 percent levels of recent years, which are predicted for the future. A main impact of this transition is in the area of tax structure and government spending—what worked during the high growth years is inappropriate for a period of sustained lower growth. A shift toward a higher level of general taxes with a greater proportion of indirect taxes and a restructuring of government expenditures may be needed. The change is politically difficult and is taking place slowly. The government's continuing deficits are met by drawing on savings through issues of government bonds, which while not inflationary under these circumstances, make for a threatening burden of government debt.

Related to this first transition is the need for governmental reorganization, in particular, the need to turn over to the private sector or otherwise rationalize the major public corporations—the telephone system, the railway system, and the government tobacco sales monopoly, among others. Also related to the shift toward lower economic growth is the shift of population during the high growth period from farm to city and the need to redistrict the national parliament to reduce the influence of the still influential rural sectors. This is economically important because to bring sense to the present problems of high land and food prices, legislation now opposed by rural interests must be enacted. Again, this change is politically hazardous, and, though proceeding, is going forward slowly.

Japan's second major transition is demographic, the maturing and aging of the population—the graying of Japan. Within only two decades, the proportion of population sixty-five years and over in Japan will have moved from less than 10 percent to more than 15, the level of Sweden and West Germany. The implications are farreaching in terms of the makeup of the labor force and consumer patterns, but are most urgently seen in the need to gain control of expanding welfare benefit programs. Japan is still able to ask the question that can no longer be asked in Western economies—is the government responsible for total care of the aged? Japanese specialists hope to learn from Western mistakes in this area and anticipate problems of funding programs before it is too late.

The third major transition having an impact on the economy is the transition to high-technology, information-intensive industries, which are based in major part on Japan's own research and development. For all of Japan's creativity in the whole range of the arts and its ability to develop a truly unique life-style, the issue remains whether this creative capacity can be transferred to the output of scientific and industrial discovery and invention.

It is not necessary to bet on one or another of the two scenarios now. It will be evident within the next two or three years as to whether real progress is made on political redistricting, tax revisions, government reorganization, and the like. It is in any event clear that the dynamism of the Japanese economy has not yet run its course. Japan's kaisha, products of fast change and rapid growth, are formidable competitors. Like the best of Western companies they have come to realize the value and meaning of market share; they are prepared to invest as necessary to capture the lead position and to reinvest the benefits in order to repeat the cycle in yet another growth sector. Given continued competent management of their political and financial environment, the kaisha will grow still stronger.

3

THE *KAISHA*

AS COMPETITOR

WITH the continuing success
of the Japanese in world markets comes an increasing interest
in their methods of competition. The kaisha are typically regarded as ruthless price cutters, willing to sacrifice short-term
profits to satisfy their relentless obsession for growth and increased market share. In the view of many Western executives,
the behavior of the Japanese is reckless when prices are slashed
in bids for increased market shares.

To the Japanese, their reach for market shares is as much
a matter of survival as it is a reach for opportunities. In the
high-growth Japanese economy a "winner's competitive cycle"
has become apparent. Those companies who establish and
maintain this cycle have consistently emerged as strong, profitable, and respected companies in both the Japanese and, within
the last decade, the world business community.

For a company to establish a "winner's competitive cycle"
it must grow faster than its competitors. This means that the
company must increase its market share so that its volume of
business will increase at a rate greater than that of its competitors. A superior rate of increase is achieved by increased investment. Increased investment can have many forms including

price cutting, capacity expansion, advertising, or product development. Once a superior rate of increase is established, a virtuous cycle begins: with increased volume, relative to competitors' volume, comes decreased costs. With decreased costs comes increased profitability and financial strength. More cash is available internally and from external sources to fund growth. This cash is then reinvested in the business in ways that will yield further increases of market share and a replay of the winning cycle. Failure to establish and maintain this cycle results in the loss of competitive position over time and ultimately a withdrawal from, or major redirection of, the business.

The "winner's competitive cycle" is evident in almost all businesses in free market economies. The power of the cycle to alter competitive positions is much stronger in high- than in low-growth markets. Because the Japanese economy has grown so rapidly since the end of World War II many examples exist of companies establishing this "winner's competitive cycle" and using it to topple market leaders or to defend competitive positions. These examples serve as powerful reminders to Japanese executives of the consequences of failing to establish the cycle.

Honda and the Winner's Competitive Cycle

THE HIGH-GROWTH YEARS

In the early 1950s the Japanese motorcycle industry had over fifty participants. Demand was growing at over 40 percent per year. The leading company was Tohatsu, with a 22 percent share of the market; Honda was second, with 20 percent. Tohatsu by most measures was the more successful of the two. Its after-tax profits were 8 percent of sales compared with Honda's 3.4 percent. Tohatsu's debt-to-equity ratio was 1.5 to 1 while Honda's was 6 to 1.

In 1955, this was the widely held view of the two competitors in Japan's financial community:

Tohatsu: With Honda, one of the two largest motorcycle manufacturers. However, it is considerably more profitable and its financial conditions are superior to Honda's.

Honda: Because of its high growth, this company can probably be regarded as one of the more successful motorcycle manufacturers. But overexpansion has deteriorated its financial condition because of an excess of borrowings.[1]

In the space of five short years, however, Honda emerged as the undisputed leader of the Japanese motorcycle industry. Tohatsu's market share dropped to less than 4 percent while Honda's soared to 44 percent. Honda reported an after-tax profit in 1960 of 10.3 percent of sales while Tohatsu registered losses of almost 8 percent of sales. Honda's balance sheet had strengthened and the company had a debt-to-equity ratio of 1 to 1. The strength of Tohatsu's balance sheet had deteriorated with a debt-to-equity ratio of 7 to 1 as Tohatsu borrowed to offset its losses. With market growth slowing to 9 percent per year, this new competitive structure appeared permanent.

The financial community in Japan—somewhat belatedly— reassessed its opinion of the two companies:

Honda: The largest production capacity for motorcycles in the world, and still aggressively expanding production at its Suzuka plant. Rapid growth is expected in both overseas and domestic markets.

Tohatsu: Business has been deteriorating since 1959 because of intense competition. Currently being restructured with support of Fuji Electric.[2]

In February 1964 Tohatsu filed for bankruptcy. Its sales had decreased sharply, its funds were exhausted, and its bills went unpaid. Tohatsu had fallen from number one to bankruptcy in less than ten years. It was not the only casualty; other motorcycle manufacturers also went bankrupt or exited the industry. The 50 Japanese manufacturers of the 1950s had shrunk to 30 by 1960, 8 by 1965, and by 1969 to today's 4—Honda, Yamaha, Suzuki, and Kawasaki.

1. *Kaisha-Yoran* (Company Handbook) (Tokyo: Diamond, March 1956), pp. 212–13.
2. *Kaisha-Yoran* (Company Handbook), pp. 233–34.

Tohatsu chose to be conservative in a high-growth market. From 1955 to 1960, it did not significantly increase volume. But Honda set its sights on increased market share and grew at about 66 percent per year in a market growing at 42 percent per year. Honda fueled this growth with heavy borrowings carrying high-interest rate penalties, but a complacent competitor like Tohatsu, coupled with the virtues of the winner's cycle, made it possible for Honda to quickly reduce costs and overwhelm the competition. As competitors fell behind, Honda's profits increased and its balance sheet strengthened.

The kaisha are often criticized by their Western counterparts for their obsession with market share. But in a growing market, competitive position and the rate at which that position is changing are the most important indices of performance. Increased market share and increased competitive advantage is obtained by preempting market growth with aggressive pricing and investment policies. A noncompetitive pricing policy and/ or the failure to add sufficient plant and equipment capacity and human resources will result in a loss of competitive position. If a competitive position is allowed to deteriorate substantially the viability of the business will ultimately be threatened.

THE LOW-GROWTH YEARS

Honda went on to become the market leader in motorcycles in all significant countries in the world. As growth in motorcycles slowed, Honda diversified into automobiles and by 1975 was obtaining more revenues from autos than from motorcycles. Honda's profits continued to increase and its balance sheet steadily strengthened through the 1970s.

Honda's entry into the automobile business was an extraordinary event. When Honda began substantial marketing of automobiles in 1967 the Japanese auto industry was in turmoil. The Japanese economy had been opened to foreign capital participation and many weak Japanese auto producers, fearing for their future, sought tie-ups with the stronger Japanese auto producers. Nissan absorbed Prince and Minsei Diesel and took control of Fuji Heavy Industries' domestic production. Toyota and Hino formed an affiliation to facilitate the rationalization of their car and truck businesses. A restructuring of the auto industry to reduce the number of participants was instigated by MITI so as to make it more competitive worldwide. It was at this time that Honda chose to enter the auto industry, a new entrant to a mature, consolidating sector.

To reduce the risk of failure Honda had to place its best resources behind the automobile venture. This meant that all available cash and technical capability, along with the most promising people, had to be directed toward the automobile business. Honda's high level of investment in the auto industry had to be supported by the resources and cash generation of Honda's motorcycle business.

At about the same time that Honda's automobile sales began to gain momentum, another motorcycle company, Yamaha, began to increase its share of motorcycle production in Japan. Honda's production share of Japanese motorcycles peaked at about 65 percent of total Japanese production in the late 1960s and then declined steadily to 40 percent by 1981. In contrast, Yamaha increased its share from less than 10 percent in the mid-1960s to about 35 percent by 1981—almost exactly matching Honda's loss.

Domestically, Yamaha had pulled even closer to Honda. Honda's domestic market share in motorcycles had declined to 38 percent while Yamaha's had risen to 37 percent. Yamaha was within reach of toppling Honda as Japan's market leader and as the world's number one motorcycle producer. Yamaha management believed an opportunity existed to overtake Honda and that their company had no option but to seize it. Honda, meanwhile, was committed to building its automobile business and was diverting a substantial amount of its resources away from motorcycles and into autos. These quotes capture the essence of the thinking of Yamaha's top management in the late 1970s and early 1980s:

> At Honda, sales attention is focused on four-wheel vehicles. Most of their best people in motorcycles have been transferred (into cars). Compared to them, our specialty at Yamaha is mainly motorcycle production . . .
> —Yamaha's President Koike, 1979[3]

3. *Nihon Keizai,* 28 July 1979, p. 7.

If only we had enough capacity we could beat Honda.
—Yamaha's President Koike, early 1981[4]

During this period Yamaha's profitability compared favorably with that of Honda. Both companies had operating profits of about 7 to 10 percent of sales in the late 1960s and about 3 percent of sales in the early 1980s. Honda's profitability was no doubt depressed by its heavy investments in research and development for its young auto business. Its R&D expenditures increased steadily from approximately 2 percent of sales in 1970 to 5 percent in 1983. Yamaha spent slightly more than 1 percent of sales on R&D throughout the same period.

Yamaha was able to pull close to Honda by focusing all its resources on motorcycles and related products to broaden the range of products offered and to continuously expand capacity. In the early 1970s, Yamaha had about 18 different models in its product line compared to Honda's 35. By 1981, Yamaha offered 60 models compared to Honda's 63. In the early 1970s Honda had introduced two new models on the market for every one introduced by Yamaha. In 1981 Yamaha introduced 18 models and Honda 17.

` In August 1981, Yamaha announced plans to construct a new motorcycle factory with an annual capacity of one million units. This factory would increase its total capacity to four million units, exceeding Honda's capacity by 200,000 units. If the new factory's total production were sold in Japan, Yamaha's domestic share would approach 60 percent. President Koike went on to announce:

The difference between us and Honda is in our ability to supply. As primarily a motorcycle producer, you cannot expect us to remain in our present number two position forever.
—Yamama's President Koike, announcing new factory plans, August 1981[5]

In one year, we will be the domestic leader. And in two years, we will be number one in the world.

4. *Shukan Toyo Keizai,* 30 April 1983, p. 86.
5. From an interview with an attendee who wishes to remain anonymous.

—Yamaha's President Koike, January 1982 shareholders' meeting[6]

Yamaha management was betting its company could achieve the leading market share in motorcycles. Since Yamaha had no other businesses with significant growth potential it was prepared to invest heavily in motorcycles. But Yamaha invested at a rate far higher than its internal cash generation could support. Yamaha turned to the banks to make up the difference, and its debt burden increased steadily.

Although it was as profitable as Honda, Yamaha and its affiliated companies[7] had a debt-to-equity ratio of almost 3 to 1 while the Honda group's ratio was less than 1 to 1. But Yamaha had almost closed the product line and volume gap between it and Honda and in June 1982 announced that it had set historic records in fiscal 1981 for both sales volume and profits. Honda continued to exhibit a preoccupation with autos as it began investing in large-scale automobile production in the United States.

HONDA TURNS ON YAMAHA

Yamaha's public pronouncements, actions, and successes did not go unnoticed by Honda. As early as 1978, President Kawashima of Honda, said "As long as I am president of this company we will surrender our number one spot (in motorcycles) to no one."[8]

In 1979 President Kawashima admitted, "From the late 1960s until recently we have concentrated our efforts on product development of four-wheel vehicles. The fact that another [motorcycle] maker could pull so close to us was an unavoidable situation."[9] When word of Koike's statements at the Yamaha shareholder's meeting in January of 1982 reached Honda's pres-

---

6. Ibid.

7. The Yamaha Motor Company owns 100 percent of all but five companies within its group of 42 affiliated companies, and it is the majority owner in these five. The principal function of these affiliated companies is the sale of Yamaha products and in 1981, approximately 70 percent of the total annual sales of Yamaha Motor were to Yamaha affiliated companies.

8. *Nihon Keizai,* 29 July 1978, p. 7.

9. *Nihon Keizai,* 28 July 1979, p. 7.

ident he was incensed. "Yamaha has not only stepped on the tail of a tiger, it has ground it into the earth!" Kawashima issued a battle cry, "Yamaha wo tsubusu!", which can be variously translated as, "We will crush [break, smash, squash, butcher, slaughter, or destroy] Yamaha."[10]

And so Honda proceeded to do just that. Over the next eighteen months Honda's production share increased from 40 to 47 percent while Yamaha's decreased from 35 to 27 percent. Honda increased its domestic market share from 38 to 43 percent while Yamaha's share collapsed from 37 to 23 percent. Honda's counterstrategy was both simple and innovative. The simple elements included massive price cuts and increases of promotional funds and field inventories. At the time of the heaviest competition between Honda and Yamaha, retail prices for popular models had fallen by more than a third. In the summer of 1982 it was possible to buy a 50cc motorcycle (the large volume cycle in Japan) for less than the cost of a 10-speed bicycle. In spite of this heavy discounting Honda was able to provide product to its dealers at costs that enabled the dealers to earn profits that were 10 percent better than the profits they could earn by selling Yamaha motorcycles.

The innovative element of Honda's counterattack was the use of product variety as a competitive weapon. In eighteen months, Honda introduced 81 new motorcycle models in Japan. Yamaha was able to introduce only 34. This is even more startling when one considers that both competitors had only about 60 models each in their entire line in the late 1970s. Yet taking these figures alone understate their effect on the market. When discontinued models are considered, Honda more completely refreshed its product line. Honda introduced 81 new models and discontinued 32 models for a total of 113 changes in its product line. Yamaha retired only 3 models and introduced 34 new models for a total of 37 changes. The consumer was seeing fresh Hondas and increasingly stale Yamahas.

The effects of Hondas's new model proliferation on Yamaha were as devastating as Honda's price cutting. New model introductions offer greater technical and design appeal to

10. *Shukan Toyo Keizai*, 30 April 1983, p. 86.

customers, thereby increasing demand, and dealers have an incentive for pushing them. But increased volumes of new models come at the expense of older ones; therefore, the life-cycles for existing models are shortened and demand for them declines sharply. This is a comfortable situation for the industry leader but a difficult one for the follower, who is less able to fund the required development costs in the time required and usually must discount heavily to move growing stocks of outdated products.

Yamaha's sales of motorcycles plummeted by more than 50 percent, and the company incurred heavy losses. By early 1983, Yamaha's unsold stocks of motorcycles in Japan were estimated to be about half of the industry total of unsold stock. At the then current Yamaha sales rate its inventories were equivalent to about one year's sales. The only way to move the stock was to forward promotional funds to the dealers and to allow cuts in prices. But Yamaha could not afford to do this, and even considered a scrapping program for the vehicles in stock.

The quality of the balance sheets of Yamaha and its affiliated companies deteriorated quickly. The debt-to-equity ratio increased from less than 3 to 1 in 1981 to 7 to 1 in 1983. Buoyed by its continued success in automobiles Honda's balance sheet actually strengthened over this period.

THE SURRENDER

By January 1983, about a year after Honda's counterattack, President Koike of Yamaha admitted defeat:

> We cannot match Honda's product development and sales strength. . . . I would like to end the Honda-Yamaha war. . . . From now on I want to move cautiously and ensure Yamaha's relative position [as second to Honda].[11]

On 14 April 1983, Yamaha announced a second half loss of 4 billion yen. The dividend was cut 80 percent and no dividend was planned for the next period. Production plans were cut 18 percent to 1.8 million units and a plan to remove 700 employees

11. *Nihon Keizai,* 23 February 1983.

from the payroll in two years was announced. Yamaha's chairman, Kawakami, who was instrumental in building the Yamaha group, said in April, "We plunged like a diving jet. My ignorance is to blame."[12] President Koike was replaced by President Eguchi.

On 28 May 1983, a reconstruction plan was announced by Yamaha. Motorcycle production was cut further, to 1.5 million units. This low level was to be maintained for two to three years to facilitate the gradual reduction of field inventories. Work force reductions were to be increased by another 2,000 employees, or about 20 percent of the total labor force. All new projects were put on hold for two years.

But even these measures could not halt the Yamaha slide. On 30 June 1983 Yamaha announced a further 30 percent decline in sales. On 6 August Yamaha reported that its losses for 1983 were expected to reach about 20 billion yen—an amount far exceeding the record profits of fiscal year 1981. In October production plans were further reduced to 1.38 million units.

Honda continued to pressure Yamaha with increased variety. From December 1983 to September 1984 Honda added and subtracted 39 models from its total offering of 110 models in Japan. Yamaha has been able to make only 23 changes out of its total offering of 106. In the all important 50cc line for the domestic market, Honda has made 18 changes and Yamaha has only been able to respond with 6.

To avoid bankruptcy, Yamaha management quickly sold off assets. From April 1983 to April 1984 Yamaha sold land, buildings, and equipment for about 16 billion yen. The average monthly salary was reduced from 239,000 yen to 216,000 yen, and bonuses were not paid. In an interview, Yamaha President Eguchi stated:

> Since Yamaha is considered responsible for the present market situation, I would first like to study our position and develop a more cooperative stance towards other companies. . . . Of course, there will still be competition. . . . but I intend it to be based on mutual recognition of our relative positions.[13]

12. *Shukan Diamond,* 8 June 1983, p. 82.
13. *Nikkan Kogyo Shinbun,* 6 February 1984 (microfilm).

Yamaha succumbed for several reasons. First, Honda is a larger company with greater product development resources. Try as it did, once Yamaha lost the initiative it had virtually no chance of keeping pace with Honda in a battle across a broad front. Second, Yamaha's welfare depended on motorcycles. Honda derived approximately two-thirds of its sales from automobiles, which continued to prosper during its counterattack. Third, Yamaha had gambled by investing in a new plant. As outsiders we cannot know when Honda began planning its attack on Yamaha, but however long the planning, the speed of execution was amazing. Honda hit Yamaha when it was most exposed: at the completion of the construction of an expensive new facility that was not yet producing products. The attack was driven home by the new product introduction which rendered much of Yamaha's line obsolete.

The timing and speed demonstrated by Honda against Yamaha underscores the importance that many of the leading kaisha place on keeping their competitors continuously in their sights. Plans are built around the anticipated actions of competitors and aim to achieve market results equal to or better than the competition. This orientation often results in a pell-mell rush of Japanese competitors into new markets or products. This tendency is sometimes derided by Western executives as "copying," but it is in fact an acceptable competitive response by companies accustomed to high growth and aware of the consequences of being left behind. ("Copying" is discussed in chapter 6.)

Many markets for new products in Japan such as floppy discs, compact discs, personal computers, and even, until recently, McDonald's and Seven-Eleven convenience stores grow 100 percent per year. The pressure of a competitive environment in a market growing at over 100 percent a year may be very difficult for a Western executive to imagine. Production capacity must be expanded at high rates and prices must be cut to whatever levels are required to create enough demand for product to fill the capacity of the plants. The executives of a company whose market is growing at 100 percent a year must plan to double production capacity *every year* just to maintain a competitive position. The original one plant must become two by year two and four the year after. Five years of 100 percent growth requires that production capacity be increased thirty-two times just to maintain market share.

From the mid 1960s to the mid 1970s production of electronic calculators grew by more than 100 percent per year. The number of Japanese companies producing electronic calculators blossomed from the first three—Sharp, Canon, and Oki Denki —to about twenty-three in the early 1970s. Unit prices fell about 27 percent per year until 1970, after which prices fell by almost 50 percent per year.

In the early years of Japan's calculator industry, Sharp had been the leading Japanese manufacturer, producing 34 percent of all the Japanese calculators. But Casio, a relatively unknown company run by two brothers, which had produced only 10 percent of Japan's calculators in the mid-1960s, charged ahead and increased its production capacity and model variety while slashing its prices. As Sharp grew at 100 percent per year, Casio grew at almost 200 percent per year. By 1973, Casio had achieved the leading position in Japan with 35 percent of the Japanese production of electronic calculators. Sharp's share had slid to 17 percent.

The intense competition in the calculator industry and the eventual decline in demand proved to be too much for many of the early entrants. The number of participants in Japan's electronic calculator industry fell from a high of twenty-three in 1970 to about nine today. Some companies, such as Vizicon and Sigma, went bankrupt. Others, including such well-known companies as Sony, Ricoh, Seiko, and Hitachi withdrew from the business. Even very strong and historically successful companies like Canon and Matsushita scaled back their participation.

When pursuing new opportunities Japanese executives, like executives around the world, rely on the lessons learned from experience. Japanese executives have experienced the competitive environment of high-growth markets. In high-growth markets investments in people and in plant are made to meet real competitive threats rather than abstract financial criteria. If the ambitions of these Japanese executives happen to collide with those of a Western executive, accustomed to say, 20 percent per year growth, the experience for the Western executive can be unsettling. For example, in a recent conversation with the executives of a leading Western manufacturer of industrial lasers, accustomed to 20 percent per year growth, there were bitter complaints about the aggressive pricing policies and capacity expansion plans of the leading Japanese competitors who have been growing in Japan at almost 100 percent per year.

The Western Competitor in Japan

The intense competitiveness of the kaisha in many of Japan's markets increases the challenge for Western companies to succeed in these markets. Many Western companies do succeed in Japan, achieving effective market entry and sustaining strategies embodying many of the characteristics of the "winners' cycle" so well understood by the leading kaisha. It is more useful here, however, to consider those Western entry strategies that proved to be weak—or even failures—to better understand the nature of Japanese competition.

Most Western entry strategies for the Japanese market are based on new products with superior product performance that enable the foreign company to obtain consumer recognition and high prices. The price is usually high enough to cover most of the expenses of the startup company in Japan and perhaps even to show an early profit. Sales volume soon begins to build, marketing and service costs decline, and profits strengthen.

The expenses of these Japan startups are often high because the product or service is new to the Japanese. This requires frequent sales calls for potential customers and subsequent calls to help the customer use the product. Sometimes marketing costs during a startup can exceed the manufacturing cost of the product. But these costs tend to decline as sales increase and time passes.

Within what is usually a short period of time several growth-seeking kaisha will enter the business. Generally, they have two forms of entry: switching the existing Japanese customers for the Western products to their adaptation of the product, or offering a product with limited features but with a low price that appeals to different customers. When the kaisha switch Japanese customers of Western companies to their product they are taking advantage of the customer education already paid for by the Western company. After one Western manufacturer had profitably convinced Toyota to use its special fluids for machinery lubrication, a Japanese competitor took over the business by offering an equivalent product at substantially lower prices. The Western company had been holding prices up to recover the cost of educating its customers, yet once educated the customers were no longer interested in paying high prices given an acceptable alternate product. The Western company moved on to educate other customers, but because it did not reduce prices to its already educated customers the Japanese competitor was able to expand volume by continuously attracting the customers of the Western company to its product.

The other mode of entry utilized by the kaisha is to compete aggressively on price to offset inferior or limited product performance (see table 3–1). Because these Japanese products are priced low and have limited features, the customers they attract may be a different group than the customers already being served by the Western company.

The market for the low price and performance products offered by the new Japanese entrants often grows much faster than the market for the higher price and performance Western goods. Even so, the high-end market usually has satisfying growth and attractive profits. The Western company will continue to believe in the strength of its advantage in product per-

TABLE 3–1

Aggressive Pricing by Japanese Entrant
Western Prices = 100

Reactive Ion Etch*	60
Electric Shaver	63
Color Photo Scanner	65
Medical X-ray Equipment†	70
Tennis Racket	70
Instant Camera with Electric Flash	73
Personal Computer	78

*Large Scale Integrated circuit (LSI) for manufacturing equipment
†Cardiovascular angiography system

formance, and the new Japanese entrants and the Western company will manage to avoid open conflict.

But beneath the surface, the dynamics of the Japan market are working against the Western company. The fast growth and increasing volumes of the low-end market will enable the Japanese to rapidly lower their costs and to expand distribution, and sales and service capabilities. As their volumes increase and their costs fall, they will be increasingly able to fund an upgrading of their technology and products. The performance distinctions between the Western and the leading Japanese products will begin to blur, but the price differences will remain very real. Soon the Japanese will not just be closing the former performance gaps but will be opening gaps to their advantage.

Medical imaging equipment provides a good example of this process of change in competitive position between Western and Japanese products. While Japanese companies have manufactured imaging equipment since before World War II, Western companies radically advanced the technology in the 1960s and began to market computer aided tomography (CAT) scanners in Japan in the early 1960s. Japanese companies responded quickly to the introduction of tomography, and others followed with additional products. Many of these Japanese products achieved only 60 percent of the performance capacity of the Western product but were priced 40 percent lower. While research institutions and government-supported large hospitals continued to buy the higher performance Western equipment, the smaller hospitals and clinics that could not afford the Western equipment purchased the less effective, but much lower priced, Japanese alternative.

From 1976 to 1980, the overall sales of CAT scanners in Japan grew at an overall rate of 47 percent annually. The Western and high-end segment of the market initially grew 20 percent per year before slowing to 5 percent, while the Japanese and low end grew 85 percent per year. The overall share of the Western products plunged from 65 percent in 1976 to 16 percent in 1980. The Japanese entries greatly expanded the market, because the smaller hospital and clinic market (the low end) grew to be ten times greater on a unit basis than the research and large hospital market (high end).

As volume increased, the prices of the Japanese systems fell at a rapid rate (see figure 3–1). Even as prices were falling, the performance level of the Japanese equipment increased to within 90 percent of the Western equipment. At this level of performance the Japanese equipment was still priced 40 percent less than the Western equipment, and the high and low end distinction in the market faded.

For medical imaging equipment the Japanese have now strengthened to the point where they are taking the initiative in introducing new products and commercializing new technologies (see table 3–2). In the 1960s and early 1970s Western companies had a six to eight-year window of opportunity before the Japanese were able to respond. By the late 1970s the Japanese were keeping pace with Western companies in new product introduction.

Western sales of medical imaging equipment in Japan have begun to falter, and in some cases decline. Profit margins are sliding. One of the world's leaders in imaging equipment which has long had a position in the Japanese market has had profit margins decline more than 80 percent in four years. Japan local

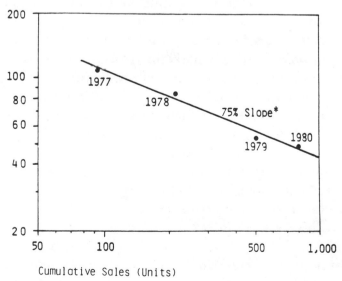

FIGURE 3–1

Price Experience Curve for Japanese CAT Scanners

*For every doubling of cumulative sales, prices decline to 75 percent of what they were previously.

TABLE 3–2

*Year of Japan Product Launches
for Medical Imaging Products*

System	Year of Western Introduction to Japan	Year of Japanese Introduction	Japanese Company	Western Advantage (Years)
Tomography	1964	1970	Toshiba/Hitachi	6
Image Intensifying Tube	1964	1970	Toshiba	6
Mammography	1974	1982	Toshiba	8
Angio-High Power	1977	1982	Toshiba	5
Angio-Poly Diagnostic	1977	1977	Hitachi/Toshiba	0
Angio-Lateral Arc	1981	1982	Toshiba	1
Digital Video Imaging	1982	1982	Toshiba/Hitachi	0
Nuclear Magnetic Resonance	1984	1983	Toshiba/Hitachi	(−1)

management has responded to pressure from headquarters to increase profits by increasing prices, but though they have been increased by over 40 percent on average, the profitability of the local operation continues to deteriorate.

In this situation the competitive position of the Japan operation of the Western company is steadily decaying. The local operation was in a high-cost position because of expensively featured product and high marketing costs. Continued pressure to achieve profit goals was met with price increases and cost cutting. Marketing and sales resources were reduced, local development projects were scaled back or eliminated, and the result was a growing price and performance gap between the Western company and the Japanese competitor. As the gap increases sales volumes decline, resulting in increased costs and further reduction in profits. With falling profits come additional pressure to improve the performance of the operation, which is met with an increase in prices and more slippage in market position.

For a Western company seeking to develop and maintain a substantial position in Japan every effort must be made to preserve and expand the original advantage that served as the wedge into the market. Western executives may find themselves making very different strategic and tactical tradeoffs in Japan than elsewhere. Strategic tradeoffs will include Japan-specific policies to restrict the kaisha's ability to enter the market. Lower priced products and those with fewer features may be required. Service and marketing may need to be expanded ahead of demand and before the operation is profitable. The goal of growth beyond the competitors' growth must be placed ahead of profit goals. In sum, the Western company in Japan must be as committed to the "winner's competitive cycle" as the kaisha are.

Anticipating the Japanese in Western Markets

Japan's leading kaisha are often its leading exporters. The patterns of competition they exhibit in Japan are often the same used in Western markets. Being in Japan and successfully competing with the kaisha is probably the best assurance a Western company has that it will be prepared to compete with them in Western markets. In doing so the executives of the Western company will be very aware of the product offerings of the kaisha, how these are marketed, the characteristic price levels, and the anticipated technological developments.

If a company does not have an operation in Japan whose staff is providing intelligence on the activities of its Japanese competitors the obvious question is, "Where will the Japanese strike next?" This is a question many businessmen in manufacturing industries across the United States and Europe are asking today. Japanese competitors have overwhelmed a succession of competitors in manufacturing industries and yet many similar industries have so far emerged unscathed. How can executives determine in advance whether or not to expect trouble from a Japanese competitor?

Successful deep penetrations of U.S. and European markets by the Japanese have characteristic patterns. If executives carefully analyze these patterns in terms of their own businesses, the nature of the Japanese economic threat can be determined while there is time to respond, and before the initial protection of marketing and distribution barriers disappears. Several patterns have consistently characterized the Japanese penetration of Western markets. First, the product will have already been used in large volumes in Japan. Second, exports of the product accelerate only after domestic demand slows. The growth-oriented kaisha will quickly seek additional sales volume to offset maturing domestic business by expanding exports.

Japanese producers have been successful in the West where two additional factors have been present—factor cost advantage and a labor productivity advantage. The most common factor cost advantage is from Japanese wage rates. Although the average wages of employees in the Japanese manufacturing sector are now almost equivalent to Western averages, many sectors of the Western economies, such as steel and autos, have wages far higher than average and higher than is justified by the skill requirements. The Japanese also enjoy a steel cost advantage due to their large, integrated labor- and energy-efficient facilities. Western steel users are generally denied access to lower cost steel by a variety of schemes, including trigger price and quota mechanisms in the United States and protectionism in Europe. In a comparison of F.O.B. prices, those for Japanese steel are 25 to 30 percent lower than U.S. steel prices. For many types of machinery, ranging from machine tools, to autos, to bulldozers, lower steel costs handily give the Japanese a 5 percent cost advantage in finished product.

As for productivity, Japanese export competitors will usually be able to manufacture an equivalent or better product using fewer labor hours per unit than will the Western rival. This can be true despite economies of scale that may favor the Western producers. The advantage is not always attributable to higher levels of investment and automation.

Among the Japanese advantages outlined, productivity is often the most important. With rare exceptions the Japanese have laid claim to a significant share of U.S. and European markets for manufactured goods—from autos to pianos—after they have first achieved a substantial productivity advantage over Westerners. The converse is also true: where the Japanese have not been able to achieve a productivity advantage, their share of Western markets has been low.

In the past few years, the Western reaction to reports of startling differences in productivity has gone through several stages. The first was disbelief, followed by glorification of Japanese management methods and the mysteries of Japanese culture. As more has been learned about differences in Japanese labor productivity, several facts have surfaced that make the productivity advantage both less alarming and more crucial to understand.

First is the realization that high productivity in Japan is limited to certain types of manufacturing processes. For example, in automobile manufacture, Japanese workers in the stamping and assembly plants are twice as productive as U.S. workers; in engine and transmission plants, they are 50 percent more productive; and in iron foundries, only 20 percent more productive. The same pattern can be seen in manufacturing processes for construction equipment, lift trucks, and musical instruments. The Japanese labor productivity advantage is enormous in high volume assembly processes where hundreds, even thousands, of interdependent steps must be coordinated. In simpler processes, such as a foundry, where perhaps thirty operational steps are required, the Japanese advantage is slight, and sometimes non-existent.

In process industries such as paper, chemicals, and metal refining, Japanese labor productivity in comparable plants is no better than can be found in Western plants. The same is true of other simple manufacturing. In other sectors as well, despite all that is said about management style and organizational effectiveness, Japanese organizations in such fields as services and distribution have low levels of productivity.

The increase of the Japanese productivity advantage with increasing complexity of the manufacturing process can be seen in figure 3–2. As the number of steps in the manufacturing process increases, the ratio of total factory labor content of the U.S. factories increases relative to the Japanese factory. Whereas the best U.S. and Japanese factories in the paper industry require about the same amount of direct and indirect labor per unit of output, U.S. factories manufacturing complex products like automobiles require twice as many factory labor hours per unit as do Japanese factories.

Higher labor productivity in complex manufacturing has

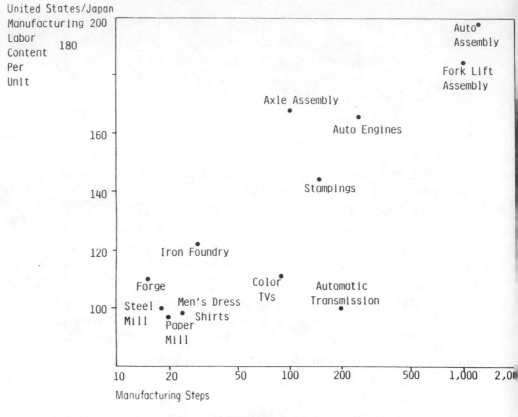

FIGURE 3–2

Manufacturing Productivity in Japan and the United States

NOTE: As the number of steps in manufacture increases, the ratio of total factory labor content per unit of output of U.S. factories increases relative to Japanese factories.

only recently been achieved by Japanese firms. For example, in construction equipment manufacturing, in 1976 Caterpillar led Komatsu in labor productivity. By 1982, Komatsu had achieved a 50 percent labor productivity advantage despite continuing improvements by Caterpillar. Similar rapid, quantum leaps in productivity can be seen at other Japanese manufacturers where the manufacturing processes also require the coordination of a large number of operations. These leaps in productivity have followed extensive changes in the manufacturing system.

The Japanese attain their productivity advantages in both obvious and subtle ways. Obvious ways include heavier investments in capital equipment, product designs that are easier to manufacture, and more focused factories. In extreme situations these alone can result in productivity advantages of 20 to 30 percent. More subtly, in the last five years many Japanese manufacturers have modified their production process from batch and semicontinuous processing to near continuous processing. This has been implemented through "just-in-time" scheduling (discussed in chapter 5), different manning configurations, changes in material flows, and related techniques. These techniques are often described as inventory reducers and quality improvers; yet they are far more. Plants with these manufacturing systems require less labor to operate even when the product variety is greater. Much of the Japanese productivity advantage in high coordination manufacturing operations can be attributed to these systems. The opportunity for the Japanese to achieve a productivity advantage in simple or continuous processes is limited because the coordination of operations is much simpler, involves balancing machinery rather than people, and does not change many times each day as the production mix changes.

The Japanese penetration of world markets has been greatest for products that have production processes with many steps. The Japanese manufacturers' share of world production has been highest for products such as bulldozers, automobiles, watches, cameras, trucks, pianos, and consumer electronics. The Japanese share of world production for these products is substantially higher than Japan's share of world gross national product would suggest it should be. Furthermore, the Japanese production share in these products is increasing. For products with comparatively simple manufacturing processes such as paper, garments, and bulk chemicals, the Japanese world production share is less than suggested by the world share of Japan's economy and the world production share of the Japanese manufacturers of these products is declining.

In sum, increased competition in Western markets from the Japanese can be expected when

- The product is produced in large volumes in Japan
- Japanese demand for the product is stagnant or declining
- The Japanese have a factor cost advantage
- The Japanese have a labor productivity advantage

If few of these apply to a particular Western business the probability of the Japanese making a significant penetration of a Western market is small. The Japanese aerospace threat, for example, is more imagined than real. The demand for aircraft in Japan is low, Japanese labor and material costs are for the most part equal to those of the Western competitors, and the existing Japanese manufacturers have labor productivity levels that are equal to or lower than Western levels. Indeed, in the case of helicopters, even though there is strong domestic demand—the Japanese civilian fleet is the third largest in the world—Japanese domestic demand met by imports has increased steadily from about 30 percent fifteen years ago to almost 80 percent today. The Japanese manufacturers are higher cost producers than their Western competitors.

If, for a particular business, the Japanese demand for product is large, growth of demand is stagnant or declining, and the Japanese have either a factor cost advantage, *or* a labor productivity advantage, the chance that the business will be successfully penetrated by the Japanese is moderate. In situations such as this the cost advantage of the Japanese may be substantial, but often it is not enough to overcome the marketing, distribution, and service cost advantages of the established Western competitors in their home markets. Products in this group include electric typewriters, consumer appliances, small and medium horsepower diesel engines, fractional and medium horsepower electric motors, vacuum cleaners, and unitary airconditioners.

Fortunately, U.S. and European companies manufacturing products similar to those just described have the opportunity—and the time, provided by home market strengths—to adjust their operations and investments to counter a Japanese threat. Products can be cost reduced and alternatives with fewer features can be developed to protect the low end of the range of offerings. Distribution can be streamlined and new channels that might be exploited by Japanese entrants can be covered with special products. Although options for responding exist in the type of businesses vulnerable to Japanese competition, actions must be taken before the kaisha build a strong enough position to begin eroding the home market strengths of the Western competitors.

For Western companies in businesses where the kaisha have a large but declining Japanese market, factor cost advantages, *and* labor productivity advantages there is virtually no time available to respond. Currently the most impressive example of this is in the medium- and heavy-duty truck industry. These large trucks are fairly complex to manufacture and the Japanese market is large but stagnant. Japanese truck manufacturers have almost the same labor and steel cost advantages that Japanese auto manufacturers enjoy over their Western counterparts. In addition, Japanese truck manufacturers are far more productive than U.S. and European manufacturers.

Evidence of the magnitude of the potential problem is alarming. Street prices for medium-duty trucks in Japan are 40 to 50 percent lower than American street prices for comparably sized trucks. Today's distribution and service strengths of U.S. truck manufacturers are not likely to withstand the pressure of these price differences for any length of time. Already Japanese truck producers are increasing their exports to the United States at rates that surprise almost all industry experts. Other products in similar situations to that of Western trucks include medium-size agricultural tractors, machine tools, large electric motors, buses, and subway cars.

The patterns described here by no means exhaust the topic, but they are applicable to many examples of significant market penetrations by the Japanese in Europe and in the United States. Exceptions exist. In recent years penetrations for products not completely fitting these patterns include typewriters, facsimiles, video cassette recorders, and 32/64 K RAM semiconductors. There is no significant demand in Japan for Western-style typewriters. Japanese domestic demand for facsimiles, VCRs, and 32/64 K RAMs has not slowed, yet even so, exports are growing rapidly. In each of these examples, even though the patterns described are not met, the Japanese are benefiting from the successes of earlier penetrations that completely fit the patterns. Brother took its typewriters to the same distribution channels that had been buying its sewing machines. The customers buying the Japanese VCRs and 32/64 K RAMs had previously purchased Japanese televisions and 16 K RAMs.

The patterns characteristic of deep penetrations of Western

markets by the kaisha are relevant today. Realistically, though, they can be expected to change. The kaisha, like Western companies, are human-based organizations and humans learn from their successes and failures. And as they learn they change their ways. The nature and the history of development of the Japanese competitors suggest that they learn very quickly and can change just as quickly. Well-regarded companies such as IBM, Texas Instruments, Eastman Kodak, DEC, and Merck have concluded that their Japanese markets and competitors require significant attention. These companies are building large organizations not only to sell in Japan but to understand the kaisha as competitors.

4

PURSUIT OF COMPETITIVE
ADVANTAGE IN
MANUFACTURING COMPETITION

IN the winter of 1980, a Western manufacturer bid on a large construction equipment contract in Malaysia. It lost. The winning bid, submitted by Komatsu, was about 30 percent less. Throughout Asia, the Western manufacturer was being consistently underbid by Komatsu by about 25 to 30 percent. To match these price levels, the Western manufacturer would have had to sell below its cash cost. The experience of this earth moving equipment manufacturer is not unique. Throughout the world, many Western manufacturers of pumps, electrical equipment, forklift trucks, and automobiles and other products are encountering kaisha which are consistently underpricing them by 25 to 30 percent for equivalent products.

Understandably, the reactions of European and U.S. businessmen to these low prices can be quite emotional. There are charges of "kamikaze bidding," "pricing below costs," "no understanding of the need for profit," "focusing on a market until all competitors have been driven to the wall," and "predatory and not competitive in the sense understood in the West."

Recently, the British Electrical and Allied Manufacturers Association reported that the "militant trading methods [of the Japanese] and [their] corporate economic strategy are far removed from the conditions under which her Western trading partners operate." Japanese manufacturers were identified as unique and diabolic in their ability "to mount highly aggressive and concentrated attacks on specific sectors of industry without any consideration whatsoever for the impact of such actions on [other] producer nations."[1] The report cites many examples in worldwide markets where the Japanese competitors are taking most of the new orders for electrical products by pricing more than a third lower than European manufacturers—sometimes below the Europeans' material costs.

Calmer discussions of the differences in Western and Japanese prices are focused on differences in manufacturing costs, but even these tend to emphasize advantages for the Japanese that are considered to be unfair or unequal. For example, estimates of the Japanese landed cost advantage in small cars range from $1,200 to $2,200 on a vehicle priced around $6,500 in the U.S. market. Spokesmen for Ford and Chrysler, quoted widely in the American and Japanese press, talk of "uneven playing fields" caused by an "undervalued" yen or differences in the national income and sales tax structures that favor Japanese exporters.[2] These differences are thought to account for about a third of the Japanese cost advantage. The remaining cost advantage is generally believed to be equally caused by higher U.S. wage and benefits and higher labor productivity in Japanese factories.

Explanations of the cause of the differences in labor costs and productivities sometimes become extreme. Lane Kirkland, former president of the United Auto Workers Union, has observed that the Japanese auto worker does not have the standard of living he deserves and that the Japanese auto companies should immediately raise their wages by a substantial amount. Anyone who has lived in Japan will no doubt be struck by the absurdity of this observation given the high levels of income, health, home ownership, and savings rates of the Japanese.

At the core of this sometimes chaotic debate is a general consensus that the Japanese worker is usually more productive

1. G. Bownas, "Japanese Competition: A Trading Strategy," paper prepared for the British Electrical and Allied Manufacturers Association, April 1981, pp. 1–3.
2. Lee Iacocca, *Iacocca: An Autobiography* (New York: Bantam Books, 1984), pp. 316–18.

than his Western counterpart. The superior productivity of the Japanese is often attributed to the style of Japanese management. William Ouchi, in his book *Theory Z,*[3] claims that the secret of Japanese success is their special way of managing people. The Japanese management style is described as having a focus on a strong company philosophy, consensus decision making, long-range staff development, and a distinct corporate culture. Lower turnover, increased job commitment, and dramatically higher productivity are believed to be the result. The explicit quantification of the relationships between cause (management style) and effect (high productivity) are gently sidestepped.

There are, of course, elements of truth in each of these explanations of the sources of Japanese cost and productivity advantages. Nevertheless, they offer little direction to the executives of a company embroiled in competition with a low cost, highly productive Japanese manufacturer. If the sources of the Japanese competitive advantage are not identified or quantified, how can difficult and expensive changes in organization, production systems, and corporate style be made with any assurance of success?

Identifying and quantifying the sources of a Japanese pricing advantage are tasks that are unique to each product, market, and set of companies involved. The sources of advantage are different today than in the past and will be different in the future. They change over time, as do those kaisha who are the leading exporters of Japan. Since the end of World War II, the primary source of competitive advantage exploited by Japan's leading international kaisha has changed four times. First, the primary source of advantage was low wage rates, then high-volume large-scale facilities, then focused production. Today, the emerging source of competitive advantage is high flexibility. In some businesses, such as automobiles, trucks, and construction equipment, the kaisha will benefit from advantages from all four sources. For others, such as consumer electronics and appliances, the Japanese benefit principally from one source—high flexibility.

3. William Ouchi, *Theory Z* (Reading, Mass.: Addison Wesley, 1982).

Low Wages as an Advantage

At the close of World War II, Japan's economy was virtually destroyed. The currency of the defeated nation was backed with no economic vitality and was worthless. The exchange rate of the Japanese yen (¥) was reduced from prewar levels of about 4 yen to the dollar to 360 yen to the dollar and 1,000 yen to the British pound.[4] This was a reduction of 98.8 percent of the prewar exchange levels and resulted in high inflation and a severe depression of wage rates and the standard of living of the Japanese—but not of their skill levels.

Japanese average labor rates at the postwar exchange rate were about one-fourth of U.S. labor rates. Large Japanese companies and entrepreneurs quickly took advantage of this and began to manufacture labor-intensive products requiring low and moderate levels of manual skills. Good examples of the industries involved were textile weaving, garment manufacturing, and shipbuilding.

The Japanese textile and shipbuilding industries grew rapidly. Their low manufacturing costs enabled them to export their products to those countries in the world having stronger economies and higher standards of living than Japan. In the 1950s, exports of textile products and ships grew in real terms at an average rate of 13 percent per year, and at their peak in the late 1950s constituted almost half of all Japanese exports.

The Japanese steel industry also emerged as a growing export industry in the 1950s. Nearly all of the Japanese steel-making capacity survived the war. The steel mills had been taken off the list of strategic bombing targets because of the effectiveness of the blockade of ore and coal shipments by U.S. submarine forces. The steel industry directly benefited from low labor rates in Japan and the rapid growth of the Japanese economy. Production grew at an average rate of 20 percent per year and exports at 28 percent per year through the 1950s.

The rapid development of the steel industry in Japan was not encouraged by the Japanese government to exploit low

4. Sidney E. Rolfe and Jame L. Burtle, *The Great Wheel: The World Monetary System* (New York: McGraw-Hill, 1975), p. 68.

wage rates but to provide an engine to pull the rest of the Japanese economy into the twentieth century. This was evident in a 1970 speech by Yoshihisa Ojimi, Vice Minister of MITI, presented to the Organization of Economic Cooperation and Development (OECD) Industrial Committee in Tokyo:[5]

> There was a great outgrowth of industries that depended on low wage labor during the pre-war period and the post-war period of transition when Japan was plagued by shortages in capital. At the same time, these industries enjoyed an advantage from the viewpoint of the theory of comparative advantage. They manufactured and exported masses of cheap articles before the war. After the war, too, Japan's first exports consisted of such things as toys and other miscellaneous merchandise and low-quality textile products.
>
> Should Japan have entrusted its future to the development of those industries characterized by the intensive use of labor? That would perhaps be a rational choice for a country with only 5 or 10 million people, but Japan has 102 million people. If Japan had adopted the simple doctrine of free trade and chosen to specialize in this kind of industry, it would have sentenced its population to the Asian pattern of stagnation and poverty. Japan would have remained a weak link in the free world, thereby becoming a problem area in the Far East.
>
> The Ministry of International Trade and Industry [MITI] decided instead to promote heavy industries that require intensive employment of capital and technology, industries such as steel, oil refining, petrochemicals, automobiles, aircraft, all sorts of industrial machinery, and electronics, including electronic computers. In terms of the comparative cost of production, these industries should be the most inappropriate for Japan. From a short-run, static viewpoint, promoting their development would seem to conflict with economic rationalism, but from a long-range viewpoint, these are precisely the industries where the income elasticity of demand is high, technological progress is rapid, and labor productivity rises fast. Without such industries it would have been extremely difficult to employ a population of 100 million and raise their standard of living to that of Europe and

5. Yoshihisa Ojimi, Vice Minister, MITI, Speech delivered to OECD Industrial Committee, 24 June 1970, p. 24. Translated and published in 1971 by Boston Consulting Group, Tokyo, Japan.

America. Logical or not, Japan had to have these heavy and chemical industries.

The participants of the Japanese steel industries received direct and indirect support from the Japanese government to encourage their growth. Capital was provided by the Japan Development Bank. The companies were granted access to special import and export exchange rates, and scarce foreign currency was made available for the purchase of materials and equipment.

As the Japanese economy recovered and productivity increased, the standard of living rose rapidly. During the 1950s wage rates almost doubled and, in the 1960s, almost tripled. With the exchange rate fixed through this period at 360 yen to the U.S. dollar, these increases negatively affected the manufacturing costs of the Japanese exporters. Many companies in Japan's leading export industries began to suffer a decline both in their international competitiveness and in their levels of employment.

The Japanese textile industry was particularly hard hit by the increase in Japanese wage rates. From 1960 through 1980, exports of cotton and cotton goods fell over 70 percent and imports to Japan approached 40 percent of domestic consumption. Employment in the silk, spinning, twisting, weaving, knitting, and dyeing mills fell more than 30 percent.

Scale as an Advantage

Substituting capital for labor is the underpinning of strategies based on "scale." In scale-based strategies, size is the objective. The strongest competitor in an industry can invest in the newest, most efficient equipment and can amortize the fixed costs of research, development, sales, and administration over its large volumes. The larger the size, or scale, of a company, the lower its costs and the greater its competitive advantage.

Under the pressure of rapidly increasing wage rates, many Japanese companies attempted to substitute machinery for labor. For some types of manufacturing processes, such as apparel manufacturing, the potential for substitution was limited. In the 1960s the output of cutting and sewing machines was still a direct function of the skill level of the people operating the equipment. Japanese garment manufacturers became increasingly less competitive in international markets, and export volume stagnated and eventually declined.

The Japanese shipbuilding companies were also pressured by the increases in their labor costs, but they were able to avoid the fate of the apparel manufacturers by investing heavily in their shipyards to maintain their growth and to ensure their continued worldwide competitiveness. These investments took two forms: raising the capital intensity of their manufacturing processes and developing ship designs that could be produced at low cost. The Japanese optimized their ship designs for low-cost production by developing standardized, modular designs. These designs could be manufactured in almost a continuous fashion with automatic and semiautomatic fabrication equipment.

The standardized designs as manufactured by the Japanese were readily accepted by Western ship operators. Despite rapidly escalating wage rates, the Japanese shipbuilding industry boomed, and from the mid-1960s until the early 1970s the industry's output grew over 20 percent per year. At its peak in 1974, the Japanese shipbuilding industry launched over 50 percent of all gross tonnage launched worldwide.

But in 1975 the Japanese shipbuilding industry experienced a severe slump which was initiated by overbuilding and later aggravated by severe price competition from companies in the Republic of Korea. With competition from lower-wage-rate countries, the future of Japanese shipbuilding became increasingly bleak. The industry was following the pattern of the textile industry with exports and employment falling almost as fast as they once grew.

The Japanese steel companies increased the scale of their facilities to preserve and increase competitive advantage. The industry was also experiencing a dramatic increase in labor rates. From 1957 to 1975 its labor cost per labor hour increased over 800 percent, while the comparable cost increase in the U.S.

was only 245 percent. The early advantage the industry had obtained from low labor costs was rapidly disappearing.

Companies in the Japanese steel industry were ruthless in their pursuit of cost reduction opportunities in an effort to maintain their growth. From 1951 to 1971, these companies built twelve steelworks that were integrated from blast furnaces through finishing mills. At the time of construction, each was the largest—or very nearly—of its kind. In the United States only two integrated steelworks have been built since 1951, and ten of the new Japanese facilities are larger (table 4–1). The two U.S. integrated steelworks represent only 5 percent of the raw steel capacity of the United States. In Japan, the twelve steelworks have over 75 percent of all of Japan's production.

The Japanese steel companies view steel production as a system of activities requiring careful integration to achieve the lowest costs. The Japanese built their integrated steelworks at deep water ports. One of the newest mills, Nippon Kokan Ohgishima Works, was built in 1975 on a manmade island. Bulk carriers bring ore and coal from Japanese-built ports in countries like Australia and deliver them to one end of the mill. At the other end of the mill, finished product is loaded directly

TABLE 4–1

Japan Versus the United States: Integrated Steelworks
(Constructed after World War II)

		Current Capacity (per 1,000 metric tons)
Japan		
1951	Kawasaki/Chiba	6
1958	Nippon Steel/Nagoya	7
1959	Nippon Steel/Yawata	12
1960	Sumitomo/Wakayama	9
1961	Kawasaki/Mizushima	10
1961	Nippon Steel/Sakai	4
1965	N. Kokan/Fukuyama	16
1965	Nippon Steel/Kimitsu	14
1967	Sumitomo/Kashima	15
1968	Kobe/Kakogawa	10
1971	Nippon Steel/Oita	12
1975	Nippon Kokan/Ohgishima	20
United States		
1952	United States Steel/Fairless	5
1968	Bethlehem/Burns Harbor	6

onto other bulk carriers. Innovations in mill siting and bulk fleet designs have enabled the Japanese steel producers to reduce the cost of transporting iron ore from Australia and Brazil to Japan to $3.50 per ton in 1973. In 1973, Upper Minnesota iron ore cost $3.50 per ton to ship to Chicago and $6.50 per ton to ship to Pittsburgh.

Contrary to the conventional wisdom in the West, and in Japan, that Japan is handicapped by its lack of natural resources, the Japanese steel industry actually benefited by not having large domestic supplies of coal and ore. The Japanese companies were forced to search the world for the lowest cost sources of supply. By contrast, the U.S. and German steel industries have self-inflicted handicaps by virtue of their heavy investment in high-cost domestic sources of supply and inland plant locations. As the Japanese have shown in a modern world of free trade, a shortage of resources does not necessarily mean that a country's population must remain impoverished.

The Japanese have equipped their new facilities and revamped their old ones with the most efficient equipment available. In the late 1950s, both U.S. and Japanese companies were building high-efficiency blast furnaces with inner volumes of 2,000 cubic meters. A decade later, the Japanese were building blast furnaces with inner volumes of over 5,000 cubic meters, while the new blast furnaces of U.S. companies had inner volumes of less than 4,000 cubic meters, and not very many of them. In 1982, 60 percent of the capacity of the installed blast furnaces in Japan had inner volumes of greater than 2,000 cubic meters. The comparable figure for the U.S. steel industry is less than 10 percent.

The labor productivity advantage once held by U.S. producers over the Japanese has been dissipated. In the mid-1960s, the United States averaged 7 metric tons of production per 100 man hours compared to a little more than 2 tons for the Japanese industry. A decade later, the Japanese were producing 9.5 tons per 100 man hours compared to 8 tons for the U.S. industry. Despite wages that were increasing at a rate two-and-one-half times faster than U.S. wage rates, the Japanese labor cost advantage increased from about $45 to $74 per metric ton.

The U.S. steel industry has faced competitive price pressures from the Japanese steel industry since the early 1960s.

Initially, the principal source of the Japanese competitive advantage was low labor costs because of its comparatively low wage rates. Today, the U.S. steel industry is still facing pressure from the Japanese because of the combination of low wage rates and high efficiencies of the large-scale Japanese steel industry. Interestingly, although the Japanese wage rates in the steel industry are about half of those in the U.S. steel industry, a Japanese steel worker earns about the same as the average of all U.S. manufacturing employees.

Both the U.S. and Japanese steel industries were affected by the rapid rise of energy costs in the 1970s. The Japanese responded with heavy investments in energy cost-reducing improvements. They have increased the use of continuous casters that directly connect the blast furnaces to the hot mills, saving enormous amounts of energy. Japanese use of continuous casters increased from 26 percent of total casting capacity in 1974 to almost 80 percent in 1980. The U.S. industry has increased its use of continuous casters from 8 percent of total capacity to 20 percent over the same period of time. In addition, the Japanese industry has reduced its cost dependence on oil from about 10 percent in 1970 to about 1 percent in 1981. Today, the industry uses mostly coke and is very efficient in its coke consumption. The Japanese industry consumes about 25 percent less coke per ton of pig iron produced than does the U.S. industry.

The competitive advantages these improvements brought have enabled the Japanese to become major exporters to the U.S. market. In the 1960s the average F.O.B. export prices of the Japanese were 15 to 40 percent lower than those of U.S. producers, and the Japanese producers rapidly penetrated the U.S. market. Since 1967, the U.S. steel industry has sought to blunt the competitive advantage of the Japanese through a variety of mechanisms, including "voluntary quotas" and trigger price mechanisms. These schemes were conceived to give the U.S. steel industry time to improve their costs, principally through modernization programs. As discussed, the U.S. industry has not modernized in any significant way, and the result has been increased prices for U.S. consumers of steel products (see figure 4–1).

The composite price per ton of U.S. steel in inflation adjusted dollars rose steadily from about $65 at the end of World War II to over $100 in 1957. This coincides with the period of rapid wage escalation in the industry. In 1957, imports principally from Japan began to increase rapidly. This placed pressure on the U.S. price structure, and the composite price fell steadily until 1967. In 1967, after Japanese imports had taken about 15 percent of the U.S. market, the U.S. steel industry was able to convince the U.S. government to negotiate "voluntary quotas" with the Japanese government. The share of the U.S. market of Japanese imports of certain categories of steel was frozen. The quotas were to be in force while the U.S. industry modernized. Instead of modernizing and reducing costs and prices to consumers, the U.S. steel industry stalled. This has resulted in a continuing cycle of increased prices, increased penetration by the Japanese in non-restricted product categories, and further import barriers and hurdles.

Today, for a wide variety of steel products, a Japanese manufacturer of steel products can buy Japanese steel at prices ranging from 15 to 30 percent lower, depending on the gauge, than his American counterpart can buy it in the United States. This handily gives the Japanese manufacturer a cost advantage

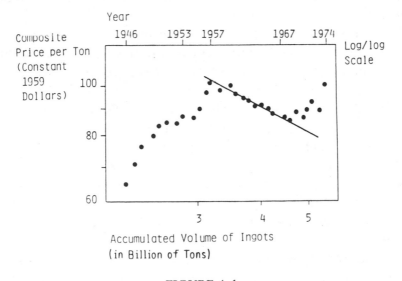

FIGURE 4–1

Price Experience Curve
U.S. Steel Industry

of 5 to 8 percent less over his U.S. competitor for products such as forklift trucks, construction equipment, automobiles, and ball bearings. Instead of importing steel in large volumes, the U.S. economy is importing the finished product and for every one employee in the steel industry that is protected, the jobs of 5 employees in other industries are placed at risk.

Not all Japanese companies have built large volume facilities that are competitive in world markets. The petroleum, petrochemical, and aluminum smelting industries in Japan are on the troubled industry list of MITI, which is actively managing the reduction of the capacities in these industries. The troubles of these industries are most often linked to the increase in energy costs in Japan throughout the 1970s. Yet even without increased energy costs, the companies in these industries would most likely still be in trouble. Their capacities per installation are far smaller and less cost effective than the capacities of the leading non-Japanese companies located outside of Japan. For example, the largest aluminum smelters in Japan are only about half the size of the largest in North America. In Japan, there are about twenty producers of polyvinylchloride (PVC) and thirty of caustic soda. Most western economies have less than five producers of each. The size of these facilities is far smaller than the facilities of the U.S. industries.

The existence of many sub-scale producers of aluminum, PVC, and caustic soda underscores two problems in Japan that are often overlooked. First, the structure of these industries is, in large part, the result of the industrial policies of MITI in the 1950s. A critical element of MITI's industrial development policies during this period was its prevention of domination by large competitors. The ministry insisted that all competitors expand their facilities at roughly comparable rates; no producer could preempt the growth of its competitors by building large-scale, low-cost facilities. The participants in the PVC and caustic soda industries were consequently saddled with high-cost, small-scale facilities.

The second problem is the inability of suffering Japanese industries to restructure themselves through mergers and acquisitions. In Japan, companies are not often acquired or merged, principally because the full consent of management must be legally obtained. The management of the vanquished firm is not readily going to give its consent to being acquired and to then face early retirement. However, merging the companies in Japan's troubled industries could close inefficient facilities and could consolidate production in larger scale, higher cost competitive facilities. Indeed, even within large industrial groups like Mitsubishi, the managements of the various companies operating PVC plants and fertilizer facilities (another industry on MITI's troubled industry list) have not been able to agree on and execute a consolidation plan.

Focused Manufacturing as an Advantage

In the early 1970s, one Western manufacturer of forklift trucks suffered intense price competition from Toyota in certain countries in Europe. Despite the fact that this manufacturer was among the world's largest producers of forklift trucks, the much smaller Toyota was still selling at prices that were approaching the Western manufacturer's material costs. Toyota did not seem to be selling the product below cost, as home market prices were equal to or lower than European prices. How could such a small company be so price competitive?

Until the 1970s, Japan has had a relatively small economy filled with companies that are small by United States and European standards. Compared to large companies, small companies typically have fewer resources to apply to their businesses, and this disadvantage results in smaller product development programs, fewer products offered, limited geographical penetration, and shortages of cash and people. To survive and prosper, smaller companies must focus their strengths on those activities that provide the most opportunities to compete successfully against larger companies.

Many of the Japanese manufacturers who began exporting from Japan in the late 1960s and early 1970s found their Western competitors to have larger, broader product lines and to be firmly entrenched in their home markets. Competing head-on with these companies required more resources than were available to the Japanese. The alternative possibilities were to focus on market niches for which there were no Western products or to focus all their available resources on those portions of the product line where market demand was the greatest and access to the customers was the easiest.

By focusing, Japanese manufacturers were able to achieve total costs that were lower than those of their Western competitors. These lower costs were used to undercut the prices of the Western competitors so that production volume could be expanded. The addition of volume caused costs to become even lower. The declining costs were then used to further reduce prices and expand volume or, if the opportunity existed, the savings were invested in expanding the product line.

Toyota followed this focusing strategy against the Western forklift truck manufacturer. In the early 1970s that manufacturer produced a broad line in a large factory in Europe which included about twenty distinctly different families of products. Toyota manufactured a comparatively narrow line of six families in its factory in Nagoya. Although Toyota was smaller on a worldwide basis than the Western competitor, these two factories were very nearly the same size at this time. Many other differences between the two companies existed, but the principal one was the level of complexity of their factories.

The challenge in manufacturing management has been to balance the desires of the production management to limit the variety of products produced with the desires of the marketing management to give customers whatever they want immediately. The balance cannot be achieved in isolation; it must reflect the approach and capabilities of competitors.

Increasing complexity is the bane of a factory manager's life. With increasing complexity comes an increased number of parts, greater material handlings and inventories, more diverse process flows, higher supervision requirements, an increase of errors and defects, and smaller batches produced in shorter runs. All of these factors increase aggravation and costs. No manager in his or her right mind, Japanese or Western, increases complexity without good reason. However, there are many good reasons for increasing complexity. Product lines are expanded to meet changes in consumer demand or to exploit a market niche where prices are higher or at least firmer. Many times, for products whose costs are principally material related, new products are introduced between existing products so as to reduce weight and material content and therefore costs.

Profit and cost reduction opportunities cause companies to increase gradually the complexity of their product offerings over time. Complexity can also be substantially increased when a new product line is introduced, but the older product line is continued for parts or to keep a valued customer. In the early stages of product line expansion, the savings from the product redesigns and from the incremental volume often offset the costs and aggravation of the factory's increased complexity. However, as the expansion continues, the factory becomes increasingly less efficient, more costly, and less profitable. Because most managerial and accounting systems are used as score cards rather than to demonstrate cause and effect, they are unlikely to show why the performance of the factory is deteriorating.

Forklift truck manufacturing is very sensitive to changing levels of complexities. The process of manufacturing a forklift truck is straightforward, consisting of metal plate and bar cutting, forming, welding, subassembly and assembly, painting, and testing. There is surprisingly little direct labor involved, as shown in table 4–2.

Direct labor—the people doing the cutting, welding, assembly, and painting—constitutes only 4 percent of the total cost of the truck. Overhead costs, which are mostly material handlers, production schedulers, expediters, maintenance people, and the like, combined with the fixed costs of plant and equipment, add more than five times the cost of direct labor to the process.

Increasing complexity significantly affects the costs of per-

TABLE 4–2

*Cost Structure of Forklift Truck
Manufacturing in Europe*

Cost Element	% of Costs
Purchased Material	75
Direct Labor	4
Overhead	21
	100

forming the tasks required to manufacture a forklift truck. As complexity increases, direct labor must be redirected more frequently to changing tasks. Each change requires the workers to prepare or setup for the new tasks. These setups usually require a fixed amount of time to accomplish. These fixed amounts of time are costs. People, sometimes specialists, are required to change tooling and other parts of the process. While changeovers are being executed, men and machines are idle.

Factory managers have a strong desire to avoid the nonproductive "down time" associated with a changeover. The longer a particular part can be machined or a vehicle can be assembled, the higher the output of the process, the greater the efficiency of the factory, and the lower the costs of the factory. For example, the larger the batch of product assembled, the lower the average setup cost per unit assembled. When setup hours per truck model were correlated with run lengths of the truck models, this effect was observed. For every doubling of the run length of a forklift truck model, the average setup hours and, hence, setup costs per truck assembled was reduced by 40 percent. Therefore, for factories of equal volume, the factory with fewer models will have longer run lengths, lower setup costs per truck assembled, and lower overall costs per forklift truck.

As factory complexity increases, greater overhead resources must be committed to ensure smooth operation. For example, the scheduling, material handling, and expediting efforts required to support a line on which only one product is assembled are significantly lower than the efforts required to support a line on which ten or twenty products are assembled. This is certainly true in the fabrication and assembly process characteristic of forklift truck manufacturing.

In figure 4–2, the effects of increasing product variety of fabrication and assembly lines on the support overheads can be seen for various assembly departments (A–H) in the forklift truck factory. The line represented by circle H is an engine assembly line that is relatively more focused than the assembly line represented by circle C, a final vehicle assembly line. The area of each circle is proportional to the total direct labor hours per year for this process step. For every 100 direct labor hours consumed on assembly line H, 8 hours of overhead support are required to ensure smooth operation. By contrast, for every 100 hours of direct labor hours consumed on assembly line C, 52 hours of overhead support are required.

The more variety of product fabricated or assembled on a line, the less focused, the more difficult to manage, and the greater the required overhead support will be. By inference, the more products a factory manufactures, the less focused, the greater the overhead requirements and costs, and the higher its total production costs will be.

A comparison of the many factories operated by the Western forklift truck manufacturer supports this observation (see

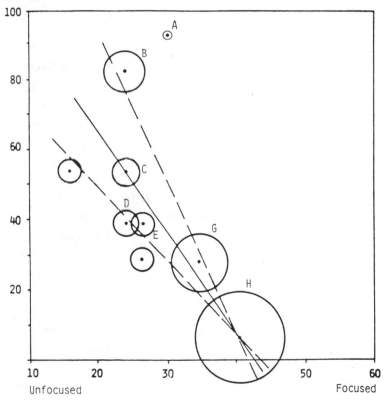

FIGURE 4–2

Impact of Fabrication and Assembly Line Focus on Overhead Costs

NOTE: The focus of assembly lines is measured by weighted average volume per model as a percentage of total volume of the line. The greater the degree of focus of an assembly line, the lower the required overhead costs.

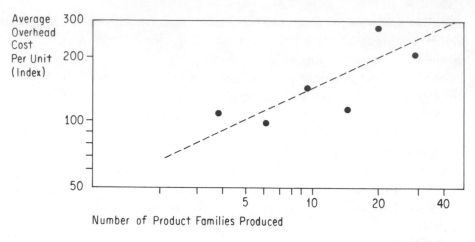

FIGURE 4–3

Effect of Product Line Variety on Overhead Cost per Unit

figure 4–3). At the time, the company had six factories manufacturing from three to twenty-eight families of forklift trucks. This comparison is crude because some differences in volume and in vertical integration exist, but the effect of increasing product variety in a factory can be clearly observed. As the number of product families in a factory increases, so does the average overhead cost per unit produced. For every doubling of the number of families produced in a factory, overhead costs per unit can be expected to increase about 30 to 40 percent.

Material costs are also affected by increasing product line variety. As the average purchasing volume per part number or commodity doubles, the cost per unit purchased tends to decrease by about 5 to 10 percent. This is principally caused by the increased yield and the improved economics of suppliers as a result of increased purchase volumes per order. Often, as is the case in forklift manufacturing, the effect on the supplier of increasing purchasing volumes is an increase in the production batch size of a large order while all the benefits observed in the forklift factory are accrued in the suppliers' factories.

The potential cost advantage to Toyota of focusing its Nagoya factory in the early 1970s on six product families rather than on twenty, as was the case of the Western manufacturer, is shown in table 4–3. The costs of the Toyota manufacturing process are estimated using the economic relationships observed in the factories of the Western forklift truck manufacturer. The material cost estimates reflect the probable effect of increased volumes per part number and commodity. Greater volumes per model and hence longer run lengths suggest that Toyota amortized setup costs over more units and had lower direct labor costs per unit. The more focused factory of Toyota implied simpler to manage fabrication and assembly lines, and as a consequence, lower overhead costs per unit.

The estimate of Toyota's total cost is very close to observed price levels in Europe and in Japan. Based only on the differences in factory complexity, Toyota is estimated to be able to manufacture a forklift truck for 21 percent lower cost than the European factory can. Labor costs, steel costs, and so forth, are all assumed for this analysis to be equal, though in reality they are not. Market prices of Toyota forklift trucks in Germany were 20 percent less than the prices of the forklift trucks from the European factory. Even with freight costs of about 2 to 4 percent of the truck cost, Toyota was able to undercut its European competitor.

Among the various responses to the Toyota challenge chosen by the Western manufacturer was focusing its European factory. From 1972 to 1975, the number of product families manufactured in this facility was reduced steadily from twenty to six. Total average cost per unit, after adjusting for the effects of inflation, declined by 18 percent. The predicted effect of reduced complexity and the actual result were quite close.

Strategies based on the cost advantages inherent in focused

TABLE 4–3

Effect of Focused Production on Competitive Costs for Forklift Truck Manufacturing
European cost = 100

	Western Factory (Europe)	Toyota
Number of Product Families	20	6
Cost Indices		
Materials	75	65
Direct labor	4	2
Overhead	21	14
Total cost	100	79
Observed Price Levels (Index)	100	80

factories have been used by many Japanese and Western companies. In the late 1960s, the companies in Japan's ball bearing industry mounted an assault on the ball bearing manufacturers of the United States and Europe. The leading Western competitors produced wide lines of ball bearings. The Japanese companies led by Koyo Seiko, Nippon Seiko (NSK), and Toyo Bearing focused on the high-volume segments of markets such as automobiles and produced a more limited line.

In 1971, SKF of Sweden and FAG of West Germany were among those Western companies producing the widest line of ball bearings. With 25,000 variants of ball bearings, these two companies manufactured about two-and-one-half times as many different ball bearings as the average major Japanese producers. The average sales per variant for FAG were less than one-fifth of the average for the Japanese, and SKF's sales per variant were less than one-half of the average for the Japanese. Even this measure overstates the comparative focus of the Japanese and the Europeans. The Swedish SKF, for example, had factories in all the major economies of Europe, and each factory produced almost the full line of ball bearings, thereby further reducing their volume per variant substantially. The effects of variety and focus are even more pronounced in the manufacture of ball bearings, and substantial cost savings are available to those competitors who focus and increase their volume per variant.

The Japanese focused not only their production but also their marketing efforts. Only the largest users of ball bearings, such as the automobile manufacturers, were pursued. Companies such as these were easily attracted by the low Japanese prices. However, rather than respond to the Japanese threat by focusing, these Western companies initially responded by adding additional variants to their line to serve special customer needs and to escape price competition in the high-volume segments of the ball bearing markets. The existing variants were not discontinued, thereby causing the complexities of their factories to increase as well as increasing marketing costs to serve more but smaller customers. Predictably, the manufacturing costs of the Western companies increased. These manufacturers attempted to recover their increased costs by increasing prices.

With increasing prices, more volume was lost to the Japanese, and the Western companies' costs were further increased (see table 4–4).

Both SKF and FAG were almost bankrupted by the Japanese competition, but SKF has managed to recover and is widely hailed in Europe as an example of repelling the Japanese through "good management." Not surprisingly, the essence of SKF's turnaround strategy was total rationalization of its production and marketing system by narrowing its product lines, closing factories, and focusing the remaining factories on those portions of the product lines in which each was most efficient.

In focused production, if the number of products manufactured is cut in half, total factory labor productivity will probably increase by more than 30 percent. Total costs, including materials, will fall by 17 percent, and break even as a percent of capacity will be reduced to about 60 percent of capacity. Some volume may be lost because of products that have been dropped, but most often this loss will be less than 20 percent of the previous volume. Generally, the increase in costs due to the loss in volume is offset by the increased efficiencies and lower costs resulting from the reduction in complexity. Volume loss is usually quickly recovered in the primary products that remain in production.

If the complexity of the product line manufactured is reduced again to one-quarter of its initial level, the effect on the key factory performance parameters is even more dramatic. Total factory labor productivity is improved by almost 75 percent, and total costs are reduced by 30 percent. Breakeven as a

TABLE 4–4
Production of Ball Bearings (1971)

	Average for Major Japanese Producers	Timken (U.S.)	SKF (Sweden)	FAG (Germany)
Number of Variants	10,000	12,500	25,000	25,000
Sales (millions of $)	1,417	820	1,492	671
Sales/Variant (in thousands of $)	141.7	65.6	59.7	26.8

NOTE: Ira C. Magaziner and Thomas M. Hout, *Japanese Industrial Policy* (London: Policy Studies Institute, 1980), p. 12.

percent of capacity is below 50 percent, assuming there are no changes in pricing.

The focus phenomenon is powerful if it is pursued aggressively. Lee Iacocca, president of the Chrysler Corporation, led a dramatic turnaround of his company with it. While his strategy had many different elements, a key element was the significant reduction of complexity at Chrysler. The product line was slashed from about seven basic car designs, or platforms, to two. Labor productivity is now said to have almost doubled, and breakeven (with prices being held up by import quotas) is said to be below 50 percent. Costs have been reduced, and the company's financial health has improved.

Competitive strategies based on focus can be risky. Although Chrysler has been spared bankruptcy, its existence is not assured. By focusing, Chrysler was able to bring its costs more in line with those of its competitors, but it did not obtain a cost advantage. Because of their larger size the U.S. and Japanese competitors can and do offer broader product lines at equal or better cost than Chrysler that appeal to more consumers than Chrysler's narrow line. More important, the broader lines enable the dealer networks of Chrysler's competitors to operate more efficiently than Chrysler's dealers, who have been forced to add the car lines of Chrysler's competitors to stay in business. One has only to look as far as the American Motors (AMC) Corporation to see the future of Chrysler. In an attempt to stay solvent, AMC substantially narrowed its product lines in the late 1960s and early 1970s. The focusing delayed insolvency, but recently the company has had large losses and only with the infusion of cash from Renault has it been able to stay afloat.

An often fatal response by Western manufacturers to a threat from a focused Japanese competitor is to offer new products. Typically, these new products will have more features and higher prices and are offered in addition to, rather than in place of, older products. The consequence of this move is an increase in factory complexity and, therefore, an increase in the overall costs of the operation. This effect is the reverse of when a factory is focused. As costs increase, the Western manufacturers find it necessary to raise prices. With increased prices, the Japanese are more able not only to penetrate the markets of the Western manufacturers but more able to increase the complexity of their own product offerings.

The phrase that best describes the competitive behavior of the Western company in this example is "segment retreat"—which can be a slow form of suicide. Triumph and Norton of the British motorcycle industry retreated from Honda. Today, General Motors appears to be retreating from the Japanese by concentrating its resources on large cars. Japanese companies under competitive pressure also practice segment retreat. As Hitachi Construction Equipment has offered larger and larger excavators to avoid competition with Komatsu, Komatsu has continued to increase the size of its largest excavators and to gain market share in all segments of the business.

Changing Sources of Advantage in the 1980s

Although today many leading kaisha manufacturers are smaller than their Western counterparts and are focused on narrower segments of demand, this is changing. While these kaisha are still smaller overall, they are increasing the variety of their product offerings, sometimes at a startling rate.

For most of the 1970s, the Japanese auto manufacturers each introduced new products at the fairly limited rate of about one, to one-and-one-half new vehicles per year. By the early 1980s, Nissan and Toyota had increased their rate of new introductions to almost five new vehicles per year, with Honda following suit. This was happening at a time when their major competitors in Europe and in the United States were trying to reduce variety of their product offerings and the frequency of new model introductions.

The rapid increase in the product variety of the kaisha is not limited to the automobile. Product variety has literally exploded for the Japanese manufacturers of trucks, audio equipment, air-conditioning equipment, home appliances, diesel engines, calculators, and more. In almost every case, their Western competitor counterparts are holding their product variety constant or are trying to reduce variety.

It is tempting to conclude that the Japanese who are recklessly increasing product variety will suffer from increased manufacturing costs accompanied by reduced competitiveness in Western markets. But this does not appear to be the case. For example, Hino, Japan's leading manufacturer of heavy trucks, has increased the number of trucks it offers by almost three times in the last ten years. The average production per model has fallen by almost four times. Yet, Hino's output per employee and per billion yen of assets has almost doubled. Hino's costs are going down, not up, with increasing product complexity. (The reason that Hino has been able to do this is the subject of the next chapter.)

The vision of the future of most kaisha manufacturers is one of increased product complexity. Product complexity has to be increased to hold existing customers and to attract new customers. The managements of Japan's kaisha have set their goals as increased flexibility, because with it comes increased capability to meet the demands of the market place. There will probably always be the Japanese factory that spits out, uninterrupted, 200,000 video cassette recorders a month, but more Japanese manufacturers are finding ways to produce smaller volumes of more varieties of product without the increase in costs so often observed in the past and still found in the West.

5

REVOLUTIONIZING

MANUFACTURING

COMPETITION

In 1975, Yanmar Diesel was in trouble. The Japanese economy was in its worst recession since before the beginning of the Korean War. Demand for Yanmar's diesel engines and farm equipment was severely depressed as were profits. The future of the company was in doubt. The management of Yanmar sought inspiration from the Toyota Motor Company. Toyota was caught in the same recession as Yanmar, but Toyota was profitable. Toyota management credited the efficiencies of its unique production system for enabling it to weather the recession. Yanmar began a crash program to convert to the production system of Toyota.

The results were stunning. Total factory labor productivity almost doubled from 1976 to 1981. The costs of most products declined, and for some parts costs were reduced 44 to 72 percent of what they were in 1976. Work-in-process inventories were reduced by 66 to 80 percent. The production volume required for the factory to breakeven fell from 80 percent of capacity to 50 percent.

These are remarkable improvements for a company that before the recession was already considered well run. The conventional understanding of competitive manufacturing economics suggests that for Yanmar to have achieved improvements of these magnitudes, production volume would have had to have been increased by more than three times or the variety of its product line reduced by 75 percent through focusing its factories.

But Yanmar had done neither. Volume increased, but far less than three times. More surprising, Yanmar did not sharply reduce the number of products it produced. Instead, the number of different engines manufactured in its main factory increased from about 250 in 1976 to over 900 in 1981—an increase of almost four times. Yanmar was able to strengthen its competitive advantage significantly without investing in larger volume facilities and without dramatically focusing its factories.

The production system adopted by Yanmar has many names including, simply, the Toyota Production System, but it is often called the *kanban* system, or the Just-In-Time system (JIT), because materials, parts, and components are produced and delivered just before they are needed. Each carry a small card, or *kanban* in Japanese, describing the part's origin, destination, identity, and the quantity required. The most obvious characteristic of the factories with the JIT system are their low level of inventories.

The JIT system is becoming an increasingly popular topic among European and American businessmen. As an inventory reduction system, JIT holds the promise of greatly reduced investments in inventories. Because of this appeal, many Western companies are experimenting with JIT. Suppliers are being asked to deliver more frequently, and in the case of General Motors, suppliers are being pressured to relocate their operations next to GM's main facilities.

Simply regarding JIT as an inventory reduction system is a serious underestimation of its significance. The JIT system changes the fundamental economics of manufacturing and, as a result, is upsetting the basis of competition in many industries. Japanese competitors who have adopted it, all else equal, can manufacture a product with only three men when U.S. and European competitors require four or five for the same task. If the Japanese competitors produce larger volumes or more limited product lines, their productivity advantages can be even greater.

The JIT system is the key to relieving the ever-present tension between the desires of the marketing organization and the manufacturing organization. The marketing organization seeks greater variety in the product line to pursue growth and higher margins. The manufacturing organization resists increasing variety because the complexity of the plant is compounded: run lengths shrink, inventories swell, and costs rise. But JIT sharply reduces the impact of product line diversity on production costs, thus enabling the marketing organization to obtain needed products at low incremental cost.

The competitive implications of increased variety at low cost can be enormous. Many kaisha have implemented JIT, and many Western manufacturers are feeling the pain of competing with Japanese companies that are taking advantage of its benefits. Western manufacturers of such products as autos, forklift trucks, power tools, motorcycles, airconditioning equipment, machine tools, outboard motors, and small appliances not only must meet increased price competition from the Japanese but also must face an increasing array of products. Usually the increase in variety comes at the same time that these Western manufacturers have been trying to reduce the diversity of their existing product offerings. Without an understanding of the Just-In-Time system, many Western companies with strong competitive positions will suffer a decline.

The Evolution of the Just-In-Time System

Toyota began development of the Just-In-Time system in the late 1930s and made substantial progress in its implementation in the 1950s and 1960s. During these years, Toyota produced fewer passenger cars than did its principal competitor, Nissan, and was less able to cost-effectively field a broad product line. Toyota's production system helped the company overcome the disadvantages inherent in its smaller size. Taiichi Ohno of Toyota is credited with developing the JIT system in the 1950s and 1960s. Mr. Ohno writes, "The Toyota production system was born out of the need to develop a system for manufacturing automobiles of many different kinds in small volumes with the same process."[1] In the 1950s, Toyota sought a way to produce greater varieties of automobiles without being smothered by increased costs.

As Toyota contemplated increasing the variety of automobiles manufactured with its factory system, productivity and inventory problems were encountered. With one model of automobile Toyota could run its factory very steadily. Production runs would be lengthy, productivity high, and inventories low. These are the virtues of a focused factory, and this is how Henry Ford ran the River Rouge factory in which the Model T was manufactured from 1908 to 1927. When additional models were introduced to the manufacturing process at Toyota, changeovers became necessary. During changeovers workers and machines were not producing autos, and increased management was required to ensure that they were carefully planned and executed quickly. While one model was being produced, inventories of other models and of parts for other models had to be maintained to meet demand until they could be produced again. Additional management was required to keep the inventories as low as possible without being caught out of stock. With increasing models came decreasing productivity, increased inventories, and higher costs.

The immediate objective of Mr. Ohno and his associates in the 1950s was to reduce the time required to change from the production of one part or model to another. If changeover time could be absolutely minimized, changeovers could be made more frequently. More models could be manufactured, run lengths could be shortened, inventories minimized, and workers would be idle for less time. The negative effects of increasing variety could be reduced.

The combined effect of significantly reduced changeover time on costs and on investments in inventory can be appreciated by its effect on economic order quantities. An economic order quantity is the quantity of production whose total cost per unit of production and of inventory handling and storage is at a minimum. A slow changeover process has high setup costs that factory managers try to absorb by producing as many units as possible before changing over again to another part. As

1. Taiichi Ohno, *Toyota Production System: Aiming at an Off-Scale Management* (Tokyo: Diamond, 1978), preface.

the run length increases, the average setup cost per unit in the run therefore declines, and the sum of setup cost and run cost declines. Typically, a process producing just one part will be producing quantities greater than that demanded and inventory will accumulate. As inventory accumulates, the time required to reduce it increases, and with this increase in holding time comes an increase in the average handling and storage cost per unit. When the decreasing setup and run cost per unit are added to the increasing handling and storage cost per unit, a run length can be determined for which the sum of these costs is a minimum (see figure 5–1).

Assume for the quick changeover process that the changeover time is instantaneous, and all setup costs are zero. The setup and run costs per unit are the same regardless of the run length. But because demand is unchanged, increasing run lengths will still result in the accumulation of inventory. When

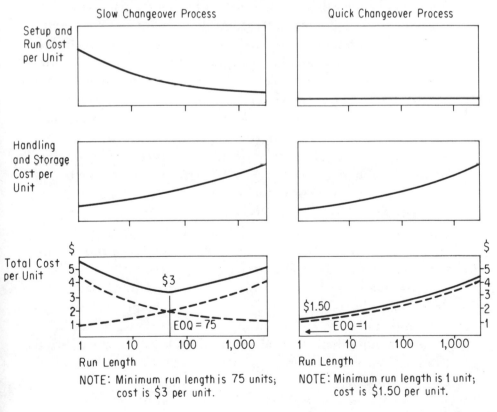

FIGURE 5–1

The Effect of Reducing Changeover Times on Economic Order Quantities

setup, run cost and handling and storage costs per unit are totaled for the quick changeover process, the lowest cost run length is one unit, and the average cost per unit is $1.50.

The implications of the differences between slow and quick changeover processes are important. The quick changeover process with shorter run lengths requires much lower inventories to operate. Furthermore, the quick changeover process produces at a lower cost than the slow changeover process. Therefore, if two factories have similar volumes and product mix, the factory with the fastest changeover process will have the lowest cost and the least inventories.

In the 1950s, the production engineers at Toyota concentrated on significantly reducing changeover times and run lengths in Toyota's factories. Toyota set one minute as a goal for the changeover of a machine from one part to any other part the machine was intended to produce. For machining operations, changeover times were reduced by investing in extra tooling and related equipment rather than in inventories. Extra machine components were purchased so that tools could be left set up to make specific parts. Jigs were fabricated so that the tools could be placed in or removed from machines quickly. The extra tools and jigs were moved from central tool bins to locations beside the machines in which they were to be used. The Japanese companies that have followed Toyota's example by adopting JIT have also first concentrated on reducing the time required to changeover their process from the manufacture of one product to another (table 5–1).

The reduction of run lengths made economic by quick setup times aggravates any existing material handling problems. In most factories, especially in the West, batches of products are moved through the various steps of production. Material handling is increased if the factory is organized by departments defined by the manufacturing technology employed, such as painting, stamping, flame cutting, grinding, welding, and machining. Components from all locations of the factory are carted from their previous storage location to a process department and then back to another storage location.

The amount of productive labor lost in material handling can be surprising. The management of a European construction

TABLE 5–1

Representative Reductions in Changeover Times

	Machine	Initial Setup Time (Hours)	New Setup Time (Minutes)	Implementation Time (Years)*
Toyota	Bolt maker	8	1	1
Mazda	Ring gear cutter	6.5	15	4
	Die casting machine	1.5	4	2
MHI	8-arbor boring machine	24	3	1
Yanmar	Aluminum die caster	2.1	8	2
	Cylinder block line	9.3	9	4
	Connecting rod line	2	9	4
	Crank shaft line	2	5	4

*The time required in some cases is overstated. Yanmar achieved reduction in setup times of 75 to 90 percent in less than two years for many of its processes.
SOURCE: Adapted from author interviews; Shigeo Shingo, *Study of Toyota's Production System from Industrial Engineering Viewpoint* (Tokyo: Japan Management Association, 1981), p. 64.

equipment manufacturer did not believe its material handling to be excessive because only 40 people out of the total work force of 1,000 were designated as material handlers. A careful analysis of the activities of factory workers in key departments, however, revealed a much different situation. In the chassis welding and fabrication department, only 50 percent of the workers' time was being spent actually working on the product. Twenty-five percent of their time was spent moving material into and out of their departments; another 25 percent of their time was spent changing over from the manufacture of one part to another. In a major subassembly department, 30 percent of the workers' time was consumed by material handling tasks. In reality, the true material handling force of this company was not 40 people as management believed, but more like 300 people.

A similar situation was observed in the factory of a U.S. hand tool manufacturer. The amount of workers' time spent actually manufacturing the product varied between 5 and 35 percent in the forging, machining, polishing, plating, and assembly departments. Between 40 and 50 percent of their remaining time was spent moving material into and out of their departments. The large proportion of time consumed by material handling was understandable given the tortuous path the product followed (figure 5–2). It was moved about from inventory holding point to inventory holding point, and its path crossed itself several times.

The Toyota engineers retained the benefits of shortened run lengths that would have otherwise been reduced by excessive material handling by drastically altering the layout of their factories to minimize the distances between processing steps. Departments based on manufacturing technologies were dismantled, and their machines were moved to newly created product departments. Great efforts were made to connect each of the subassembly and fabrication steps with the final assembly lines so that parts flowed quickly from one step to the next with limited intermediate storage. The output of each step was brought into balance, and the inventory holding points between steps were eliminated.

The inventory holding points so characteristic of factories organized by manufacturing process technologies consume considerable space. Indeed, some Western factories are better viewed as warehouses rather than factories. Many examples of factories exist in which the space dedicated to the storage of inventory and to passageways is more than 70 percent of the total space in the factory. Japanese factories using JIT often have

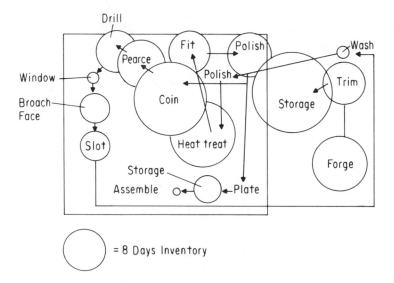

FIGURE 5–2

Simplified Manufacturing Flow—The tortuous path and inventory buildup of an adjustable wrench in a tool manufacturing factory

only one-third the floor space of a Western factory of comparable size.

Toyota further reduced inventory holding points and increased productivity by developing multimachine manning. In Toyota's past, and as it still is in most Western factories today, each machine was manned by at least one worker. The worker figuratively "waits" on the machine: bringing it its material; loading it; starting, watching, and stopping it; unloading it and being responsible for keeping the machine operating or stopping it if it begins to fail. If the worker is skilled (and lucky), management is rewarded with high machine output and utilization.

The objective of multimachine manning is not high machine utilization but high worker utilization. The machines are arranged in a "U" pattern (see figure 5–3). The machines are connected by roller conveyers to simplify material handling. Each of the workers is trained to operate several different machines. The training includes performing changeovers and providing simple maintenance. Each worker walks in a circular pattern completing tasks that include loading, starting, and unloading. The machines are rigged to stop automatically, and if a machine stops before the worker returns to it, it waits. The primary objective is to keep the worker busy. Of course, by varying the cycle times of the machines and the number of machines each worker operates, machine and worker utilization can each be maximized.

A multimachine-manned line is intended to machine many different parts in which each part has a similar geometry. An example would be the line that machines twelve varieties of crankshafts for 3, 4, 6, and 12 cylinders with three strokes. To accommodate this variety, the tooling must be easily and quickly changed. For ease of scheduling, each crankshaft must pass through the circuit in the same amount of time, and the line must always be operated at a constant speed.

Achieving a constant speed of operation for a wide variety of parts sometimes requires additional machines. As these are used only for certain parts, they become idle when the parts are not being run. To avoid the waste of idle machines, the Japanese purchase more machines that are simpler and less expensive than highly specialized machinery.

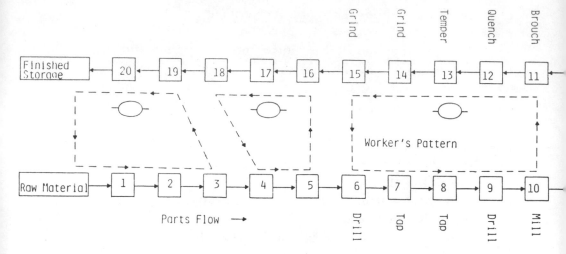

FIGURE 5–3

Schematic of Large Multimachine Manning Crankshaft Line

NOTE: Machine arrangement, production flow, and labor pattern of a multimachine line.
SOURCE: Adapted from authors' interview with Yanmar Diesel Engines, Nagahama, Japan.

The common view in Japan is that the conversion to multimachine manning should raise worker productivity by at least 30 to 50 percent. In many cases the improvements in productivity have been much higher (table 5–2). At Yanmar the labor productivity of its main crankshaft machining line improved 200 percent as the manning requirements were reduced from twelve to four people. Sanei Metal converted its press shop to multimachine manning and improved productivity by 80 percent. The improvements at Mazda were similar in magnitude.

Many Western executives naturally find the productivity potential of multimachine manning appealing. But most express skepticism that their unions would not accept such an approach without a fight. Toyota had faced the same problem in 1950, when it began its conversion to multimachine manning and endured a nasty strike that almost ruined the company. Relations between the union and management were still strained during the period Taiichi Ohno was leading the development of Toyota's new product system. Regarding multimachine manning Ohno notes:

> [In the beginning] resistance from the production workers was naturally strong. Although there was no increase in the

TABLE 5–2

Improvements from Multimachine Manning

		Multimachine Manning (Number of Men)	Output	Productivity Improvement (%)
		Before		
Yanmar	Crankshaft Machining	12	4	Same	200
Sanei Metal	Press	4	2	10% less	80
Mazda	Steering Knuckle Machining	11	4	Same	175
	Timing Gear Case and Cover	10	7	Same	43

SOURCE: Adapted from author interviews and Shingo, *Study of Toyota's Production System from an Industrial Engineering Viewpoint* (Tokyo: Japan Management Association, 1981), p. 241.

amount of work or working time, the skilled workers at the time were fellows with the strong temperament of craftsmen, and they strongly resisted change.

They did not change easily from the old system of one man, one machine, to the system of one man, many machines in a sequence of different processes—being required to work as a multi-skilled operator.

Such resistance was understandable. But, by actually trying, various problems became known. For example, a machine must be set up to stop when a machining is finished; sometimes there were so many adjustments that an unskilled operator found the job difficult to handle. As such problems gradually became clear, they taught me direction of the next move.[2]

As Toyota's production engineers sharply reduced change-over times, reduced run lengths, changed layouts to reduce material handling and connected the fabrication and subassembly processes with final assembly, the requirements for coordinating the process increased dramatically. The traditional approach of deciding weekly or bi-weekly what each step of the process should be was cumbersome and too slow to take full advantage of the processes' increasing capability to cost-effectively manufacture products in small lots. The engineers then struck upon the idea of setting the schedule for final assembly

2. Ohno, *Toyota Production System*, p. 18.

only and letting the demand for parts ripple to each upstream step. Each step would only produce what was needed to support the needs of the next step in the manufacturing process. The needs of the next step would be made known to the previous step by use of a production order card, or *kanban* (see figure 5–4).

For the kanban system to function smoothly, several requirements must be met. The production steps must be tied closely together. The process layout must be like a tree and its root system where final assembly is the trunk, and subassembly and fabrication steps flow smoothly into the trunk like the roots of a tree do. A subassembly step could encounter extreme difficulties if it must serve more than one master. The order quantities of each kanban must be manufacturable in the same amount of time. This ensures that each step is in balance. The time required to changeover from the manufacture of one part to another must be kept at an absolute minimum so that each step

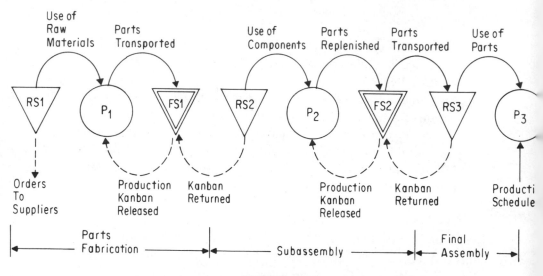

FIGURE 5–4

Use of Kanban to Control Production on the Floor

NOTE: Final assembly, P3, produces according to a given production schedule. As P3 assembles product, subassembly components stored in RS3 are consumed. Generally, RS3 storage is beside the assembly line. When a tray of components is emptied, the tray, along with an identifying kanban, is returned to FS2. At FS2 the tray is replenished and returned to RS3. The tray emptied in the replenishment at FS2 is sent with its kanban to subassembly production, P2. To P2 the tray and its kanban constitutes a production order to be filled exactly and on a first come-first serve basis. P2 draws parts from RS2 and so on, repeating the pattern for P3's production. Outside suppliers receive their purchase orders from RS3, RS2, and RS1.

can readily adapt to new orders. The changeover must be in balance with all other steps to avoid bottlenecks.

The kanban-controlled JIT process is called a "pull" system by the Japanese. The production schedule assigned to final assembly results in material being pulled from parts fabrication through subassembly into final assembly. By contrast, the material resources planning systems (MRP) that predominate in the West are regarded as "push" systems. In a push system the production schedule is provided to a master scheduler, often a computer, that determines the production schedule for parts fabrication, subassembly, and final assembly based on the needs of the production schedule and the availability of parts in inventory. The "push" system receives this name because the production of parts fabrication, for example, is pushed into inventory whether or not subassembly needs the output.

The inventories of a kanban-controlled JIT system can be reduced further by "homogenizing" the final assembly schedule. The most common final assembly sequence in the West is batch assembly. Yanmar in the mid-1970s scheduled in batches; the same product would be assembled for one, two, or three days and then a changeover to another product would occur. Today, Yanmar makes one of almost every product it offers not just every day, but every twenty minutes. This has not only reduced finished goods inventories by more than 80 percent, but the work in process created by upstream fabrication and subassembly areas has been reduced by 90 percent.

The JIT system of Toyota also includes "level scheduling," in which product schedules are progressively refined in the months prior to their execution. The final production schedule is usually frozen for two weeks to one month. During this period no changes in the schedule are allowed. The level scheduling procedure at Yanmar, for example, is as follows: A master schedule is prepared one year prior to actual production and is refined six months later. The master schedule is used for capacity planning and is released to suppliers (as are all subsequent estimates). A middle schedule is prepared three months prior to the date of production. The estimates of the volume of production are made for each model and with the understanding that in the next round of estimation the volumes will not be changed by an amount greater than 30 percent of this estimate. The next round of estimation is made two months prior to production. The procedure is the same as the estimate made at three months except that the understanding is it cannot be changed again by an amount greater than 15 percent of this current estimate. One month prior to the start of production the schedule is frozen and changes are not allowed. The product will be produced according to that schedule.

As Toyota's production engineers removed inventories and tied the steps of the process closer and closer together, the danger increased that a work stoppage at one step of the process could bring the entire factory to a halt. These could be caused by problems of poor quality manufacturing of components, insufficient quantity of parts, or failed equipment. Of all the "evil" that inventories had represented, at least they offered redundancy and time to correct problems.

Toyota reduced the risk of an isolated problem bringing the whole system down by implementing a series of programs to reduce the probability of problems occurring. Toyota was helped by the steps it had taken already. For example, reducing changeover times in machining operations was accomplished in part by investing in extra tools that could be left set up and therefore adjusted to produce at specified tolerances. No longer did five or six parts have to be machined after a change of tools to be sure the batch would be within tolerance. At Yanmar, the reduction in changeover times constituted between 70 to 80 percent of the total 80 to 90 percent reduction in defect rates. In addition to improved machining quality, operator errors had been reduced by the use of foolproof jigs. These jigs are used to ensure that parts are positioned correctly, say for drilling, and receive all the right components, such as nine inserts on the left door and seven on the right one.

The Effect of JIT on Factory Performance

The key elements of the Just-In-Time system are small batch sizes, reduced material handling, level scheduling, low inventory levels, and production control by kanban cards. These elements combine in subtle but powerful ways to enhance the performance of a factory. The total labor productivity of a factory with JIT is substantially higher than that of a factory without JIT. A careful comparison of a Japanese automobile factory with an American factory found startling differences in total labor productivity (table 5–3).

The two factories manufactured comparable vehicles at about the same volume. Both factories were considered well run by their management. Yet, even though the factories were similar in scale and in complexity, the American factory required two-and-one-half times as many people to produce a vehicle as did the Japanese factory.

An analysis of the composition of the labor productivity gap between the two factories is shown in table 5–4. The analysis indicates that fully two-thirds of the labor productivity advantage of the Japanese competitors is due to more productive utilization of overhead functions. The Japanese require about 0.2 overhead personnel per vehicle manufactured while the Americans require almost six times as many overhead personnel per vehicle produced.

Overhead is required to ensure that a factory operates as required, and overhead increases as the difficulty of operating a factory increases. If a plant made only one product, there would be no changeovers, in-process stocks, or major management overheads. Introducing variety unbalances the production process. With variety comes increased frequency of changeovers, in-process inventories, and material handling. Layers of management to "keep the lid on" are required. If changeovers require a great deal of time, the required planning and management effort—overhead—is greater than if changeovers could be accomplished very quickly whenever required.

TABLE 5–3

Labor Productivity Differences between Two Automobile Factories

	Japanese Competitor	American Competitor
Units per Day	1,000	860
Total Factory People	1,000	2,150
People per Unit per Day	1:1	2.5:1

TABLE 5–4

Labor Productivity Difference between Japanese and American Competitors

	Japanese Competitor	American Competitor	Difference
Units Produced per Day	1,000	860	140
Total Factory Workers	1,000	2,150	1,150
Workers per Unit per Day			
Direct	0.79	1.25	0.46
Indirect	0.17 ⎱ 0.21	1.0 ⎱ 1.25	1.04
Salaried, Other	0.04 ⎰	0.25 ⎰	
Total	1.0	2.5	1.5

Factory departments with machines that are difficult to changeover require more management attention and planning than departments with equipment that is easier to set up. Those departments with high percentages of setup to production hours require more overhead support per production labor hour than do those departments with low percentages.

In figure 5–5, department G is an engine block machining line that requires between two and three shifts to accomplish a major tool changeover. The time spent changing over this department is over 20 percent of the time spent for actually machining blocks. Over 50 overhead personnel are required for each 100 direct workers actually operating the machining equipment. By contrast, department A requires less than 20 overhead personnel for each 100 direct workers. The equipment in department A requires less than twenty minutes to changeover so that very little of the available run time is consumed.

If the setup times in departments B through G in figure 5–5 could be substantially reduced by investing in quick-changeover tooling, the overhead burden of the factory would be reduced by half. Total factory labor productivity could be expected to improve because half of all the employees are overhead employees.

In the West, investments in quick changeover tools are not often made. The manufacturing engineers who would like to make these investments cannot financially justify doing so, because they are only able to capture the direct cost benefits of reduced setup times. The direct cost of setup usually includes

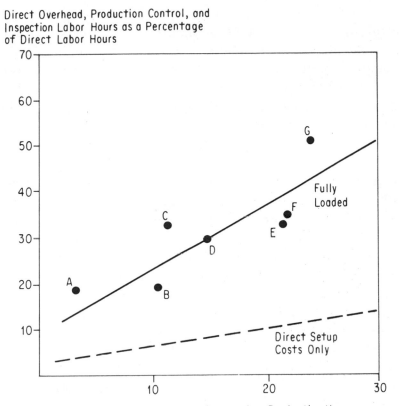

Direct Overhead, Production Control, and
Inspection Labor Hours as a Percentage
of Direct Labor Hours

Percentage of Setup Hours to Direct Labor Production Hours

FIGURE 5–5
Influence of Setup on Manufacturing Overheads

direct labor and machine down time, but does not include the
overhead cost generated by the changeover. Overhead costs are
seldom linked to specific direct costs in today's accounting systems. As can be seen in figure 5–5, the direct cost of setup is
substantially less than the cost loaded with overhead costs. If
fully loaded costs of setup are considered, investments in setup
time reduction are readily justifiable.

The combined effect of investments in quick changeover
tooling, change in layout, and multimachine manning can be
more than a doubling of labor productivity in a machining-
intensive factory like an engine facility (table 5–5). The "old"
factory with long changeover times, long run lengths, and extensive material handling required about twenty-two man-hours to
machine one ton of material of which overhead constituted

about half the cost. A "new" factory with JIT requires only eight man-hours to machine a ton of material, or a reduction of more than half the time. As in the case of the automobile factory example in table 5–4, the most dramatic differences are between the overhead functions of the "old" and "new" factories. Conversion to multimachine manning produces about one-third of the improvement. The other two-thirds of the improvement is increased overhead productivity. Costs involved in inventory management, material handling, and manufacturing management are all reduced. Machine utilization is increased, and yield losses are reduced.

The labor productivity improvements of the "new" factory are within the factory's four walls. Component suppliers can help achieve additional savings. If suppliers match their deliveries with the JIT needs of the factory, the management of the factory can be simplified even more. More important, if the supplier adopts JIT to provide this flexibility, the supplier will also enjoy savings from increased productivity, and some of these savings will be passed onto the factory.

Level scheduling, a key element of the JIT system, is often cited by many Western executives as the key for implementing JIT. In the same breath, it is also the reason why JIT is not suitable in the West as level scheduling is considered symptomatic of the rigidness and inflexibility of JIT. As one senior vice president of a U.S. automobile company said, "Our market is so uncertain that we are not sure on Wednesday what all our plants

TABLE 5–5

Estimated Labor Productivity Improvements for a Factory with JIT

	"Old" Factory (Man hours per ton machined)		"New" Factory with JIT (Man hours per ton machined)		Multiples of Productivity Improvement	
Direct Labor	12.3		5.2		2.4	
Direct Overhead and Production Control	2.6		1.1		2.4	
Inventory Management and Material Handling	4.2	10.1	0.8	3.1	5.3	3.3
General Overhead at 17 percent Loading	3.3		1.2		0.4	
Total	22.4		8.3		2.7	

will be making next Monday." Some Western executives feel that the Japanese are more willing than Americans to sacrifice sales in the short term for the efficiencies inherent in a smoothly scheduled factory: the resulting low costs can then be used to gain market share in the future.

The Japanese are likely not sacrificing much and quite likely gaining a lot. Analyses of the practice of level scheduling suggest that the Japanese can meet short-term sales needs while their factories "run level" and still minimize finished goods inventories. The effect of the level scheduling of production was investigated for a European manufacturer of industrial equipment (figure 5–6). This company has a very wide line of low and medium volume products. It also has high and increasing inventories. Because controlling inventories is difficult and the demand for most of its products is erratic, the company employs a variable production scheduling process with which it attempts to track demand with production. This is done at great expense because actual weekly production volumes can vary as much as plus or minus 100 percent of the average weekly demand. Even so, inventories of finished goods for their main product fluctuate widely. On average, the company must carry an inventory of its product equal to about seventy-four days of demand to ensure that the product is available 98 percent of the time an order is received.

A statistical analysis of the company's ability to match production schedules with demand indicates that the predictions of demand used to schedule production are as often wrong as they are right. While overall demand for the year is reasonably predictable, the distribution of demand throughout the year is almost random. The obvious conclusion is that if weekly demand is not predictable, why bother attempting to predict it? Instead schedule the factory to produce the average weekly demand for the year. With the factory running level there will at least be cost savings from production efficiencies to offset whatever increase in inventory levels that may result.

The surprising result of production leveling is that inventories are likely to be less, not more, than those resulting from the variable production schedule. The inventories required to maintain a service level of 98 percent are only equivalent to

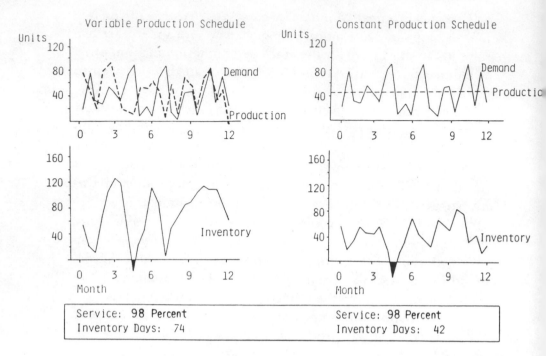

FIGURE 5–6

*Effect of Production Leveling on Inventories and Service Levels
for a European Industrial Equipment Manufacturer*

NOTE: Constant production schedules can result in lower inventories as well as smooth production.
SOURCE: Tihamer G.I. von Ghyczy, of the Boston Consulting Group's Munich Office.

forty-two days of demand or less than 60 percent of the variable schedule inventories. The company could meet its required service levels, have lower inventories, and reduce costs by level scheduling.

The more difficult it is to predict demand the more attractive level scheduling is. If demand is totally random, prediction makes no sense, and if demand is totally predictable, the factory can easily be scheduled. For those in the middle ground, techniques are now being developed to set periods of level scheduling and production volume.

Few companies, including the European company discussed, wish to run their factories level for a year. Even the Japanese do not do that. Most Japanese companies with JIT level their schedule for only a month. Some level for two weeks.

Toyota is working toward a schedule that is level for less than a week.

The minimum period that a production schedule can be leveled without increasing inventories is equal to the longest production lead time item in the factory. Sometimes this item is obtained from an outside supplier, but most often the longest lead time item is one manufactured by the company itself. In a European construction equipment company, sixty-three days are required to flame cut, weld, and machine the main chassis. Subassembly of certain components and final assembly require six weeks. Overall, more than twenty-four weeks are required from start to finish to complete a piece of construction equipment. Any attempt to level the production schedule of this company's factory for a period of less than six months will result in production interruptions caused by parts shortages, or increased inventories, or both.

The adoption of JIT dramatically reduces the time required to manufacture a product and, hence, shortens the period during which a factory can be level scheduled. A Japanese factory required about thirty days to make its product before the adoption of JIT. When setup times throughout the factory were very much reduced, the production period fell to twelve days. After the layout of the factory was changed to reduce material handling and inventory holding points, the production period was reduced to six days. Eventually, as all inventory holding points were eliminated, the period of production was reduced to two days. This is the equivalent of reducing the production lead time of the European construction equipment company from twenty-four weeks to a week and a half.

As the production period of a factory is reduced, its ability to respond to changes in demand is enhanced. Factories using JIT have production periods that can be one-fifth of those factories with slow changeovers, long run lengths, and excessive material handling time. With JIT the entire factory is more, not less, flexible, and JIT is a more suitable production system to an environment in which demand is uncertain. The Japanese have chosen not to take full advantage of this characteristic of JIT but, as indicated by reducing the period in which the schedule is frozen, the situation is changing.

The Experience of Japanese Companies with JIT

Many Japanese companies in addition to Yanmar Diesel have followed Toyota's lead in adopting JIT. The effect on the manufacturing performance of these companies has been just as dramatic as that experienced by Yanmar. Furthermore, as a group, they represent a variety of industries and accomplished their transformations in remarkably short periods of time.

Mazda, formerly Toyo Kogyo, was, like Yanmar, in trouble in the mid-1970s. Mazda was badly hurt by the recession, and its famous rotary engine-equipped vehicles were not selling well. Among the many elements of their turnaround program was a major effort to improve the efficiency of their factories.

In 1975 Mazda was Japan's third largest auto producer. Mazda was about one-third the size of Toyota and one-half the size of Nissan. Yet from 1975 through 1981, Mazda's productivity measured in vehicles produced per employee increased at a faster rate than did Toyota's productivity and substantially faster than did the improvements of productivity at Nissan (figure 5–7).

Throughout this period, Mazda was implementing its own form of JIT. Mazda began in 1976 with Operation 50, in which the objectives were the reduction of costs and work-in-process by 50 percent, reduction in setup times, and the general reduction of production delays. In 1977, Mazda began the S-Line program. Three factory lines were selected as models of the potential for further improvements. The ones chosen were a machining, an assembly, and a sand casting line. Typical improvements included further reduction in setup times, changes in layout, expanded preventive maintenance programs, and defect prevention programs. In 1980 the S-Line program was extended throughout the factories of Mazda, and the "Bumble Bee" program was begun. In this, Mazda engineers took the news of their success to the suppliers of Mazda and encouraged them to follow Mazda's example.

Mazda's vehicle production volume per employee increased from about 23 units per employee in 1976 to over 40 in the early 1980s. Work-in-process (WIP) requirements were reduced dramatically. Mazda's work-in-process turns (value of vehicles

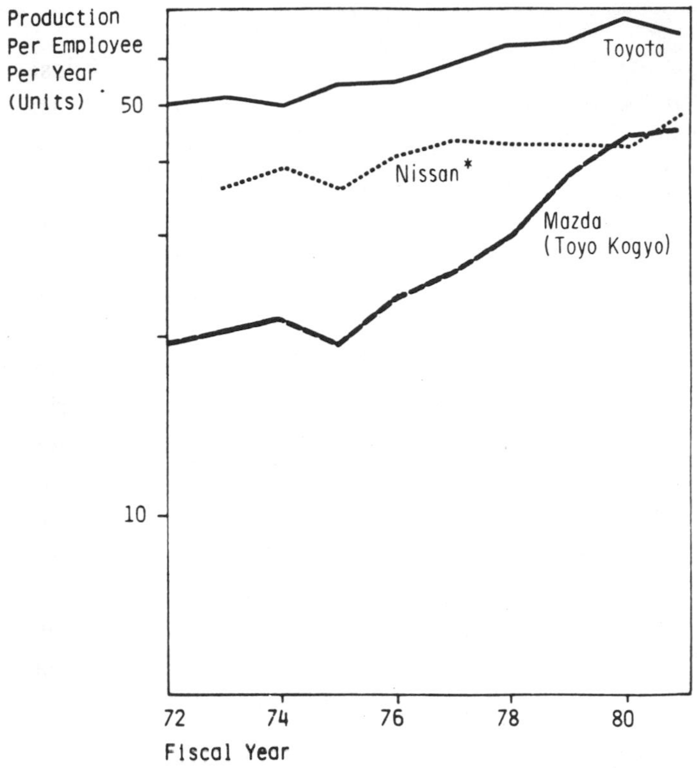

Production Per Employee Per Year (Units)

FIGURE 5–7

Labor Productivity Improvement in the Japanese Automobile Industry

*Previously known in the United States as Datsun.

sold divided by the value of WIP required by the factories) increased from about 12 times a year in 1976 to over 50 times in 1981.

Mazda was catching up. Toyota had been refining its production system since the 1950s. Nissan had its own, somewhat less efficient, version of Toyota's system. Mazda was converting from slow changeovers, long run lengths and extensive material handling to JIT. When labor productivity and improvements in work-in-process turns are compared, Mazda's catch up can be observed (figure 5–8).

The histories of Toyota, Nissan, and Mazda suggest that the improvements in the efficiencies of their operations are governed by the same economic and physical relationships. As

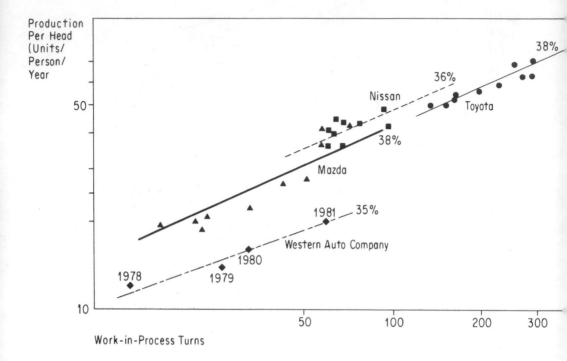

FIGURE 5–8
*Productivity and Work-in-Process (WIP) Improvements
of Selected Japanese Automobile Producers*

Toyota continues to refine its operations to reduce inventory, their labor productivity increases. Note that work-in-process turns at Toyota are greater than 300 times a year. Also note that labor productivity increases about 38 percent with each doubling of work-in-process turns. Figures at Nissan and Mazda are comparable. Interestingly, an American automobile manufacturer who is implementing JIT at certain factories is experiencing a rate of improvement comparable to that of the Japanese.

Other Japanese companies have implemented their own version of JIT and have significantly improved their work-in-process turns in a recent five-year period. Komatsu, Isuzu, a truck and auto manufacturer, and Hitachi have improved their turns by between 50 and 60 percent. Yanmar and Jidosha Kiki, an auto parts manufacturer, have improved their turns by four to five times.

As the other Japanese companies adopted JIT and reduced their inventories, they, too, experienced dramatic improvements in labor productivity. Komatsu, Yanmar, Hitachi, and Jidosha Kiki increased their output per factory worker—including direct, indirect, and all other overhead functions—by 80 to 90 percent over a five-year period.

As the work-in-process turns and labor productivities of these companies improve, so too do their asset efficiencies. The net asset turns (total sales divided net assets where net assets are total assets less non-interest bearing liabilities) of Mazda were a steady 1.2 times a year in the early 1970s. As Mazda adopted JIT, its turns increased from 1.2 in 1976 to a high of 3 in 1980 after which it declined slightly as its new factory in Hofu started up. In other words, Mazda generated 1.2 billion yen of sales in 1976 for every 1 billion yen of assets, and it now generates 3 billion yen in sales with that 1 billion yen of invested assets.

The net asset productivities of other Japanese companies also increased substantially during the period they were adopting JIT. The net asset turns of Yanmar, Hitachi, Komatsu, and Isuzu increased by 50 to 100 percent. About three-quarters of these improvements were due to increased efficiency of the plant and equipment and reduced inventories.

In Japan, the pattern has been for the factory to implement JIT first, then for the suppliers to follow. By 1962 Toyota had instituted JIT systemwide. Only then did it approach its suppliers. Another ten years passed before the JIT system had spread to all of Toyota's suppliers. Yanmar and Mazda waited about four years after they began to implement JIT before approaching suppliers to encourage them to follow their examples.

Curiously, of all the compelling characteristics of JIT, Western executives have generally been most attracted by the relationship between the Japanese manufacturers and their suppliers. Instead of concentrating efforts on those parts of the process that generate work-in-process, the Western manufacturers have been reducing raw material inventories by pressuring their suppliers. For example, a senior purchasing executive for the Ford Motor Company has said, "If we need two hundred more roof panels today, rather than keep it in inventory, we call Budd [a supplier]. Budd's got two choices: they have it in their own inventories, or they reset their dies and make them for us then and there. The supplier typically has a week's [supply], and we have a week. We're cutting back our week's worth. What we'd like to see happen is for Budd to get down to a day. It puts a lot more pressure on the suppliers. We're doing it to Budd, and we're doing it to all of them."[3]

Predictably, the executives at Budd see the situation differently. The reaction of the Budd's president to the point of view expressed by Ford was, "That's not what they do in Japan at all. If we're going to move inventory out of the car plant and into the supplier plant, the cost is still there. They [Ford] are pushing the costs onto someone else. There are times when [auto manufacturers] have forced suppliers to eat costs that, with a cooperative effort, could be eliminated."[4]

The controversy in the United States has not gone unnoticed in Japan. Toyota's Taiichi Ohno observed:

> GM, Ford and the European automobile makers have been carrying out the rationalization of the production process in their individual manner.
>
> Taking the changeover of a large type of press as an example, the European and American makers still take a long time for the job as in the past. This is perhaps because there is no need. To attempt to make parts more commonly usable was a very new approach. But still the size of a lot is large, and the effect of mass production under a planned production system is being pursued.
>
> Fast changeover is an absolute requirement in the application of the Toyota production system. Making the size of a lot small and generating the need for changeovers, the workers had to be given repeated on-the-job training.
>
> Which is in the superior position, the Ford system or the Toyota system? Each system is undergoing daily improvement and innovation and, therefore, one cannot draw a quick conclusion. However, I myself believe firmly that, naturally, the Toyota system is a method of production which is better suitable in the era of low growth rate.[5]

Many Japanese companies view the adoption of JIT as the prelude to full factory automation to further reduce costs. As one recent executive of a robot manufacturer said, "If you want

3. *Los Angeles Times,* 2 May 1982, 1, 5.
4. Ibid.
5. Ohno, *Toyota Production System,* pp. 153–54.

to know what is wrong with your process, try putting a robot in it." Factories must be running efficiently before they can be automated. Five years ago at Hitachi, their manufacturing strategy was to place their version of JIT—named MST for Minimum Stock Minimum Standard Time—in all of their factories in Japan. This was essentially completed two years ago, and Hitachi's current manufacturing strategy is to increase substantially the level of factory automation in their Japan plants over the next five years.

Competitive Implications

Late in the 1970s, many Japanese companies by adopting JIT doubled the productivity of their factory labor forces and almost doubled the productivity of the assets they employed without requiring a net capital investment. Indeed, the adoption of JIT saved or generated capital. Toyota required more than twenty-five years to achieve its remarkable level of efficiency. The Japanese companies that followed also dramatically improved their performance, but in a much shorter period (five years).

A Japanese or Western competitor that has invested time and capital implementing the JIT manufacturing system can choose to use the cost savings in two ways—it can make the same variety of products at lower cost or higher quality (or both) or it can make a greater variety of products at similar, or even lower, cost.

Komatsu provides examples of both choices. In the manufacture of construction equipment, Komatsu is second in size only to Caterpillar. The competition between Caterpillar and Komatsu is among the most intense ever witnessed. At Komatsu, a company slogan is "Maru C" or encircle Cat. So far, the statistics are in Komatsu's favor. Komatsu's volumes in the last five years have increased 40 percent while Caterpillar's volumes have fallen almost 50 percent. Employment at Komatsu has increased slightly (the slight increase a startling fact in itself, given the volume increase) while Caterpillar's employment is down by about a third.

Komatsu's competitiveness has been enhanced by its investment in the JIT system. Komatsu first invested in quick-change-over tooling for its engine plant. The production variety and the volumes of the plant have increased, but the number of employees at this plant has remained almost constant. Initially, Komatsu may have benefited from its heavy investments in low setup tooling by making the same variety of products at lower cost.

Beyond this, Komatsu has continued with investment in quick changeover tooling for its other plants. It is pursuing the benefits of making a greater variety at similar or lower costs. As a result, Komatsu has transformed itself from a short line manufacturer to a producer of a broad line of equipment. Until recently, Caterpillar produced and marketed the broadest line of construction equipment of any competitor. By 1981, Komatsu offered a greater variety than Caterpillar. Such proliferation usually weakens the smaller competitor, yet Komatsu competes vigorously against Caterpillar.

Product line expansion is of enormous strategic value. New products increase demand in old markets and enable the penetration of new markets. A company can take the initiative by introducing new products, and competitors are forced to respond. Surprisingly, today many Western competitors are paring their product lines in an attempt to focus their factories to improve production efficiency. But they are risking the decreased competitiveness and relevance in their markets. In one recent example, the leading Japanese competitor had expanded its basic model offerings of diesel engines from 7 to 12 while a leading U.S. competitor had reduced its line from 9 to 3 models.

Many of the leading manufacturing kaisha have made the investment required to benefit from JIT that most Western companies are still debating or quietly considering. Meanwhile, the kaisha continue to transform themselves. The investment focus today has moved beyond the implementation of JIT to the pursuit of the elusive goal of full factory automation and economic run lengths of one unit. As their investments continue to enhance the performance of their factories, the kaisha are using their low costs to increase the quality and variety of their products for increased world market share while many of their Western competitors remain unsure of the appropriate response.

6

THE DRIVE TO

TECHNOLOGICAL LEADERSHIP

A CHANGE is underway in Japanese industry that will alter the base on which Japan's kaisha compete with each other and with foreign companies. The competitive strength of Japanese companies has been based on price and on quality of product, driven by flexible and cost-effective manufacturing. Added now, very rapidly, is a highly competitive level of research and development expenditure, with technological innovation becoming the center of competitive capability.

This shift to technology is going largely unnoticed by the kaisha's international competitors. The long-sustained technological supremacy of the West has ingrained a sense of confidence, even of arrogance, regarding the research capability of Western companies. Japan's long-sustained role as copier and later as adapter of Western technology has reinforced these attitudes. Just as Japan's growth and competitive success have come as a bolt from the blue for Western companies and governments, so it appears that Japan's move to technological independence and self-sustained research and development may catch Western competitors unaware.

Leading firms in Japan's major industries now spend as much or more on research and development as do their U.S. counterparts. Table 6–1 presents a comparison of leading U.S. and Japanese companies in ten major industries ranging from steel and autos to electronics and pharmaceuticals, and the reported research and development expenditures in 1983 for each of the companies. In eight of ten comparisons, the kaisha spends more of its total revenues on research and development than does the U.S. company. The differences in some cases are truly startling—both Canon and NEC spend well over 10 percent of their revenues on research, more than any of the U.S. companies listed.

These kaisha are moving away from their long dependence on Western technological developments and have taken their research expenditure up to levels that are very high even by world standards. It has long been appreciated that the kaisha are prepared to sacrifice short-term profits for long-term advantage. What has not been realized, in part because it is a very recent phenomenon, is that the kaisha are now sacrificing short-term profits not only, nor mainly, for long-term market positions, but are doing so for long-term technological and competitive position.

"The First Year of the Era of Technological Independence"

In an effort to understand such a critical development better, Japanese research and development expenditures were re-

TABLE 6–1

Research and Development as Percent of Sales (1983)

U.S. Company	R&D (%)	Japanese Company	R&D (%)	Difference
General Electric	3.4	Hitachi	7.9	+4.5
General Motors	3.5	Toyota	3.9	+0.4
Eastman Kodak	7.3	Fuji Photo Film	6.6	−0.7
DuPont	2.7	Toray Industries	3.1	+0.4
U.S. Steel	0.5	Nippon Steel	1.9	+1.4
Xerox	6.6	Canon	14.6	+8.0
Texas Instruments	6.6	NEC	13.0	+6.4
RCA	2.4	Matsushita Electric Industries	7.2	+4.8
Goodyear	2.6	Bridgestone	4.5	+1.9
Eli Lilly	9.7	Shionogi	9.6	−0.1

Source: Adapted from "R&D Scoreboard: 1983," *Business Week*, 9 July 1984, 63–75 and *Nikkei Kaisha Joho*, no. 3 (Nikkei Company Information) (Tokyo: Nihon Keizai Shimbun, 1984).

viewed by the authors for 1978 and 1983 in order to examine trends over time. The review focuses on the top twenty companies in Japan and the United States ranked in terms of total research and development expenditure in 1978 and 1983. The results of this analysis are summarized in table 6–2. This is the first effort ever made to compare R&D expenditures by company between the two countries, and the results warrant close attention.

The top twenty companies in each country account for a substantial part of total research expenditures in each economy. The top twenty in Japan appear to account for about 30 percent of total national expenditure on research, and in the U.S. group, for about 20 percent. The smaller proportion for the U.S. group as a percent of national total may well result from the much larger role the U.S. government plays in research expenditure —nearly half of the national total—compared with Japan, where government research expenditure is only one-quarter of the national total.

TABLE 6–2

Top Twenty Japanese and U.S. Companies: Total Annual R&D Expenditures

		Japan	United States
Average Sales per Company, 1983 (¥220:$1.00)		$8.9 billion	$24.7 billion
Average R&D Expenditure per Company, 1983		$446 million	$903 million
R&D Expenditure as Percent of Sales	1983	5.1%	3.7%
	1978	3.1%	2.9%
Annual Increase in R&D Expenditure, 1978–1983			
Current Prices		21.2%	12.9%
Real Prices		17%	4.5%
Annual Increase in Sales 1978–1983			
Current Prices		10.1%	7.9%
Real Prices		5.9%	−0.5%
Approximate Proportion of National R&D Expenditure, 1983		30%	20%

NOTE: Real prices were calculated by deflating current prices by the increase in the consumer price index (CPI) from 1978 to 1983. The consumer price index increased during this period at an annual compound rate of 8.4 percent in the United States and 4.2 percent in Japan. The increase in GNP deflator was 7.5 percent and 2.1 percent respectively. The CPI increase is used in this analysis. Use of the GNP deflator as a measure of inflation would widen the observed differences.
SOURCE: Adapted from "R&D Scoreboard: 1978," *Business Week*, 2 July 1979; "R&D Scoreboard: 1983," *Business Week*, 9 July 1984 and *Nikkei Kaisha Joho*, no. 4, *Nikkei Kaisha Joho*, no. 3 (Tokyo: Nihon Keizai Shimbun, 1980 and 1984 respectively).

The U.S. companies are nearly three times as large in total sales as the Japanese companies, but the Japanese companies spend half as much for R&D as do the U.S. companies. Thus, R&D as a percent of sales is over 5 percent for the Japanese companies, and less than 4 percent for the U.S. companies, a more than 20 percent difference in proportion. In 1978, R&D as a percent of sales was about the same for the two groups. Thus, the relative efforts of the major Japanese companies in R&D expenditure is now considerably greater than the efforts of the U.S. companies, and have increased much more rapidly.

Yet this is not to say that the U.S. companies have been idle. Over the five year period they increased their R&D expenditure by about 13 percent per year in current price terms. During a period of high U.S. inflation rates, this translates into an annual compound increase of about 4.5 percent, a considerable increase in effort. However, the twenty kaisha increased their R&D expenditures more than 20 percent annually from 1978 to 1983. In real terms, adjusting for Japan's relatively low inflation over this five-year period, the R&D expenditure of the twenty Japanese firms increased annually at an astonishing compound rate of 17 percent per year, a rate that doubles their expenditures in real terms in less than five years. The U.S. firms real expenditures will not double over a twenty-year period at recent rates of growth. The disparity in growth rates—to the advantage of the kaisha—is enormous.

Some part of the cause of the disparity may be reflected in the relative growth rates in revenues of the two groups of companies from 1978–1983. In real terms, the U.S. group did not grow at all from 1978 to 1983, a period over which the U.S. economy as a whole also showed no growth. As any increase in research expenditure during this period was a painful one for U.S. companies, it is a testimony to their research commitment. Nonetheless, the kaisha increased their commitment to a far greater degree even than the U.S. companies.

There is, of course, no assurance that these numbers provide a precise comparison between the two groups of companies, given differences in accounting and tax treatment, for example. Also, there is no way to determine from these data which companies do more "basic" research, and which deal more with product adaptation, regulatory compliance, and the like in their research budgets. This kind of precision is not needed, however, to come to the unavoidable conclusion that Japanese firms are stepping up their R&D effort at an extraordinary rate. In fact, a good deal of what might be considered R&D is not even reflected in the R&D budgets of the Japanese companies. As noted, NEC is a leader in Japan in the proportion of R&D expenditure to total sales. But at the same time, NEC trains 1,300 foreign engineers each year, for periods of one to six months in Japan, and sends engineers to the United States annually for advanced study. These expenditures for R&D training are not in NEC's R&D budget, but come out of its personnel budget.

The Electronics Industries Association of Japan in its 1984 annual report indicated that total industry R&D expenditure increased at an annual rate of 15.2 percent from 1978 to 1982, compared with 21.2 percent in the authors' study. In addition, the EIAJ shows an expenditure increase averaging 26 percent per year for the electronics industry alone, thus increasing at a rate that doubles in three years.[1]

What are the kaisha getting for all of this money and increased R&D efforts? One answer would be that it is too soon to tell. The drive into massive R&D efforts is recent, and the effects are not likely to be evident for some time. Furthermore, R&D output is not easy to measure. But there is an available measure in patents. Table 6–3 shows the results of a review done by a major U.S. company of the number of patents issued by the U.S. patent office to six U.S. and foreign companies in the electrical equipment and electronics industries over the 1960–1982 period.

Two kaisha, Hitachi and Toshiba, compare rather well with their U.S. and European competitors in terms of 1982 U.S. patents issued. Indeed, among these companies, Hitachi is second only to General Electric. These data on numbers of patents do not provide any measure of the quality of the technology in the patents. Japanese patent performance is often belittled by arguing that U.S. companies find patents of less value since U.S. courts began to seem less willing to allow their defense, and that the cost of applying for (and the reduced value of) the patents

1. *Electronics Industries in Japan* (Tokyo: Electronics Industries Association of Japan, 1984), p. 15.

TABLE 6–3

Issued U.S. Patents 1960–1982

	General Electric (U.S.)	IBM (U.S.)	Philips (Eur.)	Siemens (Eur.)	Hitachi (Jap.)	Toshiba (Jap.)
1960	773	296	234	96	2	3
1965	1,063	537	321	161	14	14
1970	1,000	631	290	231	102	80
1975	839	519	411	451	386	90
1980	770	386	332	369	409	257
1982	741	439	386	477	544	301
CAGR*(%)	−0.2	1.8	2.3	7.6	29.0	23.3

*Compound Annual Growth Rate

have made for fewer U.S. patent applications. This view goes on to argue that Japanese companies still strive for maximum numbers of patents, which are often of limited technological value.

There seems to be no easy or precise way to deal with this last argument, although it has on the face of it a self-justifying and smug self-assurance. Perhaps Hitachi's U.S. patents in 1982 represent less technical value than do those of General Electric or those of Siemens—perhaps not. In any event, Hitachi's 544 patents issued in the U.S. in 1982 surely represent substantially more technology than the two patents issued to Hitachi in the United States in 1960. Hitachi's competitors might do well to focus more on Hitachi's relative rate of progress than on the probably moot issue of Hitachi's relative current position. Hitachi, like other leading kaisha, sees R&D as critical to its future, is making major progress in it, and is stepping up its commitment of resources to be as fully competitive in R&D in the future as it already is in product cost and quality.

Sharp increases in patents issued in the United States to Japanese nationals are not limited to the electrical equipment industry. Patents issued in the United States in recent years present an interesting pattern. From 1966 to 1984, of all patents issued by the U.S. patent office, the proportion issued to foreign nationals increased from 20 to 40 percent. From a U.S. point of view, this surely must be an alarming shift; nearly half of all U.S. patents are now being issued to foreign nationals.

But from a Japanese point of view, the change over the same period is equally interesting. In 1966 less than 2 percent of U.S.

TABLE 6–4

Real Increase in Research Expenditures (1975 = 100)

	Japan	United States	West Germany
1965	43	96	53
1970	87	102	83
1975	100	100	100
1980	130	125	132
1982	152	128	133

SOURCE: Kagaku Gijutsu Cho Hen (Science and Technology Agency), *Kagaku Gijutsu Hakusho* (Science and Technology White Paper on International comparison and Future Themes), (Tokyo: Okurasho, 1982) p. 104.

patents issued were to Japanese nationals. In 1984 the proportion was 16 percent. Furthermore, two-thirds of the increase in U.S. patents issued to foreign nationals over the period is accounted for by patents issued to Japanese nationals. The phenomenon is not simply limited to Hitachi or Toshiba, but is a general one. Are the patents issued to Japanese of a quality equal to those issued to U.S. or other nationals? There is probably no way of knowing. The rate of increase in U.S. patent issue to Japanese nationals, however, must surely be of significance as a measure of increased R&D output.

The seemingly sudden and massive thrust of the kaisha into R&D needs to be seen in a larger context. The move to independent and innovative research is the appropriate and inevitable next stage in the development of the Japanese economy. The shift to ever higher levels of output and income leads, through steady progress to higher levels of productivity and of value added in output, to a stage at which autonomous research and development is essential. In the late 1970s, there was increasing awareness of this requirement and the Minister of Japan's Science and Technology Agency referred to 1980 as "the first year of the era of Japan's technological independence."[2]

Even through the 1970s, before the current high-technology preoccupation in Japan, Japanese rates of investment in money and people for R&D were increasing rapidly (see table 6–4). Japan's progress in R&D expenditure has been quite steady, with the special feature that throughout this period (and

2. I. Nakagawa in Foreword, Kagaku Gijutsu Cho Hen (Science and Technology Agency), Kagaku Gijutsu no Hakusho. Kokusai Hikaku to Kongo no Kadai (1981 Annual Science and Technology White Paper on International Comparison and Future Themes) (Tokyo: Okurasho, 1982).

currently), these increased R&D efforts were primarily from private sector initiative rather than from government efforts. It remains the case that in Japan's R&D efforts the role of the government in staffing and funding is limited compared to that in the economies of the United States and Western Europe.

The Critical Postwar Make-or-Buy Decision

It is quite true that the Japanese economy has grown to its present status not on self-developed technology, but instead on technology imported from abroad. In the period from 1951 through March, 1984, Japanese companies and other entities entered into a total of nearly 42,000 contracts for the importation into Japan of technology from abroad (see table 6–5). These 42,000 contracts represented the best of the technology available in the world, identified after thorough and painstaking study by teams of Japanese of the relative merits of competing technologies. It has been through these contracts that Japanese industry built its position in synthetic textiles, for example, licensing DuPont's nylon patent and ICI's Terylene. Similar contracts were the basis for Japan's petrochemical industry. Bell Laboratory's transistor technology started Japan's semiconductor industry; RCA's licenses allowed entry into color television; Corning provided the TV glass tube technology, and went on to license its optical fiber patents making Japanese progress possible in that field.

This massive transfer of technology from the United States and Western Europe in fact provided the technological basis for nearly all of Japan's modern industries. Without this critical technology transfer, no amount of capital and labor could have moved Japanese companies to their present competitive positions so rapidly. Yet the cumulative cost of all of that transfer over a period of more than twenty years has been only $17 billion, a fraction of the current annual U.S. research and development budget.

It was a cost that was very high, at times, for individual

TABLE 6–5
Japan's Technological Trade: 1951–1983

Fiscal Year	Number of Cases of Technical Imports	Annual Average of Technical Imports	Payment for Technology ($M)	Receipts from Technology Sales ($M)	Balance of Receipts/Payments (%)
1951–54	880	220	47	.5	1
1955–59	1,370	274	206	2	1
1960–64	4,124	825	613	35	6
1965–69	6,779	1,356	1,278	141	11
1970–74	10,271	2,054	2,926	394	13
1975–79	9,898	1,980	5,086	1,183	23
1980–83	8,650	2,162	7,025	2,066	30
Total: 1951–1983	41,972	1,312	$17,181	$3,821	22%

SOURCE: Adapted from *Economic Statistics Annual*, (Tokyo: Statistics Department, The Bank of Japan, 1968), p. 242 and *Economic Statistics Annual* (Tokyo: Research and Statistics Department, The Bank of Japan, 1984), p. 256.

kaisha. The down-payment on DuPont's nylon patent was equal to the entire capitalization at the time of Toyo Rayon, now Toray Industries. Yet in retrospect, and especially from the point of view of the economy as a whole, this purchase of foreign technology by a country devastated by war, lagging seriously in research and development, and isolated from wartime research developments abroad, was a brilliant one. It was a historic make-or-buy decision, and the Japanese decision to buy was carried out with historic success.

From the sellers' points of view, the results have been disastrous. Technology sold to Japanese companies has come back in improved form to create competitive nightmares. Yet in the circumstances of the time, the sell decision had a certain logic. The Japanese market was very small, very far away, and felt to be hardly worth the effort of development, Japanese government entry barriers notwithstanding. Moreover, the income from the sale of technology represented a windfall return on an R&D investment already written off, a most welcome contribution to U.S. profits.

Not all foreign companies fell into the trap. A few tough-minded and farsighted firms, like IBM and Texas Instruments, used their technology as bludgeons to beat down the barriers to entry into Japan to build wholly-owned operations there. But such companies were few. The great majority sold their technology to the kaisha, with MITI standing as referee to ensure that the price paid in royalty, or contract length, or restrictions such as export limits, was not too high. The kaisha were desperate for technology and in a poor negotiating position; MITI helped improve the negotiating balance.

This pattern of purchase of critical technology lasted to the late 1960s, by which time Japanese firms were catching up in competitive ability and bargaining strength and the government surveillance of technology transfer was dismantled. By this time annual contracts for technology imports were running at a level of about 2,000 annually. They have peaked and held at that level, though there is general agreement that the level of technology in recent contracts is less significant or critical than before. Yet it is interesting to note that the pattern steadily continues of Japanese firms drawing on technology from abroad.

The Drive to Technological Leadership

The Capacity to Absorb New Technology

In a review of this history, and looking at Japan's technological balance of payments, the Economic Planning Agency made a telling point in a 1980 survey:

> Japan's technological progress has been achieved so far through the introduction of foreign technologies. This has been inevitable, it may be said, because Japan made a late start and therefore had to catch up to advanced nations in a short period. . . . In fiscal 1978, Japan's earnings from exports of technologies were equal to only 22 percent of its payments for foreign technology introduction. Nonetheless, the low ratio itself does not necessarily give cause for worry; the ratios of Britain and France stood at 100 percent (1975) and 120 percent (1976) respectively, compared with 41 percent for the Federal Republic of Germany (1977). A brisk introduction of foreign technologies may be taken as an indication that a country has a great capacity to assimilate them.[3]

Much discussion of technology in Japan focuses on the issue of creativity, which in many critical ways is beside the real point of technological progress. Technology—especially basic discoveries—is available through purchase, as Japan did through the postwar period, and through foreign study and literature search. The kaisha have shown an unusual capacity to take in, absorb, and adapt technology. This is the critical variable in technological progress, and the success of the Japanese company in assimilating technology is a main source of competitive strength.

All too often, the capacity to assimilate technology is called "copying," and dismissed. Yet economic progress by definition involves copying, in the sense of moving into industries and products that have been pioneered by others. Japanese society has historically shown a considerable freedom from the NIH syndrome—the tendency to reject what is Not Invented Here. In this context, the willingness to accept that others might have a better way of doing things appears as a strength, unlike the

---

3. Japan Economic Planning Agency, *Economic Survey of Japan 1978/1979.* (Tokyo: Japan Times, 1980), p. 135.

pejorative "copying." This openness to new and different products and processes seems characteristic of Japanese companies as well as of other institutions in Japanese society.

Still, a willingness to input new ideas and methods seems not peculiar to Japan. In the high-growth U.S. economy of the late nineteenth and early twentieth centuries, Americans took pride in what was termed "Yankee ingenuity." By this was generally meant the taking in of European discoveries and developments, adapting and commercializing them, and building on these imported technologies. (The term is, unfortunately, less often used now.) During this early period, U.S. Nobel prize winners were scarce, and U.S. universities undistinguished in their research. Today Japan has few Nobelists, but shows distinction in creative adaptation, as the United States did earlier.

There is a suggestion in this that perhaps fundamental research and pure invention occur only in relatively wealthy economies, with pure research and discovery the luxury of the affluent. Scholars became recipients of Nobel prizes in the United States as its economy reached maturity. Japan, in turn, is now the high-growth economy and is still the adapter, but with increased wealth it is moving toward greater research expenditures.

There are at least three characteristics of the kaisha that make a high rate of technological assimilation possible: the rate of capital investment, the pattern of personnel practices, and the quality of the Japanese work force. Capital investment rates in Japan have been the highest of the major economies since the early 1960s, and investment continues at a high level. Even the slowing of overall economic growth following the first oil crisis did little to change the relative rates. Equipment investment has been maintained at about 16 percent of the GNP in Japan, compared with 10 percent for the United States. Dramatic evidence of high investment rates was provided with the news that total capital investment in the semiconductor industry in Japan surpassed that of the U.S. industry in 1984, even though Japan's economy is less than half the size of the U.S. economy.

High rates of Japanese investment are primary determinants of rates of growth in productivity. High investment levels are also determinants of technological process. Rapid investment in additional plant and equipment means rapid introduction of new production technologies. In Japan's steel industry this meant construction of world-scale blast furnaces at deepwater sites in the 1950s and 1960s; the United States still has none. It meant the rapid introduction of oxygen furnaces; the United States continued to operate nineteenth-century openhearth facilities. It meant rapid conversion to energy and cost-saving continuous casting; the United States continuous casting ratio remained below 20 percent, and that capacity was largely installed by Japanese engineers.

Robotics are a contemporary example of the impact of high levels of investment on technological change. The number of robots installed in Japanese manufacturing facilities far exceeds those in other economies, with more than twice as many in Japan as in the United States. Clearly, when an investment decision is made regarding new plant and equipment, that new investment is likely to incorporate the best technology available to and within the means of the investor. Rapid investment thereby drives rapid movement to newer technologies.

While increases in capital investment make introduction of new technology possible, the issue of the willingness and ability of the labor force—at both management and shop floor level—to accept and adapt to the new technology is critical to its rate of assimilation. Resistance to the introduction of new technology is a long tradition in the West, symbolized by the movement against textile machines of the Luddites in early nineteenth century Great Britain. In a real sense, the Luddites and their modern descendants are correct in resisting new technology. In the customary system of labor relations in Western companies new technology is a threat, to employment and to income levels. Presumably the new technology is cost efficient, largely in terms of labor savings, or it would not be introduced. It is rational, then, for labor to resist its introduction.

In the customary Japanese system of labor relations that the kaisha have developed however, the inherent threat in the introduction of new technology is largely absent. Male employees in Japan's large companies have a high degree of job security, from the system of life-time employment. Further, their compensation is largely determined by length of service, rather than by the particular job they hold or their output at a given job. In addition, a good part of their compensation is in the form of a bonus related to the overall success of the company. Thus, far from being a threat to employment or to income, new technology in the Japanese case is to be welcomed in terms of the potential for increased profits—and bonus—and for the additional job security provided by improved performance of the kaisha.

It requires no great exaggeration to argue that the Western system of employment relations simply could not have accomodated the rate of technological change that has occurred in the kaisha over the past thirty-five years. Each of the contracts signed for technology introduction has in it some change in product or manufacturing process, and thereby some change in work patterns and job mix. It is the relatively close identification of the interests of the kaisha and their employees that has made this rate of technological change possible and the pattern of union relations implicit in that degree of identification.

While the willingness to accept new technology is a function of the system of personnel relations in the *kaisha,* the ability of the labor force to absorb and adapt to the new technology is a function of their education and skills. Here note must be made of one of the most remarkable and far-reaching of the many great social changes that have taken place in Japanese society over the past generation. In 1950, one percent of new entrants to the Japanese labor force had attended institutions of higher education. Nearly 90 percent terminated their education at the compulsory middle-school level, after nine years of formal education. Even as recently as 1960, less than 10 percent had entered colleges or universities. By the 1980s, nearly 40 percent of new entrants to the labor force had attended institutions of higher education, and a mere 6 percent had stopped their education at the middle-school level.

Thus, in Japan as high a proportion of young people go on to education past the high-school level as is the case in the United States, a proportion roughly double that of the countries of Western Europe. The Japanese labor force is now at least as well educated, and at least as well prepared for dealing with complex technologies, as is any labor force in the world. Indeed, if the quality of the education is considered, it seems likely that

Japan's labor force is today quite simply the best educated in the world.

In concluding a recent study of Japanese education, the American anthropologist and Japan specialist Thomas P. Rohlen, in comparing the Japanese and American school systems, states:

> The Japanese get much better results for their money. A higher percentage of students graduates from high school. One in ten young Japanese, but one in four Americans, does not finish high school. Equal proportions of students now go on to higher education, but a considerably higher proportion of males is taking a bachelor's degree in Japan than in the United States. More important, the skills and achievements of the average Japanese student are far greater for all levels up through 12th grade. The Japanese go to school one-third more time than do Americans every year; over 12 years, they have had four more years of school. They can accommodate a more accelerated curriculum. They don't lose, during long summer vacations, half of what they have learned the previous year. Elementary education takes them farther in the basics, as well as in art and music, compared with our schools. In high school all students have more required courses in math, sciences, foreign languages, and social studies. The result, I estimate, is that the average Japanese high school graduate has the equivalent basic knowledge of the average American college graduate. The Japanese clearly cannot speak English well but their knowledge of written English is certainly better than the average foreign language ability of our college graduates. It is not surprising that the Japanese do well in international tests of math and science, or that they now produce twice the number of engineers per capita as we do, or that Japanese literacy as measured by per capita newspaper circulation is higher. If we were to recalculate the costs of education up to 12th grade, comparing them with the results, there is no doubt that the Japanese system would come out at least several times more efficient then our own.

The great accomplishment of Japanese primary and secondary education lies not in its creation of a brilliant elite (Western nations do better with their top students), but in its generation of such a high average level of capability. The profoundly impressive fact is that it is shaping a whole population, workers as well as managers, to a standard inconceivable in the United States, where

we are still trying to implement high school graduation competence tests that measure only minimal reading and computing
skills.[4]

Rohlen's conclusion is supported by the analysis of the
relative performance of young Japanese on standard intelligence tests. While there is little difference among average IQs
of young people tested in the United States and various other
countries, the Japanese have an average IQ of 111, the highest
recorded for a national population by a considerable margin.
"Whereas Americans and Europeans have about 2 percent of
their population with IQs over 130, the Japanese have about 10
percent at this level. Among the populations as a whole, 77
percent of Japanese have a higher IQ than the average American
or European."[5] The Japanese educational system evidently is
providing an exceptional labor force.

This educational accomplishment, with its emphasis on
mathematics and science, and on the production of graduated
engineers, is even more formidable when viewed in terms of the
demands on the work force of the future as microelectronics and
digital technology permeates further through the manufacturing and administrative functions of the kaisha. If, as has been
argued, the principal constraint on rapid progress in microelectronics and computer-related technology depends on the supply
of engineering skills, then Japanese companies are well positioned from the direction and effectiveness of their national
school system.

Speed of Corporate Response to Market Challenge

There is a more speculative aspect of the issue of the ability
of the organization to assimilate and deal with new technology
that warrants attention. As described in chapter 3, in the famous

4. Thomas P. Rohlen, *Japan's High Schools* (Berkeley, Calif: University of California
Press, 1983), pp. 321–22.
5. Richard Lynn, "IQ in Japan and the United States Shows a Growing Disparity,"
Nature, 20 May 1982, 222–23.

Honda-Yamaha war Honda used its ability to introduce an extraordinary number of new models into the market as a principal weapon against Yamaha. In another example, from a study of the airconditioning industry, the Japanese competitors are changing their entire model line every three years, while the U.S. competitor introduces new models on a cycle of nearly ten years. In the authors' consulting practice, we repeatedly find that the kaisha are able to move products from development through production into the marketplace at a much more rapid rate than our Western client companies in competition with the kaisha can.

The speed of response of the best of the kaisha to market opportunities also appears to be unusually rapid. For example, air wave frequencies were made available for personal radio use in Japan in January 1983. By October of that year twenty-two companies were in the market with product. Again, in the video cassette recorder field, the kaisha were not first with the initial products. At least two Western companies had prototypes in hand at an earlier date than their Japanese competitors. It was the Japanese competitors, however, who managed to extract the product from the clutches of engineering departments bent on further refinements, move the product into the marketplace, cascade improved versions into the market and conclude with over 90 percent of the world output of VCRs, which are now the largest-selling single consumer electronic products in the world.

Based on our recent consulting experience, we believe this speed of response of the kaisha is a real advantage, and pervasive. If this is the case, then the kaisha have an advantage not only in terms of the rate of investment, and willingness to introduce and absorb technology, but also in organizational ability to move from development to market competition. The ability of the kaisha to react more rapidly seems to be the result of several factors.

First, the kaisha seem not as prone to vertical organizational structures as their Western competitors. It is often difficult for the Western firm to build effective communication between major functional departments—for example, between engineering, manufacturing, and marketing. Each function is prone to take a parochial view of the organization by focusing on its own narrow concerns, often to the neglect of the larger corporate interest. Similarly, product divisions focus on their own performance, suboptimizing corporate overall performance in defense of their departmental or divisional concerns. Problems that overlap or fall between functions or divisions are difficult to deal with, and reaction time of the organization is thereby slowed.

It may well be the case that the kaisha's practice of extensive job rotation across functions and divisions helps break down these provincial barriers. It may be, too, that the emphasis of the kaisha's compensation system on the performance of the company as a whole is a factor in making communication and coordination more effective. Individual workers and managers may, as a result, be more willing to view problems and opportunities in corporate terms than is the case in most Western organizations. The issue requires further study, but at this point appears to be an additional kaisha competitive advantage in the rapid introduction of technology into the organization and into the marketplace.

"Picking Winners" or Accelerating Market Forces

This discussion of the quest for technological leadership, and its driving forces, has made little mention of the role of the government of Japan. Yet, in most Western discussions, the government's role is treated as central and is the source of much controversy. Terms like "industrial policy" and "targeting" are employed in attributing to the government of Japan special powers and abilities in aiming and accelerating the economy's technological progress. Clearly, some part of the tendency to put the government in a central role is the search for a simple answer to a complex phenomenon. The causes of technological change and success are complex; yet a simple answer appeals both to would-be imitators and would-be detractors of Japan's economic performance.

Without attempting to settle the controversy, a brief review of governmental research activities may help clarify the role of the kaisha. First, the limited funding for research by the government of Japan has been noted but deserves emphasis. Nearly half of total U.S. research expenditure is with government funds —the proportion is similar for the economies of Western Europe. In the Japanese case, the government provides about one-quarter of research funds. A few years ago, Japan's Economic Planning Agency described the situation and stated the Japanese government's policy as follows:

> In Japan, the governmental contribution to the total national research expenditure stands at only 27.4 percent (as of fiscal 1977) as against 50.5 percent in the United States and 48.5 percent in the Federal Republic of Germany (both in 1977). As a matter of principle, technological innovation should be the job of the innovators—namely, businesses themselves.[6]

In a recent survey, the Organization for Economic Cooperation and Development (OECD) noted:

> It is against the fundamental principles of the United States science policy to give direct aid to industrial technology development. . . . This does not mean that the Federal government does not support industrial R&D, only that it prefers to do so via other objectives—especially Defense and Aerospace.
>
> The national government directly funds about one-third of all manufacturing R&D in the United States and in the United Kingdom, but . . . the proportions are lower in France and Germany. In Japan, manufacturing industry finances almost all of the R&D it performs.[7]

More than for companies in any other major economy, the burden of funding R&D falls directly on Japan's kaisha. Whatever may be made of the role of government in Japan's technological drive, it must be kept firmly in mind that the funds are private funds, privately directed. Furthermore, this is an explicit policy of the government of Japan. Research funding is driven by the marketplace.

Of the Japanese government's limited research funding,

6. *Economic Survey of Japan 1978/1979*, p. 137
7. *OECD Science and Technology Indicators* (Paris: Organization for Economic Development and Cooperation, 1984), pp. 98, 117–18.

one-quarter is devoted to research in agriculture with another quarter devoted to energy research. While the latter will no doubt have spillover into industry, agricultural research has little effect on industry. In contrast to Japan, with half of its government research budget focused on agriculture and energy, two-thirds of the U.S. research budget is devoted to defense and aerospace. It is primarily through these budgets that the United States government funds developments in electronics and software, air frame and propulsion, and new materials developments. These funds are aimed—or "targeted," in the current phrase—at quite specific industrial developments.

The discussion of Japanese government targeting frequently attributes to the government of Japan an exceptional ability to foresee and plan for sectors that will offer high payouts if supported—"picking winners." Much has been made of a program in the 1970s, launched with MITI support, for the development of large-scale integrated circuitry. It needs first be noted that the subsidy to that research program totaled only $100 million over a seven-year period, and was divided among a number of companies. By world standards of R&D expenditures in the electronics industry, and compared to the subsidies provided to the industry by other governments, the amount of MITI subsidy was trivial.

The electronics sector was an important one, however, and the program a successful one. Yet it hardly needed any great technological foresight to judge that larger scale integrated circuitry would be important. Nor did the government of Japan, in this same industry, show any ability at picking winners when it resisted Sony's attempts in the 1950s to license transistor technology from Bell Labs, and did not anticipate IBM's third-generation computer technology in the 1960s.

It is no reflection on the considerable ability of Japan's bureaucrats and planners to suggest that their list of promising technologies is much the same as the lists prepared by planners in other economies. Economic forces working in the marketplace determine promising technologies, not governments, and the government of Japan is no exception to this rule. Furthermore, the government of Japan does not do well in its occasional attempts to pick corporate winners. In terms of numbers of competitors, efforts by MITI in the 1960s to shape the computer industry, and earlier the auto industry, failed totally. The productive cooperation by the semiconductor industry in pursuit of VLSI (Very Large Scale Integration) technology ended abruptly with the completion of the basic research as each participant in the joint basic research program then entered into a desperate race to be the winner in commercial development, production, and marketing. Not only was there no effort to pick the corporate winner on the part of the government, but the marketplace itself has not yet picked the winner in that competition.

In terms of picking winners, two areas of special emphasis in current Japanese R&D efforts are new ceramic materials and biotechnology. These are important not only for their inherent interest in terms of new products and processes, but because they offer some relief for Japan's economy from its long dependence on imported materials and energy. More than 200 kaisha are working in the field of new ceramic materials, in current production or in research and development. In biotechnology, a MITI survey identified 157 kaisha carrying out development programs, divided about equally between recombinant DNA work and work on cell fusion. This is hardly evidence of picking winners—it is evidence of fierce competition.

The VLSI program does, however, illustrate a real difference between Japan and the United States. This is the willingness of the government of Japan to encourage joint efforts by several kaisha in support of a research objective. Interest expressed by the Science and Technology Agency, a cabinet-level government organization, or by MITI in a research area serves as a signal to the kaisha that research support will be available, even if in limited amounts. Following this initial signal, the kaisha can, if interested and willing, join in an industry-organized joint research program, with some division of tasks. This is not to say that the kaisha are entirely trusting of each other, or that they are necessarily prepared to assign their best staff to joint projects. They may have reservations about the matter, as companies anywhere would.

In the case of the Japanese government, while the dangers of monopoly and collusion are well appreciated, antitrust law is not elevated to the level of a higher morality. Rather, antitrust regulations are seen as sensible and necessary, with exceptions made as economic sense dictates. Antitrust and other related laws and policies are seen as a means to an economic end, and not as an end in themselves. Thus, limited research funds and personnel can be pooled for a joint effort toward basic development, without being seen as economically dangerous.

The antitrust policy seems eminently sensible. Indeed, a review of the role of government in the technology area suggests that it is important, but in a somewhat different fashion than is usually described. There is little evidence that the government of Japan plays a large role, or is effective in the role of director or initiator of research projects and programs. But as an effective facilitator, the government of Japan works well in recognizing and accelerating the forces at work in the marketplace. As the government of Japan does not expend resources to sustain industries that are in structural trouble, it works to smooth and speed the decline of such industries. Similarly, in terms of technological change and growth, the government of Japan seems to be at its most effective in recognizing the play of market forces, and through depreciation schedules, tax schedules, and support for joint industry efforts, helps clear the way for the growth to take place unimpeded. It is another instance of the adage that it is not in the power of governments to do great good, but rather to prevent great harm.

A review of the development of robots in Japan illustrates many of these basic facts about Japan's technological position and policies. Japan is now, by a good margin, the world leader in both production and application of robots. The first industrial robots were developed in the United States in the 1950s, with much of the work subsidized by the U.S. government, especially through air force and Atomic Energy Commission programs. The first commercial robot was marketed in the United States in 1959.[8]

The first sale of a U.S. robot to Japan took place in 1967, and in 1968 Kawasaki Heavy Industries licensed the technology of Unimation, then the U.S. industry leader, for the manufacture

8. For a review of this history, see R. U. Ayres, L. Lynn, and S. Miller, "Technology Transfer in Robotics Between the U.S. and Japan," in *U.S.-Japan Technological Exchange Symposium* (Washington, D.C.: University Press of America, 1983).

of robots. The initial market response in Japan, as in the United States, was limited as the machines were still rather crude and costly. The robot field developed slowly in Japan, and it is of note that the various agencies of the Japanese government showed little interest in the product. However, in the mid-1970s, Japanese firms came under tremendous pressure to reduce costs in every way possible, and management attention shifted from dealing with fast growth to dealing with the consequences of exploding energy costs, high inflation, and a depression. It was the era of *genryo keiei,* of slimming or dieting management. The application of robots in the factories of Japan began to take off, as shown in figure 6–1.

By the late 1970s nearly 200 hundred Japanese firms were in robot production of one sort or another, and 85 universities and other institutions—a number that had doubled in only six years—were conducting research on increased speed, size reduction, computer controls, weight reduction, and modular design. The robot market was expected to reach $1 billion in 1985 and to double again in the next five years—a Japanese technological success story.

It was not until 1980, when private sector activity and developments were well advanced that government programs in support of robot development began. These very sensibly focused on encouraging rapid growth of the field. A 13 percent accelerated depreciation write-off of purchase price was allowed, and a leasing company was set up with funds from the Japan Development Bank and commercial banks to make purchase easier. Small businesses were given special loan facilities for robot purchase. In 1982, MITI sought funding to launch a joint government-industry program to develop highly intelligent robots.

The key elements are all in place in the robotics story. The technology was pioneered in the United States, with government subsidies playing a large part. A Japanese company brought the technology into Japan through licensing. Market forces working in Japan began to drive the development of the technology at a rapid pace. Japanese investment levels made for fast growth, and there were no problems with introducing the technology into Japanese workplaces. A swarm of Japanese competitors were attracted into the field by the growth prospects,

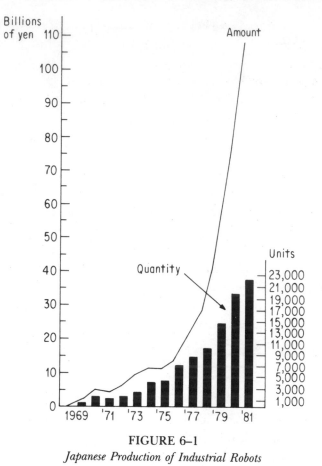

FIGURE 6–1

Japanese Production of Industrial Robots

SOURCE: Y. Machida, "Industrial Robots in Japan," in *Japan's High Technology Industries* (Tokyo: Industrial Research Division, The Long-Term Credit Bank of Japan, May, 1983), p. 8.

and the technology began to develop rapidly. Finally, the government of Japan has put programs into operation to facilitate and accelerate robotics developments, while Japanese companies emerge as world leaders in this new and fast-growing field. Although the government of Japan showed no prescience regarding the potential for robots, it reacted to the kaisha, their economics, and the robotics marketplace in a highly supportive and effective fashion.

With the increased recognition in the late 1970s of the necessity and urgency of independent R&D if economic progress were to continue in Japan, there was also an emerging general agreement on the sectors of greatest importance for it.

The Drive to Technological Leadership

One of Japan's three banks which specialize in long-term lending recently undertook a study to define these fields and assess the present competitive position of Japanese industry in each. This kind of scorekeeping, of tracking Japan's ranking in the world game, had in the past focused on growth rates and size by industry. It is an important index to changing goals and preoccupations in Japan, that "high technology" is now the dominant phrase in the business press, just as growth was the earlier theme, and that Japan's relative ranking is now not judged only by relative size but also by relative technological position.

The Long-Term Credit Bank of Japan states:

> In Japan, "advanced technology" means a high-level knowledge-intensive technology such as (1) semiconductors, (2) computers, (3) information and telecommunications, (4) office automation, (5) robots or unmanned production systems, (6) optics, (7) aerospace, (8) new materials, and (9) biotechnology . . . . Industries that make intensive use of these industries are referred to as "advanced technology industries" or "high technology industries."[9]

Japan's standing in the world competitive race in these categories is summarized by the bank as follows:

> Japan has perfected mass-production technology for the high-tech products of VLSIs, optical fiber, semiconductor lasers, carbon fibers, VTRs [VCRs], and compact disks, with the result that its market share is over 95 percent in VTRs, 70 percent in 64K RAMs, 70 percent in robots and 95 percent in compact disks.
>
> But in developing creative technology Japan still lags behind the United States, which enjoys a considerable lead in computers, aircraft, space and telecommunications equipment . . . .

In some specific areas, the bank concludes:

> [Computers] Japan is building up strength in smaller models, but in software it will not be able to catch up with the United States for some while.

9. *Japan's High Technology Industries (2)* (Tokyo: Industrial Research Division, The Long-Term Credit Bank of Japan, February 1984), p.1.

[Semiconductors] Japan's competitiveness in the field of semiconductors is expected to last. It should also be noted that Japan is highly competitive in the semiconductor manufacturing equipment industry.

[Robots] Japan is dominant in all three aspects of number of robots in operation, value of production, and technological strength.

[Office automation] In copiers Japan has an 85 percent share of the world market, and in facsimiles its exports are growing by more than 50 percent per year. In personal computers, office computers, and word processors, Japan is still weak in software, but in hardware it is competitive . . . .

[Aerospace] Developing new aircraft will be beyond (Japan's) power for at least another ten years. In space development Japan is said to be ten years behind the United States.

[Optoelectronics] Japan is thought to have overtaken the United States . . . .

[Biotechnology] Biotechnology was developed in the United States, but Japan is catching up fast."[10]

It is, of course, a task for specialists to judge the accuracy of these assessments—and for some only time can tell. But two conclusions might be drawn. First, these are the areas for research focus in most countries; there is nothing extraordinary about the list. Second, the assessments of Japan's position, however accurate, display a high level of self-confidence both about present performance and prospects for performance.

The Question of Creativity

There is a good deal of skepticism outside Japan about the ability of Japanese researchers to achieve the necessary levels of creativity that will enable the kaisha to compete in technology, as well as in manufacturing and marketing, on a world basis. The issue is complex, not least because scientific creativity is itself

10. Ibid., pp. 12–14.

not well understood. The kaisha are providing the financial resources and facilities; Japan's educational system is providing
the human material. At issue is the rather mysterious "creative
process," against a general view of the Japanese as being skilled
in adopting and adapting but not in innovation and discovery.

In some ways, it is curious that Japanese creative abilities
are denigrated so often. That the Japanese are creative seems
clear enough; the existence of a unique and distinct culture, with
special art forms and living styles, is surely testimony. In recent
years, individuals like Tange in architecture, Munakata in art,
Tanizaki and Kawabata in literature, and now a number of
Japanese in high fashion and design, are creative by any measure
and in every sense.

The point was well made by the late C. P. Snow in his
posthumously published memoir on modern physics. Discussing the information-processing industry, he remarked:

> Japan is worth particular notice. The Japanese scientists,
> technologists, technocrats, have shown skills and originality in all
> this electronic apotheosis which quite out-class the West's. That
> ought to surprise no one who has given the most perfunctory
> attention to Japanese visual art or literature or pure science. For
> hundreds of years, the culture has been wildly original, something
> oddly different from any other among the sons of men. It was an
> instance of Western blindness not to discover that simple fact.[11]

A striking perspective on Japanese creativity was offered by
Professor Harvey Brooks of Harvard University. The House of
Representative's Committee on Science, Research, and Technology was exercised about whether the United States might be
"losing the technological race." Professor Brooks remarked:

> Although Japanese success in recent years has been based on
> adaptation of Western, mainly American, technology, and on the
> capacity to commercialize it more rapidly than its competitors, it
> would be wrong to conclude from this that the Japanese are mere
> imitators who, once they have attained to the world state-of-the-
> art in a field, will not continue to move forward the frontiers of

11. C. P. Snow, *The Physicists* (London: Macmillan, 1981), pp. 159–60.

technology. On the contrary, history suggests that imitation, followed by more and more innovative adaptation, leading eventually to pioneering, creative innovation forms the natural sequence of economic and industrial development.

Successful imitation, far from being symptomatic of lack of originality as used to be thought, is the first step of learning to be creative. This is probably true of nations, as it seems to be of individuals, something which Americans may have forgotten in our almost obsessive belief in originality and individual creativity. It may be only those who try continually to reinvent the wheel that will lose out in the innovative race. In my opinion, the United States, so long accustomed to leading the world, may have lost the art of creative imitation, and is deficient in scanning the world's science and technology for potential commercial opportunities relative to what is done by its competitors, particularly Japan.[12]

In the larger sense, Japan's drive to technological leadership can only be welcomed. The research efforts of Japan's kaisha and of its government are not directed to weapons systems or the technology of destruction. They are directed toward improved and innovative products for use in raising standards of living, and toward improved and innovative methods for reducing the costs to consumers. Mankind can only benefit. In this sense, it is nonsense to speak of "losing the technological race." There will be no losers, only winners.

At the corporate level, however, there can and will be winners and losers. Leading kaisha are now spending more of their incomes on research and development than their Western competitors with the support of an informed and competent government. The labor force the kaisha deploy in their technological drive is the best educated in the world, and far from finding new technology a threat, welcomes its introduction. The organizational approach of the kaisha allows exceptionally rapid introduction of new technology to the marketplace. In a number of fields of key importance to the future, the kaisha already have strong positions. It is foolish and foolhardy to take refuge in

12. House Subcommittee on Investigations and Oversight and the Subcommittee on Science, Research, and Technology of the Committee on Science and Technology, *Japanese Technological Advances and Possible United States Responses Using Research Joint Ventures.* 98th Cong., 1st sess., 29–30 June, 1983, p. 17.

stereotypes about the Japanese as "copiers." They are already a major force in world technological competition.

Given all this, it was startling to discover in an investigation by the authors of the current activities of twelve major foreign companies in Japan that only two of the twelve had the organization and staff to study and gain access to Japanese technological developments. These two companies had already licensed products from Japan for introduction in their home markets. But most U.S. and European companies do no technology screening in Japan, and even among those that do, complacency regarding technology is the rule rather than the exception. Professor Brooks's remark is telling: "Those who try continually to reinvent the wheel will lose out in the innovative race."

The *kaisha* as competitors are driving for technological leadership. Western competitors were caught by surprise when the kaisha achieved cost and quality levels fully competitive in many industries. Will Western competitors be surprised again as technological parity, and leadership, is achieved?

7

WORKING WITH BANKS
AND SHAREHOLDERS FOR
COMPETITIVE ADVANTAGE

———————————

Low profitability of the kai-
sha, and their access to seemingly unlimited sources of borrowed funds, are commonly held to be two key competitive
advantages not available to Western competitors. The kaisha are
often described as recklessly seeking growth at the expense of
profit, using special banking relationships in order to obtain
borrowed funds for high levels of investment, and in the process
ignoring the interests of their shareholders. The pattern is seen
as unfair, in the sense that these kinds of financial policies are
not available to competitors in other countries, who have an
inherent competitive handicap from their need to achieve
higher profit levels, to keep their debt funding within narrow
limits, and to provide continued significant dividends to shareholders.

There are real differences in financial policies and strategies between Western and Japanese firms, but the extent of
these differences is often overstated. Moreover, it is within the
capacity of Western firms to reduce these differences, and con-

comitantly reduce the advantage of the kaisha. The critical issue is the value placed on growth of the company, and the drive of management to achieve growth targets that will ensure long-term competitive success. The competitive advantages of the kaisha derive as much from their selection of aggressive financial policies as from any special characteristics of the Japanese situation. Their policies are driven by their experience with and focus on growth.

Financial Performance of Japanese Companies

The controversy over Japanese financial practices is made more complex by the fact that profitability has no single, definitive measure. Western executives tend to focus on return on sales as the measure of profitability. By this measure, Japanese companies are less profitable than U.S. companies. The after-tax return on sales for the average Japanese manufacturer has been 1 to 2 percent for the past six or eight years. The average U.S. manufacturer has achieved an after-tax return of sales of 5 to 6 percent, or three to six times greater than the average kaisha company. Similarly, when measured in terms of return on assets, the profitability of the average Japanese manufacturer is lower than that of the average U.S. manufacturer.

But when profitability is measured by after-tax return on shareholders' investment, the position is reversed. The after-tax return on equity of the average Japanese manufacturer has been about 20 percent for most of the 1970s, while the return on equity for the average U.S. manufacturer has been in the range of 10 to 15 percent. Furthermore, continuing studies by the Organization for Economic Cooperation and Development (OECD) report consistently high rates of return on investment in Japan compared with other OECD economies, such as West Germany, the United Kingdom, and the United States.

The issue is, in part then, a question of the measure of profitability used. The higher returns of equity of the Japanese manufacturer are achieved at some risk. The leverage, or the amount of borrowed funds compared to the amount of equity funds, of the average Japanese manufacturing firm is much greater than that of the average U.S. company. The ratio of all debt to equity of the average Japanese manufacturer has been approximately 2:1 for the 1970s, compared with a debt-to-equity ratio of 0.5:1 for the average U.S. firm. The higher Japanese debt component in total investment funds largely accounts for the higher percent return on the shareholders' portion of the total investment.

The issue is further complicated by the fact that it is no longer possible to describe all of the kaisha in financial terms with broad generalizations. As growth has slowed in many industries, the financial performance of many kaisha has come to compare quite favorably in every respect with that of leading Western companies in similar businesses. Some comparisons are shown in table 7–1. After-tax returns on sales and on equity and debt-to-equity ratios are compared for recent, high performance years for eight companies. The return on sales and on equity of Toyota compares favorably with those of General Motors, and the two balance sheets are equally strong. In fact, Toyota is referred to in Japan as the "Toyota bank," from its aversion to debt and heavy cash position. In 1981, Toyota earned 67 billion yen more in interest and dividends than it paid out, greater than the 56 billion of net income earned in that year by the Sumitomo Bank, Japan's most profitable commercial bank.

TABLE 7–1

Financial Comparisons of Market Leaders

Market Leaders	Year	Approximate Sales (Yen Billions)	Return on Sales (%)	Debt-to-Equity Ratio	Return on Equity (%)
General Motors	1978	12,328	5.5	.06:1	21.0
Toyota	1979	3,310	4.3	.00:1	15.7
Philips	1982	3,998	1.9	.78:1	6.6
Matsushita	1981	2,346	3.6	.15:1	11.2
Black & Decker	1979	289	7.9	.20:1	18.4
Makita	1979	54	9.9	.00:1	9.9
Goodyear	1981	2,014	2.9	.50:1	10.9
Bridgestone	1979	434	5.8	.37:1	17.8

Similar comparisons can be made for many other companies. Matsushita has more impressive performance measures than does Philips of the Netherlands, the two companies being direct competitors and the world's largest consumer electronics producers. Bridgestone's performance compares very favorably with that of Goodyear, the two companies being the leading tire manufacturers in Japan and in the United States respectively. Fuji Film is now as profitable as Eastman Kodak, its great rival in photographic equipment and supplies. The U.S. steel companies, reeling under massive losses and write-offs, no longer disparage the low profitability of Japan's steel producers as they were earlier prone to do.

Just as broad generalizations about low profitability of Japanese firms are no longer appropriate, so is it hazardous now to speak of high levels of debt as characteristic of the kaisha. As seen, Toyota has no debt, and Matsushita virtually none. As growth in the economy in total has slowed, and as many industries have matured, the pattern of heavy borrowings has changed. *The Economist* reported:

> A survey by the Bank of Japan of 621 of the country's biggest companies found that in the year to March, 1984, these firms raised only 14 percent of their new external funding needs with bank loans, compared with an average of 56 percent in the previous five years and 80 percent in the 1960s. . . . Slack investment and big internal reserves mean that firms now need external funds of only the equivalent of 1 percent of sales, compared with 2.3 percent during the previous five years.[1]

In sum, it is true that Japanese firms are by some measures less profitable than U.S. firms, and it is also true that they generally have much higher leverage. But this is by no means true of all Japanese firms, many of the most powerful being highly profitable and financially strong. Western competitors need to guard against generalizations.

For all of the increasing diversity in Japan's large and maturing economy, the fact remains that these companies have been nurtured under conditions of very high growth, which

1. "Limbering Up." A Survey of Japanese Finance and Banking," *The Economist*, 8 December 1984, 21.

requires debt financing. Under high-growth conditions, market share rather than profitability is the critical measure of performance. Having been nurtured in a growth milieu, the financial policies of the kaisha under conditions of high growth are different, typically, than those of their Western competitors.

Financial Strategies and Competitive Threat

A clear and powerful statement of the competitive threat posed by the financial strategies of the kaisha was provided in a recent comparison of the financial structure of companies in U.S. and Japanese semiconductor industries:

> While the U.S. is currently the world's leader in semiconductor technology and production . . . U.S. industry is concerned that it may lack the ability to raise sufficient capital to maintain its share of the world market. Specifically the industry believes the ability of the Japanese semiconductor companies to continuously employ considerably higher debt ratios regardless of business and economic conditions places U.S. semiconductor companies at a substantial disadvantage in raising capital. The Japanese semiconductor companies' cost of capital is significantly lower than that of the U.S. semiconductor companies largely as a result of the higher debt ratios employed by the Japanese companies . . . .
>
> The lower cost of capital of the Japanese companies provides them with the advantage that their required rates of return on investment are lower than those of the U.S. semiconductor companies. As a result, the Japanese companies can accept lower profit margins and/or capital turnover ratios than their U.S. counterparts . . . . Although the cost of capital of the U.S. semiconductor companies would be markedly reduced if their leverage could be increased to that of the Japanese semiconductor industry, this reduction would still be inadequate to close the cost of capital gap. Furthermore, leverage of this magnitude would not be available from conventional banking or capital marketing sources in the U.S.
>
> In summary, the U.S. semiconductor industry is currently in a strong position as the result of its technological leadership, sound financial condition and ability to earn an adequate rate of

return on invested capital. However, the position of the U.S. semiconductor industry could be eroded by its shrinking share of the world market and its inability to raise capital as cheaply as Japanese competitors. Additionally, declining market share may adversely affect the U.S. companies' productivity and efficiency, thereby placing added pressure on profit margins and exacerbating the industry's ability to raise capital. A shrinkage in profit margins could threaten the viability of those companies within the industry that fail to earn their cost of capital over an extended period of time.[2]

In 1984, for the first time since the invention of the transistor, the total capital investment of the Japanese semiconductor industry surpassed that of the U.S. industry, and projections are for the gap to widen. The Japanese investment level has been far ahead of Europe's for many years. The threat suggested by the Chase Manhattan Bank is beginning to look real.

Accepting the premise that conventional banking and capital marketing sources in the U.S. will not allow their companies to match the financial policies of the kaisha led the management of one major U.S. semiconductor company to conclude:

> The ability of [our company] to close this gap through increased automation, better yields, more automation and assistance of indirect functions through CAD/CAM and other productivity improvements is expected to be somewhat limited as Japanese companies can be expected to pursue these same approaches at a similar rate.
>
> [Our company] in the past has shown a greater degree of flexibility than the Japanese in utilizing offshore areas to gain advantage of lower wage and benefit rates and gain financial and tax advantages. The possible next step [in closing the gap] may be to utilize areas of the world where there are available people at lower wage rates in the technical, systems, and other staff type areas in which to place functional groups that do not have to be in physical proximity to end markets or manufacturing operations.
>
> Approximately 30 percent of [our] exempt work force [are currently] offshore . . . . To close the gap requires an additional

2. Chase Manhattan Bank, *Chase Financial Policy* (Report Prepared for U.S. Semiconductor Industry Association, New York, 9 June 1980), pp. 1–10.

35 percent of the remaining exempt jobs in the U.S. to be moved offshore [for a total of 55 percent of all exempts to be located offshore].[3]

These are very serious reactions to the effects of differing financial policies of the Japanese and U.S. semiconductor companies. But as long as the kaisha are able to employ such drastically different financial policies, the U.S. semiconductor industry either has to influence the U.S. financial community to change significantly its pattern of doing business, or it has to move almost entirely offshore to low-wage countries. The option of taking no action to offset or negate the advantage of the financial policies of the Japanese is believed to almost certainly lead to the demise of the U.S. semiconductor industry.

It is in the high-growth sectors like semiconductors, and indeed in the whole range of microelectronically driven new technologies, that the differences in financial policies become critical. It is precisely in these critical competitive sectors that the growth-driven financial policies of the kaisha differ most greatly from those of their Western competitors. Japanese companies in these high growth businesses most often employ financial policies considered reckless and unmatchable by Western executives. The basis for these policies, their attraction to Japanese management, and their impact can be better understood if viewed in turn from the perspective of corporate management seeking growth, from the perspective of the banks as principal suppliers of funds, and from the perspective of the Japanese shareholder seeking an adequate return on his investment. The kaisha's financial strategies are consistent with the needs of all three major participants.

Perspective of Corporate Management

Good products and prices, growing demand, and the earning power of existing businesses provide the basis for corporate growth in Japan as in the other free market economies. Corpo-

3. Extract from confidential client memorandum to authors, 1983.

rate financial policies influence the flow of cash available to fund growth. The three key financial policies influencing the amount of funds available for growth are pricing, debt policies, and dividend policies.

Aggressive financial policies are often an important element of the strategy employed by one competitor in outperforming another. Such companies as Amerada Hess, Georgia Pacific, and Dow Chemical all changed and improved their competitive positions in large part because of aggressive financial strategies. The effect of differences in financial policies on the ability to grow aggressively can be appreciated from a study of the example in table 7–2. Call one company "Leader," and think of it as U.S., Inc. Call the smaller competitor "Follower," and consider it to be Japan, K.K. As is usual, Leader is much larger in total sales than Follower. However, in this case Follower is growing twice as fast as Leader.

The two companies have very different financial policies. Leader seeks high margins, pays healthy dividends, and scorns debt. Follower is a price cutter, with low margins, no dividends, and high leverage. Leader is very strong financially and has no

TABLE 7–2
Leader vs. Follower: Changing the Rules of the Game

	Leader (U.S., Inc.)	Follower (Japan, K.K.)
Market Share (% in units)	50	10
Growth Rate per Year (%)	15	30
Debt-to-Equity Ratio	0:1	2:1
Debt (Billions of Yen)	0	6.7
Equity (Billions of Yen)	50	3.3
Total Assets (Billions of Yen)	50	10.0
Required Reinvestment (Billions of Yen)	7.50	3.00
Sales (Billions of Yen)	50.00	7.17
Cost of Goods Sold (Billions of Yen)	20.00	4.50
Operating Margin (Billions of Yen)	30.00	2.67
Less interest (Billions of Yen)	0	0.67
	30.00	2.00
Less tax (Billions of Yen)	15.00	1.00
Profit (Billions of Yen)	15.00	1.00
Dividends (Billions of Yen)	7.50	0
	7.50	1.00
New debt (Billions of Yen)	0	2.00
Available for Growth (Billions of Yen)	7.50	3.00

debt on its balance sheet. Follower, having a debt-to-equity ratio of 2:1, is highly leveraged. To maintain growth, Leader must increase its asset base 15 percent per year and Follower 30 percent per year. These companies must fund the increase in assets using funds generated internally or obtained from outside the corporation.

Leader finances its growth entirely with retained earnings. Leader sets prices high enough to achieve after-tax profits of 15 billion yen. Half of these profits are earmarked for dividends, leaving 7.5 billion yen, the amount required to grow the asset base of Leader by 15 percent. Because of Leader's no-debt policy no additional funds are borrowed to expand the asset base faster than 15 percent per year.

Follower practices much more aggressive financial policies. The combination of deep price discounts and slightly higher manufacturing costs yields a pre-tax operating margin of 37 percent for Follower compared with 60 percent for Leader. The operating margin of Follower is reduced by interest charges on its debt and the resulting after-tax profit margin is 14 percent compared with 30 percent for Leader. The 1 billion yen of after-tax profits is not enough to grow the asset base by 30 percent. Follower elects to pay no dividend and to borrow 2 billion yen so that its asset base can be expanded at the desired rate of 30 percent per year. Follower's debt-to-equity ratio remains at two to one.

The aggressive financial policies of Follower have created significant competitive advantages. Follower is discounting prices 28 percent off those of Leader in spite of a 13 percent manufacturing cost disadvantage. Of course Follower cannot pay dividends and must borrow heavily but it is growing twice as fast as Leader, and if unchecked could eventually emerge as the real leader, with lower costs and potentially higher profits.[4]

4. The combined effect of financial policies and environment can be captured in a simple calculation of a company's "sustainable growth rate." A company can only grow if the combination of retained earnings, new equity, and additional debt is positive. The sustainable growth rate is the growth rate a company can sustain without changing its financial policies and its capital structure.

As a formula, this is $SGR = [R + D/E(R - i)] * P$, where
SGR = sustainable growth rate; R = after-tax return on net assets; D = interest-bearing debt; E = equity; i = after-tax interest rate; and P = earnings retention ratio.

(continued)

In the late 1970s and early 1980s the average Japanese company had financial policies that made possible a sustained growth rate almost 25 percent higher than its U.S. counterpart, in spite of the lower profitability of the Japanese company. The average rate of return on net assets for a U.S. manufacturer is about 12 percent. This compares to an 8 percent average for a Japanese manufacturer. The average debt-to-equity ratio for a U.S. manufacturer is 0.6:1 and for a Japanese manufacturer 1.6:1. On average, U.S. and Japanese manufacturers pay out about the same percentage of their profits in dividends, and the U.S. company pays an average 6.5 percent after-tax interest rate compared to 3.5 percent for the Japanese company. The combined effect of these differences is that the average Japanese manufacturer can grow about 10 percent per year without changing its financial structure while the average U.S. manufacturer can grow at only 8 percent per year.

If the U.S. company were to be just as aggressive as the Japanese in its choice of financial policies, it could fund a sustained growth rate of about 14 percent per year—about 66 percent faster than its average Japanese counterpart. That more U.S. companies do not use more aggressive financial policies is curious. This can partially be explained by the risk aversion policies of U.S. banks, financial institutions, and corporate management. Also, aggressive financial policies do not usually fit with desires for higher short-term profitability. With aggressive levels of debt and earnings retention comes growth, rather than short-term profitability. Finally, few companies in the U.S. have competitors who employ aggressive financial policies as a means to achieve faster growth.

The combination of aggressive financial policies and fundamentally sound product and marketing strategies can be devastating to competitors. Honda upset the leading Japanese manufacturer of motorcycles, Tohatsu, in the 1950s by aggressively

---

A company's sustainable growth rate increases with higher returns from the business (R), increased leverage (D/E), and higher earning retention. The rate decreases with lower earnings retention (P) and higher interest rates (i). A more complete discussion of the sustainable growth rate formula, and its derivation, can be found in Alan J. Zakon, "Capital Structure Optimization," in *The Treasurer's Handbook*, eds. J. Fred Weston and Maurice B. Goudzwaard (Homewood, Ill.: Dow Jones-Irwin, 1976), pp. 641–68.

expanding capacity and funding this expansion with borrowed money (as discussed in detail in chapter 3). While Honda was regarded as a good motorcycle manufacturer, many observers considered its financing policies to be reckless. Honda's profits were less than one half of Tohatsu's profits and its debt-to-equity ratio of 6 to 1 was four times higher than that of Tohatsu.

By using aggressive financial policies Honda was able to grow 50 percent faster than the market growth of over 40 percent per year, while Tohatsu grew little, if at all. Because Honda grew so much faster than Tohatsu its market share increased from 20 percent in 1956 to over 40 percent in 1961 while Tohatsu's share collapsed from 22 percent to 4 percent. Honda's comparatively higher volumes (about 10 times higher) meant that its costs were substantially lower than Tohatsu's.

Lower costs soon translated to a stronger financial position. By 1960 Honda's profits were about 10 percent of sales while Tohatsu ran a deficit of about 8 percent of sales. Tohatsu's balance sheet had deteriorated to a debt-to-equity ratio of 7 to 1 while Honda's had improved to a ratio of 1 to 1. Tohatsu was borrowing heavily in a futile attempt to maintain a viable market position. The growth of the market had slowed to about 9 percent per year and the battle was over. Tohatsu declared bankruptcy in 1964.

One cannot ignore the paradox in the application of aggressive financial policies. While successful companies have the maximum capacity to assume debt, it is usually the marginal competitor that uses the greatest leverage and hence incurs the highest financial risk. The marginal competitor often sets debt and dividend policies to compensate for an underlying and uncorrected cost disadvantage so as to defend its marginal competitive position. This phenomena can be clearly seen in the U.S. automobile industry in the mid-1970s (table 7–3). The marginal competitor, Chrysler, had less than one-third of General Motor's share of the business. Chrysler's price realization was about 5 to 13 percent lower than G.M.'s and its manufacturing costs were 8 to 10 percent higher depending on the size of the vehicle. Therefore its operating profitability was much lower. For Chrysler to defend its marginal competitive position—a must, because if it lost position these numbers only would become worse—it had to retain most of its earnings and supplement its internally generated cash flow with debt. By doing so, Chrysler was able to achieve financial growth that was about on par with General Motors and Ford, and it therefore was able to maintain its competitive position. (Ultimately, the competitive equilibrium of the U.S. automobile industry was destabilized by a severe recession and increasing Japanese imports, and Chrysler was driven to the brink of bankruptcy.)

Chrysler is not alone in using debt as a defensive measure rather than as a means of aggressive growth. Many Japanese companies also cling to marginal competitive positions in part by assuming higher debt levels than more profitable competitors. Sony is only about one-third the size of its principal Japanese competitor, Matsushita. To help keep pace with Matsushita, Sony has had to leverage up to almost three times the level of Matsushita's leverage to finance the holding of its competitive position. In Japan's beer industry, Sapporo and Asahi, the number two and number three companies, are much less profitable than Kirin, Japan's largest beer company, and have debt-to-equity ratios almost twice as high as Kirin's.

Financial risks increase with increased leverage. However, the failure to match the aggressive financial policies of advancing competitors may be even more risky. If the aggressor's financial policies are not met, pressures for higher profits and hence prices will increase. This typically leads companies into the manufacture of products that have higher gross margins but very

TABLE 7–3

U.S. Auto Industry Use of Aggressive Financial Policies
to Offset Competitive Advantage (Mid-1970s)

	General Motors	Ford	Chrysler
Domestic Market Share	52%	29%	15%
Estimate of Manufacturing Cost (Index GM)	100	104	108
Operating Margin	18%	13%	9%
Return on Net Assets	20%	12%	9%
Return on Equity	21%	14%	11%
Debt to Equity	0.1:1	0.2:1	0.3:1
Retention	27%	50%	57%
Financial Growth	6%	7%	6%

often lower sales volume and lower growth potential. Continued pursuit of higher margin products and retreat to the higher priced segments generally lead to increased costs relative to the policies of the aggressive competitor. More often than not the conclusion of these dynamics is the eventual domination of the industry by the aggressor.

Many U.S. electronic companies are facing this problem today. Their Japanese competitors have lower operating profits, lower interest rates, higher retention rates, and higher debt-to-equity ratios. The Japanese are also growing faster. While some companies have built substantial operations in Japan, and therefore benefit from the lower interest rates in Japan, hardly any have wholeheartedly matched the aggressive financial policies of the Japanese—in Japan or at home. Some of the Japanese companies that are the leaders in semiconductor manufacturing have debt-to-equity ratios in excess of 2:1. For example, NEC, a leader in the Japanese semiconductor industry, has a debt-to-equity ratio of more than 2:1. The average debt-to-equity ratio for the major U.S. semiconductor manufacturers is about 0.2:1 and for Texas Instruments specifically it is also 0.2:1. The sustainable growth rate of NEC is almost two times higher than that of TI.

The Chase Manhattan Bank analysis suggests that allowing borrowers in the U.S. semiconductor industry to raise their debt-to-equity ratio to two times is "extremely unlikely." However, the leaders of the industry could benefit from a relaxation of traditional financing principles. The debt-to-equity ratio does not have to be 2:1 to have an effect on the competitiveness of the U.S. producers. There is a precedent in the United States for more aggressive policies. Dow Chemical used debt aggressively to surge ahead in the chemical industry in the 1960s and 1970s, moving to a debt-to-equity ratio of about 1:1 for a time, with the marginal ratio (new debt to new equity) much higher for several years.

At issue then is, given that some kaisha derive significant competitive advantage by using aggressive financial policies, how can their Western competitors respond? Western companies are unlikely to change the attitudes of their financial institutions, but aggressive financial institutions that truly understand the competitive requirements of their clients do exist. Some are financing leveraged buyouts today in which companies are purchased almost entirely with debt secured by the assets of the purchased companies. Some leveraged buyouts can have debt-to-equity ratios greater than 20:1.

The larger Western companies have the additional option of going "direct" for their money by offering debentures and thereby sidestepping the growth-stultifying policies of traditional financial institutions. Also, Western companies with growth plans can stop paying dividends. Although some shareholders will withdraw, others will take their place. Digital Equipment Corporation does not pay dividends and yet attracts sufficient numbers of shareholders. Finally, Western companies can build operations in Japan where there are many financial institutions willing to back an aggressive growth company with a good history.

Perspective of Japanese Banks and Financial Institutions

The kaisha use high leverage to fund fast growth. Many Western financial executives react quite negatively to the aggressive use of debt in Japan. For example, a U.S. investment banker says "You cannot have that much leverage and still be a company," and a lending officer in the new Tokyo branch of a U.S. bank says "We have made numerous requests to our head office for permission to make loans to Japanese companies, but because of the strict balance sheet criteria imposed by our headquarters credit committee we have been unable to make more than just a few loans."

The prevailing view is that Japanese companies can take financial risks because of the relationships they have with their financial institutions. Presumably their financial institutions reduce their risk by establishing close relationships with their clients through shareholdings and access to better information. Also, some of the leading companies in the Japanese semiconductor industry such as Hitachi, Mitsubishi Electric, Toshiba, and NEC, are the lead or member companies of Japan's famed *keiretsu,* or business groups. These groups often include a bank, which will be the lead bank for the other members of the group, such as Fuji, Mitsubishi, Mitsui, and Sumitomo banks. The common belief is that with the group bank holding a share position in the company and with the financial assistance and loan guarantees from group members and the bank, Japanese semiconductor and other high-growth companies are able to pursue very aggressive financial policies.

This prevailing view overestimates the risk exposure of the Japanese financial institutions, which is less than it appears on the surface. Until recently Japanese financial institutions made loans that were collateralized with specific assets. The ability to provide collateral is usually far greater than is apparent on the balance sheets of many Japanese companies. A recent study comparing the financial structure of U.S. and Japanese companies concluded:

> This study is a reexamination, by means of a comparison of Japanese and United States corporate balance sheets, of concepts that have come to be regarded as the most remarkable features of corporate finance in Japan—namely (1) a low net-worth ratio [the predominance of borrowed capital] and (2) a high degree of dependency on financial institutions [the predominance of indirect financing]—as a preliminary to any analysis of the structure of corporate finances and corporate behaviors in Japan.
>
> We have three major findings as follows: (1) The conventional method of comparison between the two countries is superficial and one-sided, and needs to be modified. There are major differences between Japan and the United States in corporations' hidden assets, sources of funds via leases and subsidiary finance companies, and the terms of flotation and routes of sales of corporate debentures. In undertaking a comparative study of special features of the financial structures of the two countries based on corporate balance sheets, one has to make adjustments for such differences. (2) The information needed for implementing what are considered to be necessary adjustments is grossly insufficient. Consequently, it is risky to draw any hard and fast conclusions about the differences and similarities between Japan and the United States.

(3) Though such are the limitations, our own provisional adjustments for these differences significantly reduce differences in corporate financing between Japan and the United States. If that is so, then it will not suffice to settle for superficial emphasis on the unique nature of the Japanese company, as in general discussions in the past. We believe, rather, that it is necessary: (1) to account for Japanese corporate behaviors from a general theory of corporate finance instead of being too concerned about the differences between the two countries, and (2) to analyze and understand why a number of similarities do show up in the corporate financial structures of Japan and the United States even with their dissimilar environments.[5]

The authors are certainly correct in observing that "the information needed for implementing what are considered to be necessary adjustments is grossly insufficient." Fortunately, a recent filing by Hitachi yields several insights into the unstated financial strengths of the kaisha's balance sheet. A diversified manufacturer of electronic and electro-mechanical equipment, Hitachi's products include electric generation and transmission equipment, and consumer and advanced electronic products. Hitachi is in many ways similar to General Electric. Both companies are among the most profitable in their businesses, have strong growth, are formidable competitors, and are considered to be well run.

Yet the financial structures of these two companies are very different (table 7–4). Hitachi is much more leveraged than G.E. Hitachi's short- and long-term debt-to-equity ratio is greater than 1:1 compared to G.E.'s ratio of 0.25:1. Hitachi's return on sales is lower than G.E.'s. Most Western analysts would consider Hitachi's balance sheet to represent a much higher financial risk than G.E.'s. The financial risk of Hitachi, however, is much overstated. The two balance sheets have at least four major differences. Considering these differences, Hitachi can actually be regarded as an equal, or better, financial risk than G.E.

The first difference is that Hitachi consolidates its long-term credit financing and its credit company subsidiary. General Electric, like many U.S. companies, keeps its high-debt busi-

---

5. Iwao Kuroda and Yoshiharu Oritani, "A Reexamination of the Unique Features of Japan's Corporate Financial Structure," in *Japanese Economic Studies* 8, no. 4 (Summer 1980): pp. 82–83.

TABLE 7–4

1981 Balance Sheet Comparison: General Electric and Hitachi

	General Electric	Hitachi
Net Assets ($Billion)	12.0	9.3
Short- and Long-Term Debt-to-Equity Ratio	0.25:1	1.02:1

nesses off its balance sheet. Hitachi's balance sheet contains interest-bearing trade receivables not due within one year of about $361 million. This is purchase financing provided to Hitachi's customers, along with credit from Hitachi Credit, listed on the Tokyo stock exchange; G.E. provides these services through its unconsolidated subsidiary, the G.E. Credit Corporation. The result is an understatement of G.E.'s corporate indebtedness on its consolidated statement.

A second difference is that Hitachi's balance sheet includes housing loans to employees, of which G.E. has few if any. A common practice of major companies in Japan is to provide low-interest housing loans to senior employees whose future paychecks, homes, and retirement allowances are adequate collateral. Hitachi's balance sheet contains $588 million of housing loans with repayment terms ranging from ten to fifteen years.

A third difference, and a characteristic of profitable Japanese companies, is understated holdings of marketable securities. Hitachi's holding of marketable securities on 31 March 1981 were on its balance sheet at cost and were stated as being worth $243 million. Japanese companies generally do not churn their securities portfolios. Many of the securities were acquired decades ago and are holdings of the stocks of suppliers, customers, and financial institutions. General Electric constantly refreshes its holdings and states that its portfolio is valued on the balance sheet at close to market value. The current market value of Hitachi's securities on 31 March 1981 were estimated to be over $900 million. Therefore Hitachi's balance sheet reports securities whose values are understated by about $667 million.

The fourth and most significant difference is that the value of the land held by Hitachi is much understated on its balance sheet, probably far more so than G.E.'s land is on its balance sheet. Many companies across Japan have land on their balance sheet valued at cost of acquisition since the beginning of the Meiji era—the opening of Japan to the Western world, which began in 1868. For example, the Mitsubishi Estate Company is the principal owner of the Marunouchi banking district in Tokyo. The firm's predecessor acquired the land for the equivalent of $6,400 in 1892 and it is carried on the books at this cost. The land today is estimated to be worth more than $2 billion.

The exact understatements of land prices on the balance sheets of Hitachi are not publicly known, but can be fully estimated by banking institutions as the need arises. An appreciation of the potential magnitude of the understatement can be gained by comparing the general appreciation of land prices in Japan and in the United States. Increases in U.S. land prices have been led by the leap in prices of farm acreage, particularly in the last decade. The average price per acre for U.S. farmland has increased about fourteen times from 1950 to 1981. By contrast, the price of Japanese industrial acreage has increased one hundred fifty times from 1950 to 1981 and over six thousand times since just before the start of World War II. Although such a scenario is very unlikely, if Hitachi were to sell its land at market values it might realize a gain of $50 billion to $2,000 billion.

These four differences: consolidated credit financing, mortgage loans, understated securities portfolios, and understated land values make excellent collateral for lending institutions. As such, they are the equivalent of unstated net worth. Combined, the unstated net worth of the first three is well over $1 billion. The unstated net worth of land is difficult to estimate precisely. However, for Hitachi's debt-to-equity ratio to be equal to that of G.E., Hitachi's land holdings would only have had to increase in value forty-four times since the 1950s—a rate far lower than the Japan average. Hitachi, therefore, has at least as strong a balance sheet as the General Electric Company. To the financial institutions of Japan, Hitachi is no greater risk than G.E., even with Hitachi's reported debt-to-equity ratio of about 1:1.

Japanese companies have close relationships with their banks and financial institutions. The companies hold each other's equity and financial information is exchanged, and relationships are reinforced by continuous financial dealings. For example, Hitachi's balance sheet contains large amounts of cash and marketable securities. The cash deposited in interest-bearing time deposits totaled $640 million on 31 March 1981. These deposits are made to "maintain satisfactory relationships with the banks, although not subject to any restrictions on withdrawal." For Hitachi these deposits represent an inexpensive insurance against possible needs for banking support. At the same time, because of its strength, Hitachi can balance its funding activity equally between four major banks to ensure that no one bank will exert undue influence on the corporation.

When kaisha encounter severe trouble, it is their bankers who step in to reconstruct the corporation. Japan's distinguished long-term credit bank, the Industrial Bank of Japan, has played a notable role in such reconstructions, from the early postwar period with Nissan Motors, through the 1960s with Yamaichi Securities, and over the last decade or so for Chisso Chemical and Japan Lines. Indeed, the bank's principal troubleshooter in several especially difficult cases, Kaneo Nakamura, has moved rapidly to the presidency in part because of his successes in these reconstructions.

The Industrial Bank of Japan has focused on financial reconstruction and has inserted many of its own executives into management positions in troubled companies. It is reported to have several hundred such executives in place in client companies, a tribute to the quality of its personnel and to the forcefulness of its interventions. In some cases, the reconstruction role of the bank is more directly managerial. For example, Tsutomo Murai, who led the return of Toyo Kogyo (Mazda) from the brink of bankruptcy in the mid-1970s was a former managing director of Toyo Kogyo's principal bank, the Sumitomo Bank. Murai was the leader of what is called in Western banking circles the bank's "work-out" team or the collection of banking executives charged with forcing the financial restructuring of troubled companies, and he was very successful.

By contrast, in the spectacular bankruptcy in 1984 of the

trading company Osawa Shokai, it was argued that a major cause of the company going into bankruptcy was the fact that it had no "main" bank, and that therefore no single bank felt sufficient obligation or financial pressure to rescue and reconstruct the company. While there were clearly a good many other reasons for the Osawa failure, the argument that it lacked a main bank is an interesting commentary on the Japanese view of the value of close ties to a powerful financial institution. There is something in this of the Western view that if one owes the bank a little, the bank controls; if one owes the bank a great deal, one controls the bank.

Perhaps it might more accurately be concluded that it is possible to merge the interests of the banking institution and its clients through mutual interdependence. This assumes a good deal of flow of information and mutual consultation on major investment decisions. It is clear enough that Japanese management prefers independence from banks when possible. It is clear too that Japanese management is prepared to become dependent on banks if that is the price of achieving corporate growth targets. Once achieved, the profitability from having reached the targets offers the prospect of independence from the banks.

In any case, it is clear that whatever Japanese bankers are, they are no greater risk takers than Western bankers. Until recently, almost all debt instruments in Japan were collateralized. Since the early 1980s, Japanese companies have been allowed by the Ministry of Finance to sell uncollateralized debentures. The standards of quality for such debt issues are so high, however, that some Japanese bankers believe that less than ten Japanese companies and fewer than one hundred companies worldwide can meet the criteria.

From the perspectives of management and of the Japanese financial institutions, the aggressive financial policies of the kaisha support growth without necessarily incurring high risks. This is more true given a governmental monetary policy that aims to maintain low interest rates and to avoid a liquidity crisis. In this generally supportive economic environment, growth, and the bank financing of growth, is in the interest of both parties.

Perspective of Japanese Shareholders

Of the corporate financial policies—aggressive pricing and low profits, high rates of profit retention in the firm, liberal use of debt to fund growth, and special company-bank relationships —it is the seemingly powerless position of the Japanese common shareholder that is often the most perplexing to Western executives.

Without protest, Japanese shareholders seem to accept low profits and meager dividends. The average dividend paid by all major Japanese companies over the last five years was equivalent to a return of about 1.8 percent of the average share price. Toyota's return of dividends for the last five years was only 1.3 percent compared to 7.1 percent for General Motors. Hitachi's return was only 1.7 percent against 4.7 for General Electric. The dividend return of Texas Instruments was 4.6 percent, or more than four times higher than the 1.1 percent return of NEC.

In the United States, the view is that dividends are part of

TABLE 7–5
Industry and Country Leaders

Industry	A Japanese Leader	A U.S. Leader
Machine Tools	Toshiba Machine	Cincinnati Milacron
Tires	Bridgestone	Goodyear
Beer	Kirin	Anheuser Busch
Measuring Instruments	Yokogawa Electric	Hewlett-Packard
Pulp and Paper	Oji Paper	International Paper
Glass	Asahi Glass	PPG Industries
Steel	Nippon Steel	U.S. Steel
Sewing Machines	Brother	Singer
Computers	Fujitsu	IBM
Communications	Nippon Electric	Texas Instruments
Synthetic Fibres	Toray Industries	Monsanto
Copying Machines	Ricoh	Xerox
Bearings	Nippon Seiko	Timken
Construction Machinery	Komatsu Ltd.	Caterpillar
Specialty Steel	Daido	Carpenter Technology
Automobiles	Toyota	General Motors
Film	Fuji	Eastman Kodak
Cameras	Canon	Polaroid
Heavy Electronic	Hitachi	General Electric
Pharmaceuticals	Fujisawa	Merck
Forklift	Komatsu Forklift	Clark Equipment

the total return a shareholder expects to receive. The aim is to increase dividends along with earnings per share year in and year out. Cut the dividend and there will be hell to pay sooner or later. In Japan, dividends are paid to reassure shareholders that the company is healthy. The common practice is to pay a dividend equal to about 10 percent of the par value of the stock. Most Japanese companies try to pay this and will borrow or even sell assets to do so because missing this payment risks their ability to attract additional future funding from banks as well as from shareholders. But the common shareholder can do little to influence the decisions of management regarding dividends or other corporate policies.

In spite of an apparently weak position, the fact is that the Japanese shareholder does quite well. This can be seen when the stock performance of twenty-one industry leaders in Japan and the United States are compared. The leaders, listed in table 7–5, were selected from industries in which comparable Japanese and U.S. market leaders could be identified. Included are Kirin and Anheuser-Busch, Texas Instruments and NEC, and General Motors and Toyota. The industries represented by these leaders account for more than 25 percent of each country's gross national product and 70 percent of manufacturing sales.

Median stock prices for 1973, 1978, and 1983 adjusted for splits are used as a basis for measuring stock returns in figures 7–1 and 7–2. An Eastman Kodak shareholder who bought in 1973 has seen the investment decline steadily through the late-1970s and has not enjoyed much of an appreciation since then. The yearly median stock price of Eastman Kodak has decreased 36 percent since 1973. Shareholders in Fuji Film, Japan's largest manufacturer of photographic supplies and Kodak's principal worldwide competitor, benefited from a dramatic appreciation of their investments throughout the 1970s. On the other hand, shareholders in Cincinnati Milacron, a large U.S. manufacturer of machine tools, have experienced a greater appreciation of their investments than have Japanese shareholders in Toshiba Machine.

Over the past ten years, Japanese shareholders fared better than their U.S. counterparts in sixteen out of twenty-one comparisons of industry leaders (see figure 7–3). On average, Japa-

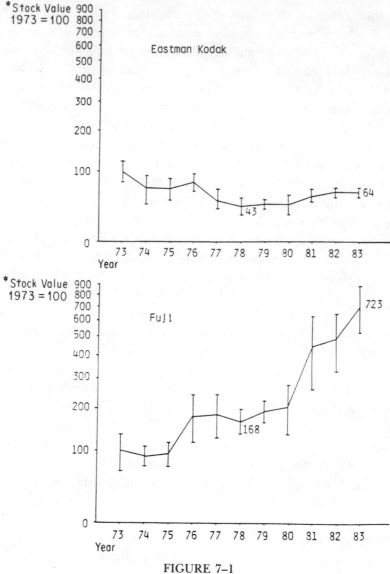

FIGURE 7–1

Annual Stock Price Medians*: U.S. and Japan

*1973 median price equals 100

nese shareholders outscored Americans 175 percent to 39 percent in pre-tax appreciation plus cumulative dividends expressed as a percentage gain over the original price for an average share. On average, for a stock chosen from among the Japanese industry leaders, a 1,000 yen investment in 1973 in these companies would have returned a total profit of 1,750 yen

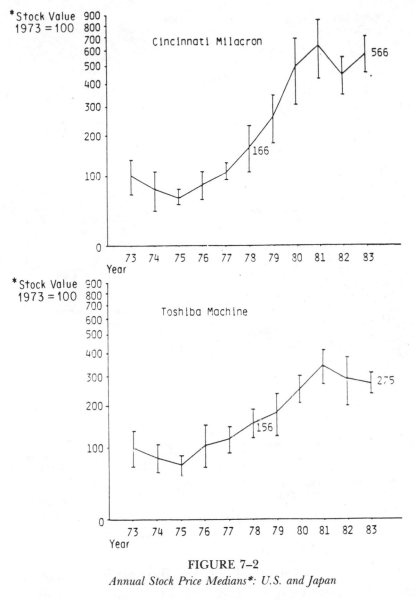

FIGURE 7–2

Annual Stock Price Medians*: U.S. and Japan

*1973 median price equals 100.

by 1983. A $10.00 investment in the average U.S. leader would have returned only $3.90. Dividends would have accounted for only 11 percent of the total profit to the Japanese shareholder, but would have been 85 percent of the U.S. investor's profit. On a pre-tax basis, Japanese shareholders fared more than four times better than their U.S. counterparts.

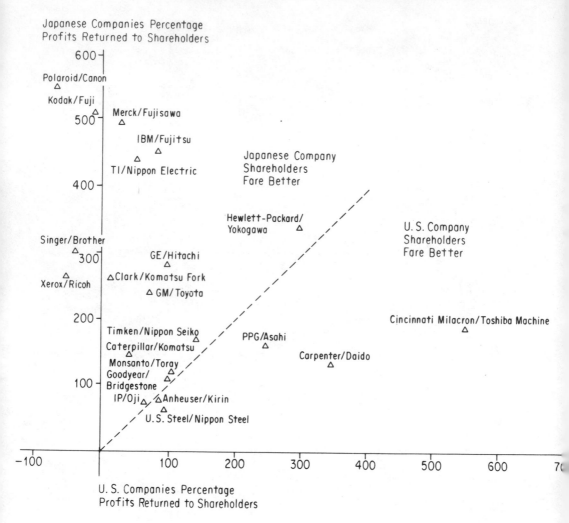

FIGURE 7–3

Comparison of Pre-Tax Capital Gains and Dividends: 1973–1983

When the comparison is limited to the past five years—to increase the weighting of the 1982–1983 U.S. bull market—the profits of the U.S. shareholders jump from 39 to 76 percent, or a $7.60 profit in 1983 on a $10.00 investment in 1978. Nevertheless, the Japanese result is still superior, returning a total profit of 940 yen on a 1,000 yen investment—a 94 percent return—even before considering Japan's 1984 bull market.

When the returns are subjected to taxation the distinctions are magnified. Although dividends paid to individuals are heav-

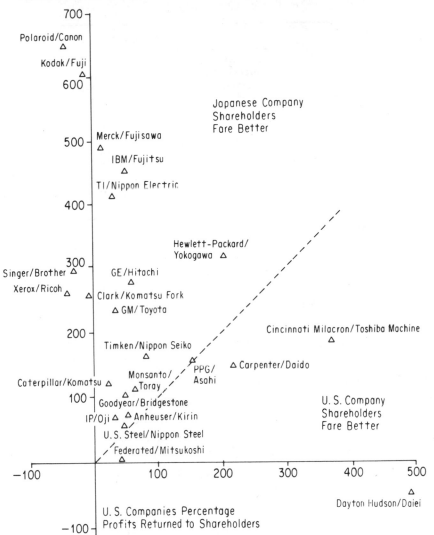

FIGURE 7–4

Comparison of Post-Tax Capital Gains and Dividends: 1973–1983

ily taxed in both countries, capital gains are not usually taxed in Japan. In the past decade, Japanese stock returns after tax outperformed comparable U.S. stocks 170 to 20 percent (figure 7–4). Over the past five years, the Japanese stocks returned 92 percent compared with only 48 percent for the U.S. stocks. Almost 95 percent of the total return to the Japanese shareholder would have been from capital gains. Capital gains to the

TABLE 7–6

International Comparison of Shareholders' Returns 1971–1982

	Total Return*	
	Local Currency Based (% annually)	U.S. Dollars Based (% annually)
Singapore	16.04	18.93
Japan	14.01	16.73
Hong Kong	13.32	12.26
Canada	11.81	10.22
England	11.02	8.14
Holland	10.72	12.66
France	8.35	6.47
Australia	7.05	5.56
West Germany	6.95	9.87
United States	6.95	6.95
Italy	4.73	0.57
Switzerland	2.45	8.78

*Average annual compounded rate of return, comprising dividends and capital gains.
SOURCE: New Japan Securities Research Institute, Pamphlet (Tokyo, February 1984), p. 42.

U.S. investor would have constituted only about 20 percent of the total for the last ten years and 70 percent for the last five years. The remainder of the U.S. investor's return would have come in the form of highly taxed dividends.

These averages mask the performance of certain industries in which the stocks of the U.S. leaders fared better than the Japanese. But of the twenty-one industry leaders compared, the shareholders of only two U.S. industry leaders in the past decade and seven in the last five years were more prosperous than their Japanese counterparts.

These results are corroborated by a recent study by the New Japan Securities Research Institute. The institute compared dividends and capital gains across major free-market economies from 1971 through 1982. Japanese stocks averaged better than a 14 percent compounded annual return and ranked second only to Singapore (table 7–6). By contrast, Great Britain came in fifth with 11 percent compound annual growth, and the U.S. tied West Germany for ninth place with 7 percent annual increase.

The role of the Japanese shareholder in the management of

TABLE 7–7

1983 Financial Statistics for Three Japanese Companies

	Hitachi	MELCO	Toshiba
Overall Competitive Position	Strong	Medium	Weak
Return on Sales (%)	3.8	2.2	1.6
Return on Assets (%)	3.8	2.5	1.6
Debt-to-Equity Ratio	0.7:1	1.4:1	1.9:1
Interest to Operating Income (%)	27	44	50
Dividend to Net Profit (%)	14	27	45
Profits Available for Reinvestment (%)	86	73	55
(Billions of Yen)	540	110	90
Investable Profits plus Incremental Debt			
(Billions of Yen)	917	260	260

his company is similar to that of a preferred shareholder in a U.S. company. The Japanese shareholder has a right to a dividend, albeit small, if the firm has the capacity to pay one. Beyond this, the Japanese shareholder has few rights. The management of the Japanese company is free to do what it pleases with the cash remaining after the payment of the dividend.

The right of a Japanese shareholder to a dividend has a strong influence on the ability of a company to compete, particularly if the company is weak. Short of being on the brink of bankruptcy, management must pay the dividend before it can invest cash back into the company. Therefore, the weaker the Japanese company, the lower its profitability, and the less is the cash left over after payment of the dividend. The financial implications of this can be seen in a comparison of Hitachi, Mitsubishi Electric (MELCO), and Toshiba. These companies are Japan's leading producers of electrical and electro-mechanical equipment, and they all seek high growth. Hitachi is the strongest competitor, Toshiba is relatively weaker, and MELCO is in between. Their financial statistics reflect these different positions (table 7–7).

Toshiba has the least portion of profits available for reinvestment in its businesses, Hitachi has the most, and MELCO is in between. Note that the debt levels of these companies increase with worsening competitive position, a sign that the weaker companies are borrowing to defend their competitive positions. Toshiba and MELCO must borrow many more yen for each yen of retained earnings to have the substantial amounts of cash needed to fund growth. Also interesting is the reduction of Hitachi's debt-to-equity ratio from about 1:1 in 1981 to 0.7:1 in 1983, as it is able to fund growth and also pay down its debt position.

The Japanese financial policies described have a growth bias. Aggressive pricing, high profit retention in the firm, low dividends, and aggressive use of debt are mechanisms that enable a growing company to grow faster. The welfare of the employees, of the management, and of the shareholder is improved with continued strong growth—therefore, growth is the principal goal of all parties. Because the Japanese shareholder generally pays no capital gains tax, the benefit is great if the company invested in grows rapidly. Growth also increases the income and job security of employees and managers, as they benefit from the increased power of their company.

Almost all executives, Western and Japanese, would claim growth to be one of their principal goals. However, the goals of Japanese and Western management can be quite different. In a recent study reported by the Japanese government, the corporate objectives of about 500 major U.S. and Japanese companies were compared (see table 7–8). On a scale of one to ten, the responding executives of U.S. companies ranked return on investment as their principal corporate objective. Share price increase was ranked second and market share third. Many Western executives who have seen the results of this study agree with the rankings, though some consider share price to have precedence over return on investment.

The U.S. ranking is in sharp contrast with that of the responding executives of the Japanese companies. Market share was ranked first, return on investment second, and the refreshment of the product portfolio third. Share price increase was last among Japanese corporate objectives. Indeed, the responding Japanese executives placed the objective of share price increase no higher than the U.S. executives placed improved working conditions.

Judging from the realities of competition, the elevation by U.S. management of the return on investment goal over the goals of market share and refreshment of the product portfolio

TABLE 7–8

Ranking of Corporate Objectives: U.S. and Japan*

	U.S.	Japan
Return on Investment	8.1	4.1 (2)
Share Price Increase	3.8	0.1
Market Share	2.4	4.8 (1)
Improve Product Portfolio	1.7	2.3
Rationalization of Production and Distribution	1.5	2.4
Increase Equity Ratio	1.3	2.0
Ratio of New Products	0.7	3.5 (3)
Improve Company's Image	0.2	0.7
Improve Working Conditions	0.1	0.3

*291 Japanese companies and 227 U.S. companies ranked factors weighted 10, for first importance, to 1, for least importance.
SOURCE: Adapted from Economic Planning Agency, Japanese Government, *Economic Survey of Japan 1980/1981* (Tokyo: *Japan Times*, 1982), p. 196.

would seem to be illogical. In the West, as in Japan, high profits and hence high return on investment come with superior competitive position. Superior competitive position is achieved with good products and maintained with new products, and the measure of superior competitive position is market share. Although there are debates as how to measure the value of market share, in Japan superior market share means "I sell more than you where it counts." If in the pursuit of market share Japanese companies find that they must make certain capital or expense investments to hold or gain share, the investments are made with little regard for the short-term returns of the project. Not making the investments risks a loss of competitive position; the business may well never earn much money.

If a Japanese company is successful in its pursuit of market share, the return on investment will follow. This is readily apparent in the success of such companies as Toyota, Matsushita, Bridgestone, and Makita. Toyota and Matsushita, for example, have a history of adding increments of capacity that are equal to or significant portions of total industry capacity and then pulling the rug out from under prices to fill the capacity. Very soon after starting this process they often announce their plans for their next capacity addition.

The aggressive investment behavior of Matsushita and Toyota is difficult for many Western businessmen to accept and deal with. Faced with these investment challenges, few Western companies, with the notable exceptions of some U.S. electronics companies such as IBM and Intel, are willing to make as big a bet as many kaisha seem routinely to make. The "numbers" do not seem to justify such behavior.

Discussion of the investment issue generally proceeds along two lines. First, what is the cost of capital of Japanese companies? Second, how do the kaisha evaluate and manage their capital budgeting? The assumption behind the first question is that the Japanese use a capital budgeting procedure similar to that used by Western companies. The key number is cost of capital, used to set the minimum return expected of investments, often called the "hurdle rate." Hurdle rates are crucial in discounted cash flow calculations that constitute the heart of most Western capital budgeting procedures. If the Japanese cost of capital is lower than that of Western companies, the logic goes, their hurdle rates can be lower and thus the otherwise irrational behavior of the Japanese can be rationalized.

Cost of capital is a complex topic. Taken at its simplest, interests rates might be used as a surrogate for cost of capital, or at least differences in interest rates might serve as a surrogate for differences in cost of capital. In this sense there is a sharp contrast between Japan and the United States. The policy of the Japanese government is, and long has been, to hold interest rates to industry at as low a level as prudent monetary policy management allows. Fiscal policies are adjusted to match this objective. In the United States real interest rates are, and have for some time been, nearly double those of Japan. The effects on investment are obvious, and greatly to the disadvantage of U.S. companies that are attempting to compete with the kaisha in capital-intensive, high-growth sectors like semiconductors.

Few Japanese companies employ the elaborate capital budgeting processes widely practiced in the West. Indeed, few Japanese companies have the massive organizational apparatus called "Finance" which is characteristic of Western companies. The Japanese capital budgeting analysis is often a simple estimate of the number of years required for an investment to be paid off by profits (payback analysis), with the cost of funds arbitrarily set at 10 percent annually. Japanese analysts will use discounted cash flow techniques, but are uneasy about what they see as arbitrary and hazardous pricing and return assumptions. The simplicity of a payback analysis allows a sustained focus on the business issues involved in the investment and avoids the elaborate assumptions and artificial constraints of Western analytic financial techniques.

In any event, the analysis of an investment decision in a Japanese company is rarely done to obtain approval of "Finance." The analysis is done to help the managers responsible for the success of the projects make their decisions. The function of the executives in the finance department of most Japanese companies is to maintain accounting standards, manage banking relations, process capital requests, and find the necessary money. Finance does not hold veto power over business decisions for the kaisha.

However, this approach can present problems, especially when the sum total of capital requests by all of a Japanese company's divisions is greater than the amount the finance group can raise. The kaisha are susceptible to the problems of "democratic" management. At Hitachi, for example, senior management appears to try to be fair when allocating capital. Indeed, the chief executive of Hitachi is said to be chosen for an ability to develop compromises among the powerful heads of Hitachi's divisions rather than for individual qualities of leadership. The result is often that the allocation of budgets for each of the company's individual divisions is made in equal proportion to the rate that senior management wishes the entire company to grow. For some divisions, the capital allocation enables them to grow faster than competitors, and for others it may prevent them from growing as rapidly. At Hitachi, this appears to have contributed to a characteristic pattern of gaining an early competitive lead, often from technological innovation, and then moving into the number two or three spot in the marketplace over time. This move to second or third place has occurred in almost all of Hitachi's divisions, although the current drive in semiconductor memories may represent a departure from the traditional pattern of the company.

One approach to the problem of limits on capital given massive and wide-ranging growth opportunities is to set up subsidiaries partially owned by the parent company, and requiring these subsidiaries to seek their own capital sources. Fanuc, the world leader in numerical control equipment and a leader in robotics, was a division of Fujitsu until 1972. The division that became Fanuc was, and still is, growing at a spectacular pace. The competition with the other high-growth divisions of Fujitsu for financial resources had become too great. The management of Fujitsu spun the division off into what is now a 43 percent owned Fujitsu subsidiary that has fended for itself very successfully in Japan's capital markets.

Western executives need to ask themselves which of the financial policies of the kaisha are relevant and applicable to their businesses. The greatest leverage for increased total return to the company and to shareholders lies with growth rather than with dividends or reported profits. Dividend payments are implicit statements to shareholders and to the capital markets by management that shareholders can better invest the cash after tax than management can, on their behalf, before tax. For the company with growth opportunities, dividends might well be reduced to zero and the shareholders encouraged to match their interests with that of the company.

Increasing leverage to support a competitive, growth-oriented strategy is difficult for Western management to implement. But should management of, say, a U.S. semiconductor company, really believe that increased leverage will enhance their ability to compete, particularly against the Japanese, they should press their financial institutions to increase their lending limits, perhaps in return for more information on the degree of risk being undertaken. If this is not sufficient to provide the necessary funding, then management should consider private placement with more sympathetic sources of cash, including Japanese and other Asian sources.

In competition, all performance measures and goals are relative. If one competitor, Japanese or Western, is growing faster in a key business but is getting lower returns on sales and assets, then its competitor may well have no choice but to accept its goals and policies. To do otherwise will help the first competitor gain position, and will threaten the future of the other companies that are trying to compete.

8

WHOSE COMPANY

IS IT?

A PHRASE much used in
Japan is *Nihonteki keiei,* or Japanese-style management, referring
to what the Japanese see as considerable differences between
Japanese management methods and those commonly used in
the West. The differences cited are usually those having to do
with personnel practices—career job security, unions that include all the employees of the company, pay and promotion
systems heavily weighted toward seniority, and group approaches to decision making. There is now considerable pride
in this Japanese-style management.

The basis for pride is apparent as Japanese productivity
levels continue to rise rapidly. Reporting OECD data on productivity growth from 1964 to 1983, *The Economist* noted that
"the old truth remains: the pace of economic growth depends
largely on the growth of each worker's output. Among industrial
countries, the big winner by far is still Japan. Though its productivity grew more slowly in the 1970s than in the 1960s, it is still
rising as quickly as West German productivity did at its postwar
fastest."[1]

1. *The Economist,* 20 October 1984, p. 107.

Not only are the Japanese working effectively, but they are working long hours. Hours worked per person annually declined in every major industrial country from 1975 to 1982, except in Japan, where they increased over the period. This was despite steadily increasing income and living standard levels in Japan. The Japanese worker puts in an average of more than 2,000 hours per year, while the average in Great Britain and Sweden is less than 1,500.

There are many other indicators of a higher level of worker commitment. Absentee rates in Japan are lower than in other major countries. Days lost to industrial disputes are fewer than in any other industrial nation except West Germany. Suggestion systems for productivity improvements are in place in almost all Japanese companies, with quite extraordinary rates of participation. Quality Control Circles, which organize workers to study and deal with production problems on their own initiative and time, and their high level of participation and output are the envy of Western managements.

Indeed, there are so many of these indicators of a work force that is more dedicated and concerned than others that the conclusion of a real difference in performance is inescapable. Many Japanese attribute the difference to national characteristics—diligence; a preference for working hard; a sense of loyalty to the group. There may well be aspects of Japanese society and Japanese character that contribute to their impressive performance, but the causes may also lie in more basic and universally relevant explanations.

The kaisha have dealt effectively with the fundamental problem of all organizations, that of tying together the interests of the individuals that make up the organization with the interests of the organization as a whole. The kaisha system of management has gone farther than others to minimize conflicting interests and to integrate each of the members of the group into a whole that works in the common interest. This achievement results not from special diligence, loyalty, or other special characteristics of individual Japanese. Rather, it results from a total system of employment and corporate governance that combines to produce exceptional results. The system is, as a whole, unique to Japan, and perhaps could only have taken shape in the context of Japanese society. But it is a system whose elements can be introduced into any management system given adequate understanding, conviction, and effort.

Does the Shareholder Own the Japanese Company?

Whose company is it? In the West, as in Japan, the answer provided by legal convention is clear. The company belongs to the shareholders, to those who provide the capital that makes the company possible. Because the company belongs to the shareholders, benefits accruing to the company from successful performance belong to the shareholder who has undertaken the risk of investment.

With ownership separate from the management of corporations, the board of directors represents the interests of the shareholder-owners. Thus, in U.S. companies, directors are named to the board from outside the company in the majority of cases. A strong chief executive of the company may well control board membership and build a friendly and relatively accommodating board. Nonetheless, the board is expected to maintain surveillance of company affairs, and step in as necessary in cases of mismanagement (even though the precise legal responsibilities of the board members remain unclear).

This has also come to mean generally that the U.S. shareholder is to receive a significant share of profits in the form of dividend payments. While a few companies, like Digital Equipment Corporation, retain earnings and do not pay dividends in order to command less expensive capital, most U.S. companies view a dividend payout rate of about 50 percent of earnings as appropriate. Dividends are taken to be a sign of successful operations and competent management. Share price is strongly influenced by the rate and level of dividends paid.

In order to help ensure that management works in the interests of the shareholders and to link the interests of management with that of the shareholders, profit-related bonus plans for management (and stock options and similar plans to reward

183

management for improved earnings and increased share price)
have become widespread and even recognized in U.S. tax codes.
As Western stock markets tend to be highly sensitive to trends
in earnings per share, management has a strong motive to maintain steady improvement in earnings, even on a quarterly basis.
A faltering in earnings trends lowers share price, which lowers
the value of stock options and similar compensation programs
of management. Management is expected to maintain earnings
trends and provide increasing rewards to shareholders. This
pattern is so familiar and accepted in the West, especially in the
United States, that it is taken for granted as the natural and
proper state of corporate affairs.

The Western corporate pattern might be described as an
alliance of senior management and shareholders to optimize
current earnings from the company to mutual benefit. The company becomes a vehicle for profit optimization, or, at worst, for
profit maximization. Implicit is the view that the success of the
company depends critically on a single executive or small group
of executives. Thus, if they achieve success through their individual efforts their compensation should be appropriately increased. Not surprisingly then, lower ranking employees, especially as represented by their trade unions, also seek to optimize,
and in fact seek to maximize their share of current earnings. In
this process, the company becomes an organization external to
the interests of its members, to be used to further their earnings
advantage to the maximum.

Against this pattern as it has developed in the West, the
common stock shareholder of the Japanese company is more in
the position of a preferred shareholder in a Western company.
Having made an investment that is at risk, the shareholder is
entitled to a return on that investment. Therefore dividends are
paid, but not as a percent of earnings but as a percent of the par
value of shares in the company.

Dividend yields as a percent of market value of Japanese
shares are low, typically only one to two percent. Nevertheless,
it is critically important that the dividend be paid, and Japanese
companies in some earnings trouble have been known to borrow to cover the dividend payment and thus meet the investor's
expectations and maintain their ability to raise equity funds.

Yet, when the shareholder's claim to a return on his investment is met by the Japanese company, the shareholder has little or no further voice in corporate affairs. The board of directors of the Japanese company consists almost entirely of inside board members, that is, of the senior management of the company. They achieve board member status as they move up in the executive ranks; they are career employees. To the extent that they might be seen as representatives of a constituency, their constituency is the career employees of the company itself. In a few of the companies that are members of the traditional groups of companies, such as NEC as a member of the Sumitomo group, there will be an occasional outside director representing and symbolic of group membership. In cases where the company has become deeply obligated to a commercial bank, and the bank feels at some risk, it may well second an executive to serve as financial officer in the company and sit on the board. But in no event are outside directors either a majority, or even truly outsiders to the company.

A recent and colorful case was an interesting exception to these rules of continuity and control from inside the company. Shigeru Okada was dismissed as president of the Mitsukoshi Department Store through the offices of an outside director. Mitsukoshi has long been Japan's most prestigious department store group, the proper place to buy gifts for special occasions. It was also once the largest retail operation in Japan, losing that pride of place with the onslaught of supermarket chains. Its special prestige stems largely from its being the source of the fortunes of the Mitsui family, the initial firm in what became the Mitsui Group, once Japan's largest combination of companies.

Okada assumed the presidency of Mitsukoshi in the early 1970s, and soon established a reputation as both a flamboyant and a one-man operator. His one-man style was evident as executives began to leave the company for other firms (in itself very unusual) and his flamboyance was displayed in his rental of the Versailles Palace for a night, with guests flown to Paris to celebrate the fame and position of Mitsukoshi.

The trigger for Okada's downfall in 1982 was a store-sponsored display of Persian treasures, many of gold, and many of

which turned out to be fakes produced in a workshop not far
from Tokyo. With the press in full outcry, management rose up
and removed him, reportedly by a unanimous vote of the sixteen
directors, on the grounds of the ruinous inventory position of
the store. Most of the excess, unsaleable inventory had been
supplied to the store by companies organized by Okada's mis-
tress. This proved the last straw in a long sequence of mismanagement.

The Okada case is of interest in this discussion in two re-
gards. First, it has been widely reported as the first in recol-
lected Japanese history where a chief executive has been voted
out of office by his board of directors in direct confrontation.
In itself, the rarity of this case supports the view of succession,
continuity, and lack of shareholder control as being the Japanese pattern.

Second, other players in this drama are of interest. The
coup that unseated Okada was engineered by Goro Koyama,
retired executive of and still advisor to the Mitsui Bank. Koyama
served on the Mitsukoshi board as banker and group representative and arranged the overturn to defend the good name of the
Mitsui Group, as well as to defend the financial interests of its
bank and department store. Even so, some reports indicated
that the actual vote to dismiss Okada was close, despite the
appearance of unanimity.

A final observation on the Mitsukoshi case is important.
Okada's successor was not an outsider brought in to clean up the
situation, nor a bank executive sent to defend the interests of the
Mitsui Bank. The successor was another company officer who
had been running Mitsukoshi's Nagoya store, and thus was not
involved with Okada's operations. For all of the drama, the final
note was the continuity and integrity of the organization.

Along with the pattern of inside directors, with no specific
shareholder representation on the board, goes a quite different
approach to dividend payments in the case of the Japanese company. As noted, dividends are paid as a percent of par value of
shares. This means that a highly profitable company can meet
its dividend requirements with only a small percent of its total
earnings. Most of its earnings will be available for reinvestment
in the company. To meet the same dividend requirement, a less

profitable company must pay out a large share of its earnings in dividends.

In 1984, Matsushita Electric Industries, the world's largest appliance company and highly profitable, paid out less than ten percent of its earnings in dividends, retaining the balance for reinvestment. As one consequence, Matsushita has been growing in sales nearly 15 percent a year and doing so without incurring the risks and costs of bank borrowings. Conversely, Toshiba, in a less favorable market position and therefore less profitable, paid out nearly 50 percent of its earnings in dividends and has a 2:1 debt-to-equity ratio, borrowing heavily to maintain a growth rate of less than 10 percent per year. The Japanese approach to dividends is a powerful factor in separating corporate winners and losers in the Japanese economy. The winners are able to become very strong companies indeed.

With the shareholder in the position of investor rather than controller, and with dividends not critical to share price, Japanese management has developed a different view of the importance of share price. In the survey presented in chapter 7 regarding corporate objectives of U.S. and Japanese managements, U.S. executives ranked return on investment as their first objective and share price second. In reviewing these survey findings with U.S. executives, there is usually agreement that these are the top two objectives for U.S. management, though there are some who argue that share price is the first objective, even taking precedence over profitability. In the same survey, of the nine corporate objectives presented for rating, Japanese executives rated share price as the least important objective in managing their companies. Few cited share price as an objective of their company at all. The survey data do not provide an explanation of this result. Several explanations are possible: first, that Japanese executives simply do not care about the price of their company's shares. Few Japanese executives hold significant amounts of shares and because treasury shares owned by the company cannot be held, there are no stock option programs in Japan, or even similar plans such as "phantom stock" for executives. Second, Japanese shareholders have little voice in corporate affairs, so again perhaps share price need not rank as a corporate objective. Perhaps this is the explanation of the seeming indifference of the Japanese executives surveyed to the price of company shares as an objective in managing their companies.

A third explanation is also possible. Perhaps Japanese managers believe that if their companies achieve market share and profitability targets, and continue to grow through introducing new products that allow the cycle of market share and profit to be repeated, the stock market will recognize their performance by supporting the shares of the company, thus leading to higher share price. In this view of objectives, a high and increasing share price is not an objective of the company, but is rather the consequence of good management of those companies that get their basic objectives right, and work to achieve them.

There is a real competitive advantage in this pattern of shareholder relations for the successful Japanese competitor. Managements of the kaisha are freed from the tyranny of accountants, and from the terrible pressures throughout the U.S. organizations for steady improvement in earnings per share. It is rational for U.S. managers to be preoccupied with short-term earnings. Their job security depends on it, because the board, the top executives, and the shareholders demand steady earnings improvements. Moreover, their personal income and estate depend on it, because their principal potential asset is likely to be in the form of options and other plans dependent on stock price. Earnings can always be improved in the short term by sacrificing those expenses and investments that build long-term position. The Japanese manager is able to look further into the future and is freer to do what is necessary to ensure a successful future. This is possible only because of the system the Japanese executive operates in, not from any natural tendency to take the longer view. At the same time, the shorter time horizon of the U.S. executive is a function of the system he operates in, and is not necessarily from a lack of understanding or concern over the company's future.

During the 1950s and 1960s period of very rapid growth of the Japanese economy, with capital in short supply, something of the role of the Western common stock holder was played by the banks of Japan. Most investment funds came not from equity or retained earnings but from bank borrowings. Furthermore, most of these were short-term loans that were "evergreen," or regularly renewed. Under these circumstances, it was hardly surprising that the main supplier of funds—the banks—became significant factors in corporate decision making.

With greatly increased liquidity in the Japanese economy, and with stronger company balance sheets, this system has changed. Banks must now solicit attractive borrowers, and find themselves providing funds to the weaker companies, in which their powers remain considerable. The most successful of Japan's companies work to maintain good relations with key banks, but are hardly under bank control. The leading companies have little debt, and they can choose their bank sources. Companies like Kubota (a major manufacturer of farm machinery) and Hitachi are careful to balance their banking business between two or more banks, rather than relying on one main bank. By recent law, bank shareholdings in companies will soon be limited to a maximum of 5 percent. The conclusion is that dependence on a bank is no more to the liking of Japanese management than management in other countries, and for leading Japanese companies no longer a significant issue.

A rather similar situation has developed with respect to Japan's historically important groups of companies, the former *zaibatsu,* or giant holding companies, like the Mitsubishi, Mitsui, and Sumitomo groups. Members of these groups are often large and important companies in their industries. Impressive maps of group memberships and affiliations are often drawn up by observers of Japanese industry. There are some industries—housing and related equipment is a good example—where group membership and affiliation is crucial to success, because the important customers are for the most part group members.

Yet, when a list is made of the companies that have led the growth and success of the postwar Japanese economy, few are group members. Toyota, Honda, Hino, and Suzuki in vehicles; Kubota in farm machinery; Shiseido, Kao, and Lion in personal products; Hitachi, Sharp, Sanyo, Matsushita, and Sony in electronics; Shionogi and Fujisawa in pharmaceuticals; and Fuji

Film, Canon, Ricoh, and Seiko are neither group members, nor bank dependent. Some have become so large and successful that through subsidiaries and affiliates they now control groups of their own. They are highly independent companies, with recent entrepreneurial origins. They are the kaisha that have succeeded in the sectors of fast-changing consumer markets and high technology.

Companies in the traditional groups are large, ponderous, and slow moving. Their businesses are mostly in declining industries. By an irony of history, these group companies have major positions in those raw material processing and heavy industries that are now in trouble in Japan. In sectors that require a good deal of long-term financing, that have long engineering lead times, and that often require good government relations—the export of industrial plants would be an example—the group member companies remain strong. Where the technology changes fast, and where the market changes fast, they do not do well. The trading companies of the groups, with which the manufacturing companies have been so closely associated, are also a troubled group of companies.

There are exceptions: NEC, a high technology leader, is a Sumitomo group member; Kirin, with the leading domestic share in beer, is a member of the Mitsubishi group. But the exceptions are few. Furthermore, whether traditional or bank- or trading company-centered, these groups are in no sense centrally controlled or closely coordinated. All things being equal —quality, price, and delivery—a group member will be favored in purchase decisions. But because things are often not equal, group affiliation does not provide a captive market nor assured support. Group membership may be an important starting point, but it will more often than not be irrelevant to corporate policy and business decisions.

It is interesting to see references in the Japanese business press to the Morgan group, Mellon group, or Rockefeller group of U.S. companies, and to IBM's close government-business relationship, inferred from the flow of personnel between that company and Washington. These misconceptions parallel the U.S. tendency to see plots and plotters in the Japanese business community. There are some plots, and some plotters, and some feelings of paranoia—on both sides—are not neurotic. They must be kept in proper proportion, however, on both sides.

In sum, the shareholder in the kaisha is in the position of an investor, but is in no operational sense in control of the company. With adequate return on investment, the shareholder's role is largely ended. Furthermore, it is no longer useful nor accurate to view the kaisha as being under the thumb of their banks, soliciting borrowings and deferring to bank judgment on decisions. The successful kaisha are as free of bank control as are their Western counterparts. Finally, describing the kaisha as group members and thereby under some form of control from that membership is of limited value. Those kaisha that have led the postwar international competitive thrust are generally separate from Japan's traditional groupings of companies, and operate independently.

How the Money Is Distributed

If the shareholders' control is limited, and banks and groups have little influence on the most successful kaisha, perhaps it is possible for the chief executive officers of these companies to operate essentially without check. A useful way of examining this possibility is to look into the pattern of compensation in the kaisha.

With increasing debate over levels of executive compensation in U.S. companies, the pattern of compensation in the Japanese company provides both an interesting contrast and a measure of some basic differences between the kaisha and Western companies. In 1982, Nikkeiren, the Japan Federation of Employers Associations, reviewed the differences in compensation between the presidents of large Japanese companies and newly employed college graduates in those companies (see table 8–1). In the prewar period, in the late 1920s, the spread in total cash compensation between the newly employed and the top ranking officer was one hundred times more for the latter. In those halcyon days of low income taxes, both pre-tax and post-tax differences were of the same magnitude. In the postwar period, the difference in compensation

TABLE 8–1

Annual Cash Compensation of Company Presidents and Newly Hired Employees
(in yen)

Year		President Compensation	New Employee Compensation (Male, College Graduates)	Difference
1927	Pre-tax	165,000	1,500	110.0x
	After-tax	151,000	1,500	100.6x
1963	Pre-tax	6,082,000	257,900	23.6x
	After-tax	3,013,000	252,500	11.9x
1973	Pre-tax	15,676,700	825,500	19.0x
	After-tax	7,181,400	797,400	9.0x
1980	Pre-tax	23,593,000	1,623,000	14.5x
	After-tax	11,543,000	1,546,000	7.5x

SOURCE: Rodo Mondai Kenkyo Iinkai Hokoku (Report of the Research Committee on Labor Problems), *Senshinkoku Byo ni Ochiiranai Tameni* (In Order not to Succumb to the Advanced Nations' Disease) (Tokyo: Nihon Keieisha Dantai Renmei [Federation of Japanese Managers Associations, 1982]), p. 6.

has been steadily diminishing, and on an after-tax basis is now only eight times less.

The level of pay of the lower ranks of the Japanese companies has been rising much more rapidly than the level of pay of the top executives, a thousand-times increase for the new entrants compared with a hundred times increase for the top executives. Not only has the disparate spread in compensation narrowed, but it is also clear from the Nikkeiren report that the pre-tax annual compensation level at the top of the Japanese company is low—about $100,000. This generally low level of pay for Japanese top management is borne out by other reports; for example, *Fortune* of 19 March 1984 reported on "salaries of Japanese chairmen and presidents, which range from $50,000 to $250,000 depending on company size." *Fortune* also commented on U.S. executive salaries. "In 1982 at least 85 American chief executives earned more than $1 million. In contrast, the highest paid foreign bosses rarely earned more than $500,000."[2] *Business Week,* reporting on 1983 executive compensation levels in the United States noted that there were twenty-five U.S. chief executive officers with total annual compensation of more than $2.3 million.[3]

2. Lisa Miller Mesdag, "Are You Underpaid?" *Fortune*, 19 March 1984, pp. 15–19.
3. "Executive Pay: The Top Earners," *Business Week*, 7 May 1984, pp. 60–65.

There are Japanese who report very high levels of income —farmers benefiting from the leap in postwar land prices, individuals with substantial shareholdings, baseball players, film stars, and the like. The executives of the kaisha do not join this happy group on the basis of their salaried compensation.

The large differences in salaries between the executives of the kaisha and those of U.S. companies cannot be explained on the basis of profits—as has been seen, the top companies in both economies enjoy similar levels of profitability. They also cannot be explained in terms of greater perquisites of office paid one group compared with the other. The Japanese executive's generous expense accounts, company-provided housing, Mercedes and driver, luxurious office, and deferred retirement impress foreign visitors with the benefits of his position. However, the U.S. executive also has his or her expense account, a jet plane or helicopter, company apartment, deferred compensation, special insurance program, golden parachute protection against dismissal if the company is taken over, and special retirement benefits. It is not clear which group of executives does better; perquisites do not begin to close the compensation gap.

The differences in executive compensation cannot be explained in terms of low overall levels of pay in Japan either. Studies of relative levels of workers' pay indicate that the average Japanese worker is well remunerated compared to workers in other advanced countries. Reports by the OECD indicate that the typical Japanese worker was about as well paid in 1982 as was the U.S. worker, even with the distortions from an over-valued dollar, and was considerably better off in after-tax take-home pay than the workers in the United States, as well as those in West Germany, France, and Great Britain (see table 8–2)

In evaluating the data in the OECD report, it is clear that they differ from the usual reports of "average wages." The 1983 average wage per hour in manufacturing in Japan was about the same as in West Germany, higher than in Britain or France but only two-thirds of the U.S. average hourly wage in manufacturing. Three factors make for the difference between "average wage" and "annual earnings of a typical worker." First, the Japanese worker puts in a good many more hours, part of them at overtime rates. Second, the average encompasses all workers, including temporary workers and women, who in Japan are

TABLE 8-2

Annual Earnings of a Typical Worker,* 1982
(in U.S. Dollars)

	Annual Gross Earnings ($)	Payments to Government ($)	Cash Transfers from Government	Disposable Income ($)
Japan	17,099	$1,966	—	15,133
U.S.	17,136	3,587	—	13,549
West Germany	14,918	4,027	$742	11,633
Great Britain	13,070	3,781	996	10,285
France	10,458	1,418	2,436	11,476

*Male, manufacturing sector worker with two-child family, wife not working.
SOURCE: *The 1982 Tax/Benefit Position of a Typical Worker in OECD Member Countries,* (Paris: Organization for Economic Cooperation and Development, 1983), p. 8.

lower paid. Third, seniority weighs heavily on the Japanese pay scale. Thus a "typical worker" in Japan—on closer examination than is possible through the use of averages—turns out to do very well relative to foreign counterparts.

The pattern of relatively high pay to lower ranked employees is not limited to Japanese manufacturing workers. The Union Bank of Switzerland reported on the earnings of several different categories of employees, including production department managers in large manufacturing firms in different cities. In table 8–3, the disposable income of the Tokyo department manager is higher than in other major economies. The disposable income advantage at this level in the company is also about 10 percent. In terms of pre-tax income, the Tokyo manager is behind the New York manager, though well ahead of counterparts in other major industrial cities.

These data help make clearer the indication of a compression in the range of company compensation that the earlier Nikkeiren data in this chapter—on the spread from CEO to newly hired graduate—suggested. Both within the kaisha, and in comparison with compensation levels in other countries, the lower ranks of the kaisha do well and the higher ranks do not do as well in total cash compensation.

It should also be noted that the kaisha provide perquisites in terms of housing support, commuting allowances, access to vacation facilities, family allowances, and the like at all levels of employee. This suggests that the proportion of compensation

TABLE 8–3

Earnings of Department Managers
(in U.S. dollars)

	Gross Earnings per Year*	Net Earnings after Taxes and Social Service Contributions†
Tokyo	$41,600	$30,700
New York	46,500	28,000
Paris	31,600	21,100
Dusseldorf	31,400	20,600
Stockholm	28,900	13,000
London	16,700	11,600

*Technical manager of a production department in a sizable company (more than 100 employees) of the metal working industry; completed professional training with many years of experience in the firm; about 40 years old, married, no children.
†Including all supplements such as additional monthly salaries, bonuses, and vacation money.
SOURCE: *Prices and Earnings Around the Globe, 1982—UBS Publications on Business Banking and Monetary Problems*, vol. 81 (Zurich: Union Bank of Switzerland, 1982), p. 40.

provided through perquisites is similar at all levels of the kaisha and does not work to broaden the range of total compensation from the bottom ranks to the top.

Put simply, the employees of the Japanese company share more equally in the cash benefits available from the company than is the case in other countries. The Nikkeiren report states, "Rather than seeking increased personal income, the objective of the [Japanese] executive is the growth and development of the enterprise."[4] Given that by all reasonable measures, Japanese executives, and indeed the Japanese in general, show a considerable interest in increased personal income, this statement has a rather sanctimonious air about it. Surveys of executive attitudes indicate that Japanese executive pay levels are set with a conscious awareness of the need to stay within reasonable ranges with regard to other levels of compensation in the kaisha. Organizational pressures work to limit executive pay at least as much as do self-sacrificing impulses by the executives themselves.

There is an interesting parallel in this to the pattern of income distribution in Japan as a whole. Income distribution in Japan, while far from equal, is more nearly equal than in most countries:

4. *Senshinkoku Byo ni Ochiiranai Tameni*, p. 10.

Depending on which of the measures [of income] is preferred, three countries (Australia, Japan and Sweden) would seem
to record the lowest degree of inequality for a post-tax distribution. At the other end of the scale, France is consistently ranked
as the country with the most unequal distribution. The rankings
given by pre-tax inequality are not very different. Australia and
Japan, in that order, rank as the least unequal countries on most
measures. And France is joined by the United States at the opposite end of the scale.[5]

The conclusion seems inescapable that some part of the
cause of the political stability of postwar Japan is a consequence
of this relative equality in income distribution. Not only have
incomes been rising rapidly, but the sharing of the total has been
reasonably equitable. Similarly, in the Japanese company, income distribution is more nearly equal than in companies in the
other major industrialized countries. It seems likely that within
a corporate organization, all else being equal, a relative equity
in distribution of benefits results in a higher degree of integration and sense of common purpose.

One feature of the kaisha's compensation system that deserves special attention in terms of its potential for application
in other systems is bonus payments. Generally, about one-third
of total annual compensation is paid in the form of a semiannual
bonus, paid out at the traditional gift-giving seasons at mid-year
and year-end. In the case of very successful firms, bonuses are
paid that are the equivalent of a full year's basic compensation.

The bonus has many advantages for the kaisha. It is a deferred payment system, allowing the company use of the cash
until the bonus is paid. Through increasing the bonus rather
than base compensation, those allowances including retirement
benefits that are a function of base pay can be held down. From
a national point of view, the bonus has served as a major factor
in bringing about the high rate of savings from the Japanese
household. There is a clear-cut tendency to live within the base
monthly pay and a propensity to save at the time of bonus
payments.

5. Malcolm Sawyer, "Income Distribution in OECD Countries," in *OECD Economic Outlook, Occasional Studies.* (Paris: Organization for Economic Cooperation and Develop-ment, July 1976), p. 16.

In terms of managing the company, the bonus payment system has a further advantage. It is, in principle at least, and in practice to a good degree, a payment made contingent on the continuing adequate financial performance of the company. The bonus is paid at all levels of the kaisha, and can be reduced when circumstances demand without forcing the company to consider reducing the total labor force.

This, of course, is not the bonus system that Detroit made notorious—bonuses paid executives while negotiating with the union for reductions in total worker compensation. This is a company-wide system, in which all levels of the management and work force participate. Reductions in bonus affect all, proportionately equally, as do increases. Given all of its potential advantages, it is clear why the kaisha use a bonus system, but it is not clear why the system has not been more widely adopted in other countries. If bonuses serve to motivate management personnel, they presumably would serve the same function in motivating workers on the shop floor.

Still another feature of the compensation system in Japan conveys something of the nature of labor relations within the kaisha. This is the approach to wage-cut negotiations with the union and work force. When a Japanese company is in deep trouble, it can cut its temporary and part-time workers. There are no contracts or other constraints against reducing that part of total labor cost. The next step is to limit bonus payments. Following this, the next step will be to seek to reduce wages. At this point the general pattern is for management to announce across-the-board cuts in executive compensation. Having made these cuts, management, then and only then, approaches the union to open discussions of possible wage reductions.

This pattern was followed recently by Mitsubishi Corporation, Japan's largest general trading company, with annual sales of $85 billion. Like nearly all of the general trading companies, Mitsubishi Corporation's financial performance had been deteriorating for some years. Labor costs are an especially large part of total costs in the trading business and Mitsubishi Corporation was forced to act to lower labor costs of its regular work force. The first step in the process was the announcement of a 20 percent salary cut by the management of the company, preparatory to negotiations for a wage reduction across the company.

There is a common theme in these several compensation patterns. The kaisha provide more equal compensation throughout their organizations than is the case for companies in other countries. Extremes of compensation are avoided, and thereby a good deal of anger and conflict within the organization is presumably avoided. A good part of compensation at all levels is in the form of a bonus, proportionately equal for all employees, with some minor differentiation for individual performance. This provides a reward system for all that is tied to total performance of the organization, rather than to the performance of an individual in it. It also provides a cushion against a downturn in the economy or for the company. Finally, when the company is in trouble, the top executives of the organization sacrifice their compensation first, before asking for sacrifices from the rest of the employees.

This system of compensation assumes that the organization is a unit in which all members share in its success or failure. In terms of its compensation system, the kaisha is a more integrated and egalitarian organization than most companies in the West. The competitive advantages that are in part a result of these facts are reflected in the productivity performances of its members—to a considerable degree, the company belongs to its employees.

The Bases for the Kaisha's Integration

Just as the kaisha have been shaped by the fast-growing and fast-changing economic environment of Japan, so have they been shaped by their social environment. Japan's is a notably group-centered society, with far less emphasis on individualism as a value than in the West. The Confucian ethic, with its emphasis on respect for rank and age, has provided much of the value system. The view of the family as paradigm for nation and for organization has carried over to the postwar business organization as well.

The three main elements of what has come to be called

Whose Company Is It?

"Japanese-style management" are career employment security, a system of pay and promotion based on seniority in the firm, and the enterprise union system whereby all employees of the corporation belong to a single union with no differentiation by job skills. Each of these elements is worth examining, as they affect the capability of the kaisha as competitors, and as they affect the nature of the company itself. The high quality of the Japanese labor force has been noted earlier. It is in the recruiting, training, motivating, and organizing of this work force that Japanese-style management comes into play.

CAREER EMPLOYMENT

The Japanese system of career-long employment, which applies only to men, has several key elements. First, the employee is hired directly from school, rather than from an open job market. Second, he is hired for his general characteristics and abilities, rather than for a particular skill or a particular job. Third, he is expected to remain with the company for a life-long career, and in turn expects not to be laid-off or discharged.

The consequences of this pattern of employment are profound. In terms of selection of new employees, the company needs to exercise considerable care, for a recruiting error is not easily corrected and has long and expensive consequences. Thus, academic examinations of the candidate, personal interviews, and investigations of the individual and family background are well warranted.

From the new employee's point of view, great care is also needed in deciding where to apply for employment. His commitment is not for a single, particular job, but for a career. The best performing companies can recruit the best students into employment. The best students seek out the company that appears to have the most promising long-term prospects. Allocation of the labor force from an overall economic point of view is thus made highly efficient, with the most able young people tending to move from school into the faster-growing and most promising sectors of the economy.

There is a real exchange of obligations in this process of selection. The individual is taking considerable risk in linking his future fortunes with those of the company. The company for its part is obliging itself to care for the recruit for his entire career. This concept is only meaningful when in fact the company is prepared to make real sacrifices on behalf of its employee, and is willing to incur losses when it is necessary to protect the individual's job security. The crisis of 1974, when the real growth rate of the economy plunged in a single year from 9 percent to minus one percent, provided a severe test. Japan's corporations as a whole showed losses in that terrible year, yet pay increases fully covered the explosive inflation, going up an average of nearly 30 percent in only one year. There were no significant lay-offs or discharge of permanent employees. The mutual obligation was real, not a matter of lip service.

All too often the U.S. company will piously announce that "our employees are our most valuable asset," and promptly waste that asset with sudden plant closings, "head count programs," or arbitrary staff dismissals to demonstrate the power of the new chief executive. These things simply do not happen in the kaisha. It is hardly surprising that as a result the kaisha's employees show a greater degree of commitment to the company than is customarily the case in the United States.

It is in the context of the exchange of commitments between employee and employer that the notion of the kaisha as family becomes a meaningful one. The leaders of the kaisha can speak, and do, of entry into the company as being born again into another family. Furthermore, rather like the family, there is a real socialization process that takes place following entry into the Japanese company. The first years of employment are largely a process of initiation—moving between departments to learn the nature of the company's activities, its history and its culture, as well as learning job skills. The employee may reside in a company dormitory, and will certainly focus not only working hours but social hours as well on relationships in the company. The employee will not be differentiated from others in his age cohort in these first years, in terms of rank or pay. The first differentiations will be slight and gradual. The indoctrination will be thorough; the calibration of the employee's skills and abilities will be fine; mutual knowledge of members of the organization, and of each others' strengths and weaknesses will become detailed.

It is in this employment process that the kaisha becomes a

different social institution than the corporation in the West. Involvement is more total; options are more limited; commitments are more difficult to revoke. The West has institutions that share these patterns—religious orders, professional armies, professional bureaucracies. Western corporations are rarely among them.

In the ideology of Japanese management, this employment pattern is held out as the proper one, as the ideal model to be emulated. As the pattern of employment of major Japanese corporations, it is the pattern that the Western firm operating in Japan is expected to adhere to (and deviation from which will prove costly).

There is, however, a sizable part of the Japanese labor force that is not involved in this system. Women are expected to—and usually do—end their period of initial employment at marriage or on the birth of the first child, perhaps reentering the labor force later. Also, some part of the labor force of many large companies is made up of temporary employees, often seasonally hired, who are outside this system unless or until they become regular employees. Finally, small firms with limited resources will aspire to follow the permanent employment system, but may find it uneconomical to do so. They will, however, be expected by employees to adhere to it within the limits of their resources.

It has been suggested that some 30 percent of the Japanese labor force is covered by the system of permanent employment, but it appears that this estimate derives from the fact that 30 percent of the labor force is unionized. The system is by no means coterminous with unionization. An accurate estimate of the proportion of labor force included in the system is not possible both because of the pervasiveness of the concept of permanent employment and because of gray zones where its application is uncertain.

There are real costs and competitive disadvantages to the system. Compared to U.S. companies in particular, the Japanese work force cannot quickly be adjusted to downturns in demand. The kaisha have to depend on reduction first of temporary workers, then on a reduction in subcontracted work, then pulling that work back into the plants of the company, then offering special retirement allowances to encourage workers to withdraw from the work force, and finally allowing attrition to do its work. Only in acute crisis, only after exhausting other approaches, and only with full agreement of the union and work force, can actual layoffs or dismissals take place.

Even short of crises, there are immobility costs. Both NEC and Fujitsu report that some 10 to 15 percent of their electronics workforce is redundant, despite the fact that these firms continue to hire new recruits at a rapid pace. What is happening is that there is an accumulation of less-than-competent staff that these kaisha find redundant but cannot discharge.

A further cost of the system is the extreme difficulty of bringing about acquisitions or mergers. The kaisha in a real sense belongs to all its employees. By law, merger or acquisition is possible only with the unanimous consent of all its directors, who with few exceptions are career employees. Sale of the company has about it the sense of buying and selling people, with implications of immorality and social irresponsibility. Merger raises nearly insoluble problems of combining two entrenched work forces, and under Japanese conditions of employment offers little scope for concentration of facilities and reduction of work force.

As a result, the Japanese economy suffers from the fact that mergers are very difficult to bring about even in fragmented industries with facilities that are not world-scale. Despite years of effort, the several Mitsubishi group companies in the distressed chemical fertilizer industry have not been able to merge, even given their common group affiliation. Personnel barriers are too great to allow merger. Yet merger of these and other companies in industries in trouble would make very good economic sense.

For the kaisha themselves, the difficulties of merger and acquisition pose special problems in terms of diversification. In the West, entry into a new business area can be greatly facilitated by acquiring a firm already in the new sector. The kaisha confronted with a mature or declining business must grow its way out of the problem by internal diversification efforts—a more risky and time-consuming route—though perhaps a route that in the long-run, if successful, makes for more secure diversification.

In any event, the career employment system has its costs to the kaisha. Again, there is a trade-off—the kaisha trade flexibility in personnel management for maximizing employee involvement and commitment to the company. Their Western competitors choose the opposite.

In many of these employment patterns, the situation of the Japanese company is not greatly different from that of firms in West European economies, who are similarly restrained, often by law, from arbitrary work force reduction. However, in the Japanese case, the system has been embraced by management, and is used as a positive factor in building personnel relations. Full advantage is taken by the kaisha in identifying the interests of the work force with those of the company, and using the system as a basis for increasing motivation and morale of the work force. European firms tend to incur the penalties of the system, without exploiting its potential strengths.

SENIORITY PAY AND PROMOTION: A SYSTEM UNDER PRESSURE

Closely related to the practice of career employment, and the second characteristic of "Japanese-style management" is the importance of length of service with the kaisha in determining pay and promotion. The linkage to career employment is a natural one if the kaisha have responsibility for the career of the individual, then compensation needs to increase as the individual's responsibilities increase. Japan remains, in important respects, an age-graded society, and the concept of compensation and position being determined by age is deemed appropriate. When the employee is hired directly from school, age and length of service become parallel, and seniority becomes an appropriate basis for reward.

The competitive effects of a seniority system in the context of career employment have been powerful. The fast-growing industry or company is hiring large numbers of new staff members. In the Japanese case, these are necessarily younger people. The result of high levels of hiring is to reduce the average age of the work force. As average age declines, so then does average wage level. Whatever forces were responsible for rapid growth are now reinforced by a wage advantage. The slower growing company, hiring few if any people, is experiencing a steady increase in the average age of its work force. Its competitive disadvantage is reinforced by rising wage rate levels.

It is a unique feature of standard information on the kaisha that the average age of the work force, reported separately by male and female workers, is published along with the usual financial data on the company. Most Western companies would probably not have the data available, much less consider it important information. For the kaisha, age data are an important index of the competitive position of the company.

The seniority-based pay system has come under considerable pressure in recent years, however. With slower overall economic growth, the economic advantages of the system have lessened. Moreover, as life expectancy has lengthened, the earlier retirement age of fifty-five has been extended. The average retirement age from large companies will soon reach sixty.

Pay increases granted automatically with each additional year of service become more and more costly as seniority increases. Therefore, a number of experiments are underway in various kaisha, seeking to flatten the wage curve at some earlier point. The rationale is that family and other responsibilities lessen past the mid-forties, and therefore a flattening of the wage increase curve need not work a hardship. This is the sector of Japanese employment practices that is most liable to change in the near future.

Promotion is also a function of age in the Japanese firm, being provided within a predictable and narrow age range. Not everyone gets promoted—the escalator cannot carry everyone to the top floor—but promotion will rarely if ever take place until adequate seniority has been attained.

Western businessmen are prone to overestimate the frustrations that this seniority-weighted system engenders in young (especially Western-trained) Japanese. For many of these young people, the frustrations early in their career are real. There appears to be increasing mobility from job to job. Yet the frustrations appear to diminish sharply as the system begins to reward the young person reaching the early thirties. Further, few of the complainers feel a sense of frustration so extreme as to cause them to risk the security their job provides by hazarding a new career in another, especially Western, company.

Seniority-weighted pay and promotion systems are by no means peculiar to Japan. Most societies have some degree of age-grading, and most personnel systems pay some respect to length of service in their reward systems. It is the degree of weighting, the systemization of the seniority factor, and its pervasiveness as a major issue in the Japanese company that warrants giving it place in the complex of Japanese-style management.

THE UNIONS

The third aspect of Japanese-style management is the enterprise union, which includes all employees of the company with no differentiation as to skills or job category. As an employee is promoted to a management position, he ceases being a union member. Nearly one in six of the major kaisha executives have been executives of the company's union. The trade union and the kaisha are coterminous in that the worker does not have a separate skill identification outside of or differentiated from his job assignment in the company. The union does not exist as an entity separate from, or with an adversarial relationship to, the company. The union includes all company members, and only company members. Its future and the kaisha's are identical.

Not surprisingly, there has been little interest in the issue of co-determination, of demands that the union and management share executive authority. The notion of co-determination implies basic differences in objectives between company and union, an adversarial interaction, and a need for the union (and workers) to have better knowledge of and control over company affairs. This confrontation of interests and objectives is far less likely to happen given the kaisha's enterprise union system.

The linking of the fate of union and company puts limits on the extent to which the union is prepared to risk damaging the economic situation of the company. Employees have no illusions that management is entirely benign; union membership is seen as a counterweight to potential abuses of management authority. However, damage to the company risks damage to the employees' own interests in a clear and immediate sense. Thus, the wearing of armbands with "solidarity" written on them is a meaningful statement to management of worker and union purpose, as is a lunch hour demonstration, or an after-hours protest meeting.

An especially high economic value of the enterprise union system results from the fact that the union structure poses no barriers to the movement of worker from one job to another. Unlike the situation where workers are organized by skills or job categories, there is no institutional restraint within the kaisha against reassigning workers to the limits of their capabilities. This fact is an important balancing factor to the limited mobility of Japanese workers between companies, which by itself would impose an economic cost in restricting the efficient allocation of the labor resource.

In addition, the enterprise union system means that the kaisha deal with a single negotiating unit. In an adversarial context this might provide exceptional power to the union, but this is mitigated for the kaisha by the identity of union and management interests in preserving and strengthening the company. It means that the kaisha are free of the plague of jurisdictional disputes and multiple union bargaining situations so common in the West.

The union in Japan is important, but its organizational pattern raises the question of why Western managements, instead of resisting unionization of the work force, do not work to encourage the formation of a union with which management can cooperate. It is a curious fact that the Western company in Japan often resists formation of a union, from its Western experience. The best move would be to encourage early formation of a union in the Japanese subsidiary and facilitate communications with the work force, ensuring that the union could be dealt with in a constructive fashion. Rather than taking this initiative, Western management in Japan usually attempts to forestall unionization. As a result, when the number of employees reaches a certain size, usually about 200, professional organizers, often of a distinctly leftist persuasion, organize a union that management finds difficult or impossible to deal with.

It needs to be noted that the influence of the trade union in Japan as elsewhere appears to be diminishing. The year 1984 marked the thirtieth anniversary of Japan's unique approach to wage negotiations, the *shunto,* or spring struggle, a pattern of settlement of wage negotiations during a concentrated period in March and April of each year. The anniversary was observed with widespread comment that the *shunto* is losing its meaning. Settlements are being reached at reasonable levels, without disputes, with general agreement that wage increases should reflect productivity improvements plus inflation.

As in the United States, the proportion of the work force in Japan that is organized into unions is declining. It is now 30 percent in Japan, compared with 20 percent in the United States, in contrast to more than 40 percent in Western Europe. As the Japanese company shifts further toward the tertiary sector—toward services and away from manufacturing—this trend will continue and union influence, both in the workplace and in national politics, is likely to slowly but steadily diminish.

In Japan, the three features of Japanese-style management, career employment, seniority-based pay and promotion, and the enterprise union, are referred to as the "three pillars" of the system. The three are mutually reinforcing, and as a system, the results are remarkable. To a degree unmatched by any other organizational system, the *kaisha* of Japan have achieved an identification of corporate and individual interests. This is not the result of some special inclination of the workers of Japan toward feelings of loyalty, or toward diligence, or toward hard work. It is the result of a system that imposes close identification of corporate and individual interests. The costs of confrontation are minimized. Investments made in training of staff can be fully amortized over the career of the employee. Thus, the company can invest in the individual—in recruiting, training, and retraining—to the limit of its resources. The individual in return has every reason to work on behalf of the company, without concern over arbitrary discharge or capricious abortion of his career. The company can call for, and reasonably expect, levels of effort and quality of output that are only exceptionally available in most other employment systems.

The kaisha becomes in a real sense the property of the people who make it up. It will not be sold, in whole or in part, without the specific approval of all of its directors, acting on behalf of all of its employees. Earnings of the company go first as a return to investors, with the entire balance going to ensure the company's future and thus ensure the future of its employees. The kaisha is not simply an economic institution, but is a deeply social institution, working out its destiny in a competitive economic environment.

The Process of Decision Making

In discussing Japanese-style management, some reference needs be made to the issue of decision making, and differences in the process between the kaisha and Western companies, if only because the topic is so often raised. There is a general view that the kaisha have a special approach to decision making, consensual in nature to an exceptional extent, as symbolized by the formal *ringi seido,* in which a memorandum summarizing the decision is circulated and signed by all concerned.

Much attention has also been paid to the informal, predecision processes of discussion and accommodation of views, called in Japanese *nemawashi.* The kaisha are felt to take a relatively long time to arrive at a decision as these informal and formal processes are worked through, but are seen as able to implement decisions very rapidly once a formal decision is arrived at.

This is no doubt a reasonable description of the usual Japanese decision-making process. It is self-evident that the organization of the kaisha, with tight integration of individuals into the group and an emphasis on group values and behavior, would emphasize group-centered decisions as well. The entire culture of the kaisha mitigates against the spectacular individual making his way against odds and general opinion and finally drawing the group after him. (Japanese politics are similarly free from this man-on-horseback model.)

The problem with this characterization is that it sets up a polarity between all Western decisions made rapidly by an individual and all Japanese decisions made slowly by groups. Neither extreme describes either universe very well. Japan has its occasional one-man companies. Not all Japanese decisions are long drawn-out ones. Indeed, the Western negotiator who believes negotiations with a Japanese company are taking a long time has probably been politely refused and is unable to comprehend the fact.

Many Western organizations have elaborate procedures for study and review before decisions are made, and it is a rare and usually unsuccessful Western executive who fails to sound out his or her organization informally before making a decision. The usual contrast between cultures in terms of decision making seems not to be a very useful one. One might conclude that the culture of most kaisha will ensure group discussion before decisions are made, with the corollary that responsibility for any decision tends to be shared, and that all concerned understand and act on their role in implementation once it is made.

When Will the Employment System Change?

The system of organization and personnel relations of the *kaisha* is not an old system in its present, integrated form. Essentially a product of elements of earlier systems and of the conditions prevailing after World War II, it dates from around 1950. It is a product of a special set of circumstances, history, and events coming together in a particular social and cultural setting. As such, it is liable to change, if and as it becomes dysfunctional under the pressure of changed needs and conditions.

Western journalists are given to writing periodic articles on how the Japanese employment system is changing, based on anecdotal reports or rumors of changes. Some job changes have always taken place between Japanese companies, and continue to; the occasional exception in no way negates the rule, nor signals an end to the general pattern. The Japanese system of employment has proved to be quite durable, through periods of high growth and no growth, in flourishing industries and declining industries. It offers very real advantages to both employees and to the kaisha. It is not surprising therefore that it has survived periods of difficulty.

Viewed in terms of individual motivation, the Japanese system of employment is a trade-off of opportunity for security. It provides security above all, at the loss of opportunity for unusually high reward. It is often remarked by Westerners that security has a high value for the Japanese, and that preference for security against opportunity and risk can be inferred not only from occupational and job preferences but from savings and consumption patterns, as well as political choices.

A security preference is usual for most Japanese, which is not surprising. Until quite recently Japan was a very poor country. The long period of war, the experience of total defeat, and the desperate conditions of the early postwar period would alone make a preference for security over risk entirely understandable. Seen from a historical view, there has been in Japan the sense of a country limited in land, terribly poor in resources, and subject to an exceptionally unpredictable and violent geographic environment. It is not surprising that under these conditions there would be a need to husband limited resources and invest those resources carefully. A strong preference for security over risk would be a natural response.

But as these conditions are changing in important ways, it would not be surprising to find that the security-risk trade-off is also changing, with young people prepared to take career chances their parents did not. Patience with and satisfaction from seniority-based pay and promotion systems would then be likely to wear thin, and the opportunity to change jobs might appear to be a reasonable exchange for the security of the present job.

Changes in attitudes and values may well erode the system over time, but are likely to work slowly. More immediately, the system is under real and continuing economic pressure. It has been the case from the earliest applications of the system that companies in declining industries in Japan, facing a steady falling off of demand, come under severe pressures. As noted earlier, these companies have an aging work force, and thus rising wage levels. The technological level of their work force tends to become obsolete as young graduates are no longer hired. As the age cohorts remaining in the work force move up in seniority, their promotion opportunities dwindle as growth stops and younger workers are not hired. Titles indicating career progress must be created to preserve an illusion of advance.

From point of the economy the results are entirely beneficial. Pressures on declining sectors are increased, accelerating their decline. The labor force shifts to growth sectors, as young people are drawn into the growth industries. Pressure on companies in the declining industries to find growth in new products is intense.

Just such a picture was presented by one of Japan's major shipbuilding companies in a recent study. Its employment peaked in 1973, and fell off sharply after that bulge in employment. Those hired in 1973 are now in their mid-thirties, moving inexorably, like a pig in a python, in age and in wage cost, their morale little improved by a proliferation of titles that are empty of the substance of authority or responsibility. A very hard fate for the company, its employees and its shareholders, but very sound for the economy. The company is being driven out of shipbuilding and toward new kinds of engineering businesses out of desperation—but to Japan's overall advantage.

Yet under the pressures of lower economic growth and of automation, this pattern and this problem is no longer limited to Japanese companies in declining sectors. Figure 8–1 shows the age structure of one of Japan's largest, best-managed, and fastest growing electronics companies. One would have expected hiring to continue at a high level in this company, and the age bulge problem to be nonexistent. In fact, until about ten years ago, the age pattern was perfect—a smooth triangular pattern, with hirings increasing, average age declining, and all the resulting advantages. But even in this fast growth sector, hirings of male workers has dropped off steadily and sharply in recent years. Female workers do not present a problem, as they tend to leave the company as they marry, or have children, and generally therefore do not pose a problem in terms of long employment. But the pattern for male workers is an ominous one.

It is worth noting that table 8–1 was available from the company in essentially the form shown in a matter of minutes after requesting it. It was in the personnel department's computer in chart form. Similarly, the shipbuilding company's age structure data were immediately available upon request. This fact is itself a measure of the importance of the problem to the kaisha management.

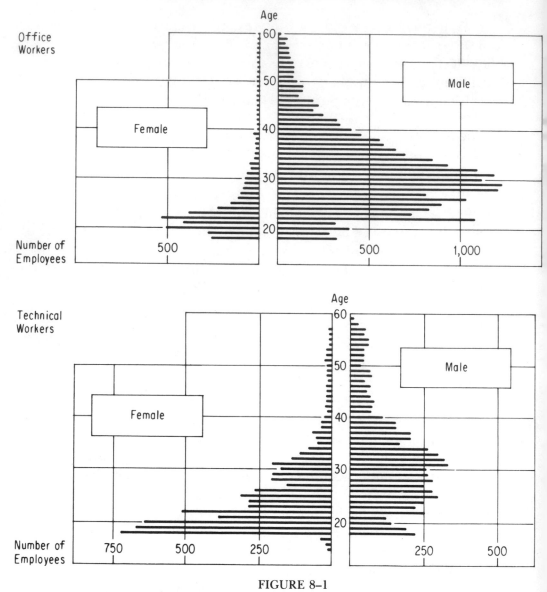

FIGURE 8–1

Age Structure of Employees in a Major Japanese Electronics Company

A survey of a number of major Japanese companies reveals a similar pattern of age structure. The electronics company's personnel manager predicted that the effect would be an end to the current Japanese system of employment by the end of the current decade. The general view is that the seniority-based pay and promotion system will need to give way to a job- and output-based system, but that security of employment will continue.

212

Whose Company Is It?

It seems likely that the benefits to the kaisha of the current system, and the system's fit to the attitudes and expectations of employees, are such that Japan's employment system will change only slowly—and not necessarily in the individualistic, confrontational and, in human terms, costly U.S. or Western system. However, just as the retirement pattern has already changed, so changes in the compensation system are underway and likely to continue. The enterprise union and career employment security are likely to give way last, and continue longest in the manufacturing sector. It may well be that in the service sector, where the emphasis is likely to be on specific professional skills, and where the organizational unit is smaller and more mobile, employment practices will be more individualistic and the employee more mobile. In manufacturing, however, the kaisha have developed a powerful and effective approach to dealing with the human problems of the organization. The approach is not likely to change quickly in significant fashion.

9

THE FOREIGN COMPANY

IN JAPAN

_____

IN industry after industry, from steel to television to autos, the competitive thrust into world markets of the *kaisha* has followed a similar pattern: rapid growth of the Japanese market; fierce competition in Japan for market share; steadily improving cost and quality position of the leading Japanese companies; then an export drive by the domestic winners from "Fortress Japan's" maturing industry, their base position protected from the lack of foreign competition in the Japanese market.

Competition from the kaisha can best be met, and in many cases can only be met, by market competition *inside* Japan. All too often, by the time Japanese products begin to appear in volume in Western markets, the competitive advantage has already shifted away from the Western competitor. The strategic battleground is the Japanese economy: it has been yielded by too many Western competitors without a fight.

The effective strategy is to invest in Japan, taking full advantage of the market's rapid growth, matching Japanese price and quality standards, and controlling the competitive choices available to the kaisha before they are in a position to enter world markets. Although some Western companies have moved aggressively into Japan, to their considerable competitive and profit advantage, all too many have not.

214

The Paradox of Foreign Investment in Japan

The question of why Western companies have not been more aggressive in their attempts to enter the Japanese market is one of the more complex and vexatious issues concerning economic relations with Japan. In discussions by Western government officials and businessmen, the topic is heavily laden with myths, stereotypes, and conventional wisdom: "Japan is closed to investment"; "Foreign companies cannot enter Japan"; and more often, "Foreign companies cannot succeed in Japan," accompanied by citations of discrimination and restrictive regulations, a road blocked by informal and formal obstacles.

More than 1,500 companies in Japan are "foreign-capital related," to use MITI's phrase. That is, foreign companies hold 25 percent or more equity positions in some 1,500 Japanese companies or foreign subsidiaries. This large number takes no account of the proliferation of branch offices and other noncorporate forms of foreign position in Japan. Two-thirds of the top 200 U.S. industrial firms are in this group of foreign investors in Japan.

And the numbers continue to grow. Among the forty fastest growing companies in Japan in the period from March 1980 to March 1983, one in five were foreign related. Four were wholly foreign-owned, in a range of fields from health foods to electronics. Three involved Japanese firms as partners, while one was the extraordinarily successful licensing of Seven-Eleven to a leading Japanese supermarket chain.

While there have been failures, a study in the late 1970s by the American Chamber of Commerce in Japan—prone to criticize Japanese regulations—indicated that U.S. investment in Japan had been exceptionally profitable, with an apparent average investment of 19 percent annually, twice as profitable as the U.S. return on investment in France and Great Britain.[1]

There are more recent indicators of the success of foreign investment. Of all Japanese business entities, including the Bank of Japan, five foreign-related companies are among the most

---

1. *United States Manufacturing Investment in Japan* (Tokyo: The American Chamber of Commerce in Japan, 1979), p. 65.

profitable hundred. Toa Nenryo, a petroleum refiner founded by the Standard Vacuum Oil company and now owned 25 percent each by Exxon and Mobil, reported pre-tax income in fiscal 1983 of $450 million. Nippon IBM, wholly owned by IBM, ranked 22nd in profit among all Japanese business entities ($357 million). Matsushita Denshi, 35 percent owned by Philips N.V., is a power in the semiconductor field ($168 million). Nestlé's wholly owned Japan subsidiary ranks with Suntory as Japan's most profitable company in the food and beverage industry ($153 million). Finally, the Xerox joint venture with Fuji Photo Film is also in the top hundred with pre-tax reported income of $136 million.[2]

A listing of the most profitable privately held companies in Japan includes twelve companies with 50 percent or more foreign ownership. This list takes in not only the companies just mentioned but also includes such successful foreign ventures as Pfizer's Japan subsidary, Coca Cola's Japan company, and the joint ventures in Japan of Caltex, Caterpillar, 3M, and Hewlett Packard. All reported more than $30 million in pre-tax income to the Japanese tax authorities.[3]

These listings include only individual foreign-owned companies. They do not include the substantial positions in Japan of such companies as DuPont, Hoechst, and Bayer whose total sales in Japan are divided among several joint ventures as well as wholly owned companies. A statement of their considerable total positions is thus not publicly available.

The stereotype that the Japanese economy is closed to foreign investment, and that it is an economy where foreign firms cannot succeed, is clearly inaccurate. But the fact is there has been little foreign investment in Japan. An annual survey conducted by MITI of foreign capital-related companies indicates that sales of these companies as a percent of total sales in Japan have remained over the past two decades at about 2 percent. In manufacturing alone, foreign-related firms account for less than four percent of total manufacturing sales. Bearing in mind that

2. These data are drawn from "Henshin Kigyo ga Kaeta Gyokai Seiryoku Zu" (Map of Changing Companies in Changing Industrial Dynamics), *Nikkei Bijinesu,* 7 May 1984, pp. 51–56.

3. *Daimondo Kigyo Rankingu: Shukan Daimondo Bessatsu* (Diamond Company Rankings: Special Issue of Weekly Diamond) (Tokyo: Daimondo Sha, 1984), p. 35.

much of this foreign investment has taken the form of joint ventures, with the foreign equity holding half or less of total equity, it is evident that the position of foreign companies in Japan makes up at most only 2 or 3 percent of total economic activity in Japan.

This low foreign investment is in contrast to Western Europe, where foreign firms account for about 20 percent of sales in West Germany, France, and Great Britain. The foreign investment position in Japan is even less than the position of foreign investment in the United States, where foreign companies account for some 10 to 11 percent of total sales.

The position of foreign investment in Japan is small despite the fact that by any measure of country risk, Japan is surely an attractive site for investment. The market is enormous, second in size only to the United States. The economy continues to grow rapidly relative to most other economies. The labor force is of highest quality and available for moderate cost. The infrastructure of banking and other supporting services is fully developed. The currency is stable. The government is exceptionally stable, and sympathetic to private business. The list of positive factors for substantial foreign investment is a long and impressive one.

Protection by Regulation and by Indifference

Why, then, is the level of foreign investment in Japan so low? For an answer, a brief review of the postwar history of foreign investment is necessary. The pattern that emerges is curious: the Japanese economy has been protected from foreign investment in two ways. The first type of protection was—but is no longer, and has not been for some years—from Japanese government regulations and restrictions on foreign investment. The second type of protection—no less effective and much more lasting—has been provided by the indifference and ignorance of possible foreign investors regarding Japan, and their unwillingness in many cases to pay the price in effort and patience to make the investment. The postwar investment pattern reveals both types of protection.

The first phase of direct investment into Japan was from 1952 to 1964. During this period, Japan's was essentially a siege economy, with all flows of goods, capital, and technology subject to specific government approvals. Thus, even those companies established before the war required specific approval in order to transfer goods, capital, or technology to their ventures in Japan. If capital was transferred into Japan without government assurance and approval, capital and earnings could not be repatriated unless or until the yen became convertible.

Still, it was possible during this period to move capital into Japan freely and undertake direct investments in the so-called "yen companies." These were established with converted foreign funds, and there was little restriction on the sector for investment and no restriction on percent of ownership. Coca Cola established its operations in Japan in the late 1950s through such a yen company, as did a few other companies, including General Foods and AMP.

Some of these yen companies have done very well. The success of Coca Cola is well known; at one point in the late 1960s, the Japan operation alone accounted for more than one-quarter of Coca Cola's world-wide earnings. There are some pleasant ironies in the Coca Cola Japan story, and it is no reflection on the competence or efforts of that company's management to note that its success was due in no small part to the restrictions placed on it by the Japanese government.

Coca Cola had been introduced into Japan via the U.S. armed forces, and the local bottler, Tokyo Coca Cola Bottling Company, was soon on its way to its present distinction as the world's largest beverage bottling company. As the yen company was established to enter the domestic Japanese market, the Japanese government was concerned over the possible impact of Coca Cola on the hundreds of local bottlers of a cider-like drink that was then Japan's dominant soft drink. Coca Cola was under pressure to price its product at a high level in order to protect the local small businesses. Because the product was foreign, and thought to be likely to attract only the more sophisticated consumers, the high price was agreed to (a price so high it was not raised for fifteen years).

Coca Cola, of course, proved to have broad appeal despite

its high price. As the company was a yen company, and could not repatriate its earnings until after the 1964 move to yen convertibility, the profits were aggressively reinvested in distribution and promotion, which in turn generated more popularity and profits. In a real sense, Coca Cola was the beneficiary of the Japanese government's pricing requirements and the restrictions on repatriation of earnings. If Coca Cola could have pulled profits out of Japan from the beginning, would it have become so extraordinary a success story?

AMP also set up its electrical connector business in Japan as a yen company. Despite competition from an NEC subsidiary and from fast-growing Hirose Electric, AMP remains the market leader in the vastly expanded electrical connector market of Japan today. Not all yen companies were successful: General Foods, after a long struggle, gave way under Nestlé's competitive pressure and sold a half interest in its wholly owned company in Japan to Ajinomoto, Japan's leader in processed foods. As a joint venture, the operation has performed reasonably well since.

The critical point about the yen company route to foreign direct investment in Japan is the small number of companies that chose to take advantage of this largely unrestricted mode of entry. Odd as it may seem today, very few foreign managements in the 1950s and 1960s were prepared to take a chance on the economy succeeding and the yen becoming convertible. The Japanese economy was small, remote, and unfamiliar. Its strategic position and prospects went largely unnoticed. Gambling on Japan's success was not to the taste of Western boards of directors.

An alternate route to direct investment in Japan during this period was through application to the Japanese government for investment approval, which brought with it guarantees of repatriation of earnings and capital. Not surprisingly, the Japanese government chose to attach strict conditions to such approvals. The proposed venture had to be seen as being in Japan's national interest, which came to mean the introduction into Japan of unique technologies that could not otherwise be acquired. The investment had to be into a new company rather than an existing Japanese company, and the foreign equity participation was to be no more than 50 percent. (In a few cases, minor equity positions in existing Japanese companies were obtained through sales of technology).

The majority of foreign companies were prepared to invest in Japan during this period only with government approvals and guarantees. Thus, the joint venture came to be the modal form of foreign investment into Japan. Some of these ventures, like Fuji Xerox, have done very well. But in general, the joint venture form of investment posed problems for both sides in the investment, and as will be seen later in this chapter, many of the most successful of these joint ventures have been dissolved in the last few years.

It might be argued that the stiff requirements of the Japanese government before approving investments during this period was a barrier to greater investment. No doubt this was the case, but the yen company route went largely unused. Furthermore, most Western companies were content during this period to forego the problems, and risks, of government approval procedures, and simply sold their technology to interested Japanese firms. A technology sale represented a windfall income to the U.S. seller from fully amortized research investments. The Japanese buyers were seen as representing no competitive threat. Thus, there was a massive shift of technology, particularly out of the United States, into a Japanese economy starved for technology. In the process, Japanese competitors were helped to grow and become formidable; U.S. companies, by having sold off their principal competitive advantage, lost the lever that might in a few years have been used to move to positions inside the Japanese market.

Failure of foresight regarding Japan, and indifference or ignorance regarding Japan, was by no means limited to potential new investors into postwar Japan. Neither Ford nor General Motors made any substantial effort to regain and rebuild their considerable prewar positions inside Japan. Until the late 1950s ITT was a one-third equity holder in Nippon Electric Company, a legacy of the founding of that company by the old International Western Electric. But ITT dumped its holdings in Nippon Electric onto the Japanese market in the late 1950s, holdings in what has become NEC, Ltd., a $9 billion world leader in semiconductors, computers, and telecommunications equipment.

Both Otis Elevator and Carrier Corporation introduced their product categories into Japan and dominated the prewar Japanese market in those products. Both egregiously failed to invest and compete adequately in the postwar period and suffered dramatic losses of position to such Japanese competitors as Hitachi and Mitsubishi Electric, which now dominate the market. Only lately, under the aegis of United Technologies ownership and with aggressive management, have these companies begun the difficult and long struggle to regain Japan position.

Other companies that inherited prewar positions did in fact make the necessary efforts to keep pace with Japan's economic development. Nestlé is one example; IBM is another; NCR is still another. Each did what was necessary by way of capital, products, and manpower to rebuild and expand its prewar positions. It needs be noted that the introduction of technology into Japan was no less tightly controlled in the case of these established companies than was the case with newcomers. The introduction of IBM's computer technology to Japan in the late 1950s required a prolonged and stormy round of negotiations with the Japanese government, permission being given only after IBM agreed to licensing the technology to local firms. Again, looking at companies with prewar histories in Japan, it is clear that Japan's protection even in this early period derived no less from the failure of foreign investors to make necessary efforts than from the constraints of the Japanese government.

The next phase of foreign investment into Japan was from 1964 to 1973. With yen convertibility in 1964, the yen company route for direct investment was closed, and all direct investment required specific government screening and approval. The requirements remained that these investments in manufacturing be into newly established companies, with foreign equity participation no more than 50 percent. Even these restrictions yielded on occasion to sufficiently determined, able, and powerful potential investors. The case of Texas Instruments (TI) was one where despite restrictions, a U.S. company, using its technology as a weapon, was able to establish a wholly owned position in a key sector of the Japanese economy.

In the early 1960s, TI held a basic patent in semiconductor technology, one that could not be designed around to evade the patent protection, and one that the Japanese had to have access to if they were to build an export position in electronics. Fairchild Semiconductor, with an equally basic patent in the field, chose to license Japanese producers, foregoing the opportunity to invest directly into Japan. But TI was determined to invest and it applied to the Japanese government for a 100 percent investment, arguing that under treaty obligations between Japan and the United States, nationals were entitled to equal treatment. Because Japanese firms could invest in wholly owned operations in the United States, TI argued, so by treaty rights, U.S. nationals were entitled to the same treatment in Japan.

After a long period of attempting to ignore TI's application, and then only under direct pressure from the U.S. government at cabinet level, the Japanese government announced its position. Texas Instruments could invest in Japan, but only in a 50-50 venture, its partner to be one of six specified Japanese companies. Further, as a condition of such investment, TI's key patent was to be made available for licensing by Japanese firms at a fair price. But TI remained adamant—it would consider only a 100 percent investment and continued to withhold patent access. Under U.S. government pressure, but far more important, under pressure from the Japanese industry to resolve the patent issue promptly, MITI asked Akio Morita, then president of Sony, (who was believed to have some advantage in understanding and dealing with U.S. businessmen) to serve as special ambassador to Texas Instruments.

A compromise was reached, in which TI would set up a joint venture, with Sony as partner. However, Sony would provide no support to the venture in terms of personnel or technology, and would at the end of three years sell its shares back to TI at cost, with TI thus achieving its wholly owned position. As part of the bargain, TI would license at reasonable fee its patent to Japanese firms (which already had the technology but required patent access for its full application).

Texas Instruments faced no small task in establishing itself in Japan. Far from being considered locally made, its products were deemed imports. A wounded bureaucracy was not inclined to provide favors, but the company moved aggressively, among other things recruiting a senior MITI official as officer (now chairman) of its Japan company. That company now has four factories operating in Japan, with productivity levels reported to be the highest in the TI system, and TI uses its Japan operation as a principal source to world markets of its most advanced semiconductors.

The key elements of success in Japan are well illustrated in the TI case. Top management was determined to be in Japan for strategic as well as operational reasons. Technology was husbanded to ensure its availability as the base on which to build a Japan position. Patience and ingenuity were exercised in building a local position. Aggressive investment followed to realize fully the benefits of the Japan operation. All of this was done in the face of determined resistance from the Japanese authorities.

That resistance began to crumble not long after TI's success. Around 1966 a great debate began in Japan about liberalization—the opening of Japan to foreign trade and investment. It was clearly in Japan's economic interest to dismantle its controls on the flow of goods, capital, and technology. Further, Japan's commitments to the International Monetary Fund and the Organization for Economic Cooperation and Development required liberalization. Nonetheless, real fears remained of being engulfed by giant foreign companies—Nabisco for example, which was described, accurately, as larger than the entire Japanese biscuit industry combined.

The process of liberalization began in 1967, slowly at first, but quickly gaining momentum. Within only six years, the apparatus of controls had been dismantled, with Japan as open to capital investment as any other of the OECD member countries. The change in policy was completed and formalized on 1 May 1973, when the principle of 100 percent direct foreign investment in new or existing Japanese companies was put into effect by the Japanese government.

If Japan's protection from foreign direct investment derived only or even principally from government restrictions, during and after this process of removing restrictions a surge of foreign investment into Japan would have been expected. But in fact, nothing of the sort materialized. Foreign investment into

Japan has increased, but at about the rate of growth of the economy. The total position of foreign firms in the economy has not increased. Japan's attractiveness as a site for investment has in no way diminished. However, foreign investment has not expanded, despite the removal of controls.

In terms of competitive balance, however, there is a difference in the situation of foreign investment in Japan today compared to the earlier period. In the more traditional industries, foreign companies, by bad planning or bad luck, failed to establish or reestablish themselves in postwar Japan. In heavy electrical equipment, giants like General Electric and West Germany's Siemens all had had major positions in Japan earlier. Indeed, GE and Siemens were founders of Toshiba and Fuji Electric respectively, as ITT's predecessor company had been of NEC. They have never regained their prewar positions in that industry. In tires, as another example, Dunlop was forced by declining market position to sell a majority of its long-established company to members of the Sumitomo Group some years ago as Bridgestone moved to dominance in the Japanese industry. Now Sumitomo Rubber is buying a substantial part of its European tire-making facilities from Dunlop—the relationship has come full circle. Goodrich has withdrawn from Yokohama Rubber. Goodyear's technology helped Bridgestone become the dominant Japan producer, but Goodyear has no significant position in Japan now.

In contrast to these more traditional industries, the position in Japan of foreign companies in the newer, higher technology industries is substantial. As noted, IBM Japan is a major company, with sales of more than $2.5 billion. But IBM is far from alone as a major foreign company in Japan's electronics industry —NCR owns 70 percent of a Japanese company that is a substantial one (the balance of NCR Japan's shares are publicly traded). Hewlett Packard holds 75 percent of a sizable venture with Yokogawa Hokushin. Like TI's major investment in Japan, Motorola now has a wholly owned subsidiary in manufacturing and marketing. Intel has a design company, Burroughs has a wholly owned company, and Fairchild is building a plant for semiconductor manufacture.

The list of wholly owned or majority-owned foreign operations in electronics in Japan is a long one. It is interesting for two reasons: first, it is the sector that the Japanese government is seen as most determined to support and defend. Yet the electronics sector is penetrated by perhaps more foreign investment than any other sector except petroleum. Second, whatever the outcome of competition between Japanese and Western companies may turn out to be, the pattern will not be a replay of the earlier steel, consumer electronics, and auto industry cases. There is and will be real competition in the Japanese market itself. There will be no "Fortress Japan" for Japan's electronics producers.

The pharmaceutical industry, and by extension future developments in biogenetics, is another area of high technology where foreign firms have major positions in the Japanese market. This is an especially government-oriented industry, both from the fact that product approvals are required from the Ministry of Health and Welfare, and from the fact that payments for pharmaceuticals are almost entirely financed by tax monies through the National Health Insurance program. Pfizer and Merck have major positions in the Japanese industry, and in addition every major pharmaceutical firm in the world has a venture in Japan, a number of them wholly owned operations. The Japanese industry is fragmented, and is only now becoming a significant producer of new products. Yet no special protection has been extended by the government of Japan to shelter this industry from foreign investment, despite its weakness and the government's important role in its development. Here again, as with electronics, a replay of the competitive trade pattern of the 1960s and 1970s is not possible given the position of foreign firms in the industry in Japan.

It seems that companies in these newly developing, higher technology industries have the advantage of being able to take a look at the pattern of world competition as it is emerging, rather than as it has been in the past. They can, and have, benefited from the errors of omission or commission of the older industries. Their pace of technological change means that they tend to have a basis for competitive advantage when moving into the Japanese market, a competitive edge not available to companies dealing in more mature technologies.

The End of the Joint Venture Era

In terms of type of investment, throughout the postwar period the principal form of foreign investment has been the joint venture. Japanese government restrictions were one reason why the joint venture became the most common pattern of investment. Even after the restrictions were lifted, operational issues and needs often made the joint venture the selected pattern of foreign entry and investment.

In certain industries, the joint venture is turned to because of distribution problems. The food and beverage industry is a good example. Japan has 750,000 retail food and beverage outlets, mostly tiny, poorly financed, and difficult and costly to reach in physical distribution. A foreign company entering the industry faces almost insurmountable problems in achieving competitive cost position against established competitors. The new entrant typically has a narrow product line and cannot spread the costs of distribution over a full line. This was essentially the problem for General Foods; the solution was to ride into the market on the wider distribution apparatus of Ajinomoto. Coca Cola is no exception, as it distributes through its bottlers, independent Japanese companies with considerable resources. Nestlé worked through the trading companies' systems. Nabisco, Del Monte, Kellogg's, CPC, and United Biscuits have all done well, and have all worked through a Japanese food company's distribution system.

Another major operational problem that makes for joint venture solutions is the personnel issue. It is simply not possible to recruit first-class experienced managers from the open labor market in Japan. It is difficult enough for the foreign firm to recruit youngsters to fill its lower ranks, much less find factory managers, sales managers, and other senior personnel to manage its Japan operations. The Japanese joint venture partner is seen as a source of supply of key personnel.

This solution is burdened with hazards, however. Unable to discharge its less able staff because of its system of permanent employment, the Japanese partner may take the occasion to fob some of them off on the joint venture, allowing the partner to share the cost of carrying incompetents. Personnel inherited from the Japanese partner remain the partner's men, not the joint venture's men, much less the followers of the foreign partner. Under these conditions, whatever the balance of equity ownership in the venture, it is the Japanese partner who is in fact managing the venture. Despite these hazards, the issue of finding qualified personnel may still favor a joint venture solution to direct investment.

For all these factors that contribute to a joint venture approach, developments over the last few years suggest that the era of the joint venture is drawing to a close. The joint venture has always been an awkward compromise of conflicting interest. From the Japanese side, it has come about from the firm seeking a technology that it cannot obtain through a simple license. Therefore, it is often a clumsy and costly way of getting access to a needed technology. For the foreign side, the joint venture is entered into in order to obtain a position in the Japanese economy that it could not—or felt it could not—achieve in any other way, either because of early government restrictions, or because of barriers to entry on its own, such as distribution or personnel. To the foreign partner, the joint venture is a beachhead in Japan to be used for further expansion. For the Japanese partner, the joint venture is nothing of the sort, having ample alternatives for expansion in Japan.

The problem of conflict of interest between partners is made more severe when, as is usually the case, the partners are in the same industry or even in the same business within an industry. Not surprisingly, a partner is usually sought who knows the business, is experienced in it, and has a position already established. Unfortunately, this also means that as the venture expands over time, and especially as the separate interests of the so-called partners expand in world markets, the two parties to the venture are likely to come into conflict with each other.

But this need not be the case, and is not always the case. Certain joint ventures, such as that of Dow Corning with Toray in silicones, have represented a true diversification for the Japanese partner with little likelihood of long-term conflict of interest from competing market positions. Expansion of the venture is in the interest of both parties, and poses no threat to the base business of the Japanese partner. However, these kinds of ventures, where the Japanese partner is entirely new to the business, are all too few.

There is yet another problem area for joint ventures which results from the nearly inevitable slowness of decision making in a situation in which two vitally interested parties must participate in all major decisions. The result is delays in reaction time, that can, in a business subject to rapid changes in product design and market conditions, effectively doom the joint venture to steadily diminishing market share.

There is no doubt that in recent years, Japanese companies that once were very open to discussions of possible joint ventures have as a matter of policy decided against entering additional ones. Part of this attitude is due to increasing self-confidence regarding the ability of the Japanese firm to develop its own technology and products. Much is due, however, to negative experience with earlier joint ventures from developing conflicts of interest and decision-making problems.

There is no clear pattern of either success or failure of joint ventures. The balance of equity in a venture—either foreign minority, 50-50, or foreign majority—is not by itself the critical factor in determining a venture's success or failure. Such 50-50 ventures as Fuji-Xerox in copy machines, Yamatake Honeywell in process control equipment, and Sumitomo 3M in a diversified range of products have all done well, and continue to prosper.

Other joint ventures have been disasters. Some, like the Heinz venture with Nichiro Fisheries and the Unilever venture with Honen Oil ended with the foreign partner taking control of the venture in order to salvage it. In others, like the joint ventures of Kraft Foods with Morinaga Milk in processed cheese products and Campbell Soup with Toyo Suisan in canned soups, the foreign investor withdrew.

Mixed results with joint ventures have been the case over many years. Some businesses and relationships were well conceived and executed and others were not. Their successes and failures no doubt reflect normal business risks rather than the results of inherent advantages or disadvantages of the joint venture form of investment. Yet in the last few years, a distinctly different pattern has emerged. A number of large and successful joint ventures have been terminated, not owing to business difficulties, nor to bad relations between the partners, but rather to diverging interests of the partners. Table 9–1 lists some recent cases of the break-up of joint ventures, with one taking controlling position. In each of the cases, there is a special set of circumstances leading to the changes in ownership. Asahi Dow was one of the largest and oldest joint ventures in Japan with sales well over $800 million in petrochemical products. Dow Chemical was in the process of liquidating several of its international positions for cash. In this case, Asahi Chemical, the Japanese partner, bought most of the venture for $90 million, with Dow retaining two of the venture's plants to integrate into its rapidly growing and wholly owned Japan operations.

It is interesting to note that Dow Corning appears on both sides of the listings in table 9–1. Dow Corning held a 45 percent position in Shinetsu Silicon, and a 50 percent position in Toray Silicone. The products of both ventures are now global products, and supply and pricing strategies need to be integrated on a worldwide basis. In metallic silicon, the basic material for the manufacture of semiconductors, Shinetsu Chemical is rapidly becoming a world leader, competing with Wacker and with Monsanto in all markets. Dow Corning sold its interest in this

TABLE 9–1

Recent Ownership Changes in Successful Joint Ventures

Japanese Side Takes Control	Foreign Side Takes Control
Asahi Dow (Dow Chemical)	Yokogawa-Hewlett Packard (Hewlett Packard)
Shinetsu Silicon (Dow Corning)	Toray Silicone (Dow Corning)
Komatsu International (International Harvester)	Showa Oil (Shell)
Atlas Kao (ICI)	Proctor & Gamble Sunhome (Proctor & Gamble)
Ebara-Infilco (Westinghouse)	Aizu Toko (Motorola)
Japan Automatic Transmission (Ford)	Tokai TRW (TRW)
Bristol Banyu (Bristol Myers)	Nippon Data General (Data General)

venture to Shinetsu Chemical. In silicones, Dow Corning is world leader, and Toray agreed to reduce its position to a one-third equity interest, thereby yielding control to Dow Corning. The change in joint venture equity positions thus was the result of changing corporate objectives rather than problems in the ventures themselves.

International Harvester cashed in its position in its successful joint venture with Komatsu under pressure of financial problems at home. In the process it filled out Komatsu's product line, strengthening Komatsu's position as it moved into the U.S. market. And ICI could see little future for its surfactants joint venture with Kao Soap; the venture was imbedded in Kao's facilities, with little prospect for expansion. Westinghouse has long since divested itself of the Infilco businesses. The Ebara-Infilco Company was a remaining piece of Infilco investment and had become Japan's largest engineering firm in the field of water treatment, but the venture had no place in Westinghouse's long-range plans. With an increasing commitment to Toyo Kogyo (now Mazda), Ford's transmission venture with Nissan presumably raised conflict problems. When Merck announced the acquisition of a majority of the shares of Banyu, Bristol-Myers's joint venture with Banyu became untenable.

The common themes in these disinvestments by Western companies from successful joint ventures in Japan seem to be changes in corporate objectives and changes in the evaluation of the venture within the changing context of the Western partner's business plans. Over time, joint ventures for various reasons became marginal to the strategy of the Western partner. The disinvestments appear in all cases to have suited the purposes of the Japanese partner as well, and the ownership changes appear to have taken place without rancor or special problems.

Disinvestments by Western companies from joint ventures in Japan seem to be balanced by a similar number of cases in which the Western firm moved for control or full ownership of the ventures. In each of these cases, the Japanese venture is central to the strategies of the Western company, comprising a key part of an aggressive Japan strategy. Again, all of these changes in ownership geared to equity control by the Western company seem to have taken place without any difficulties apart from the usual hazards of negotiation. In most of these cases, the Japanese partner to the original venture has retained some interest in the operation and management has continued largely unchanged.

The joint venture in many ways represents a low-cost, low-risk mode of entry to a market. The foreign partner lowers exposure by sharing capital costs with a local partner. Indeed, because often the Western equity is in the form of technology sale for shares in the new venture, the principal capital risk is often for the local partner. Cost and risk is further reduced by drawing on the staff of the local partner, employing his distribution system, and often operating from the local partner's land and facilities.

The joint venture mode of entry was appropriate when the stakes of the game in Japan were seen, correctly or not, to be low. A great many companies now appreciate that the stakes in the Japan competitive game are greater. A higher cost, higher risk position in Japan is not only justified, but is indeed required. Wholly owned operations in Japan are high-cost, high-risk operations, but an increasing number of firms are willing to undertake the risks. Japanese firms also see joint ventures as less appealing or necessary. Thus it seems possible to speak of the end of the joint venture era. There will be more joint ventures, of course, but they will no longer be the dominant or customary form of direct investment in Japan.

Acquisition as an Option to Enter the Economy

The shift in the pattern of foreign direct investment in Japan was made more probable by the emergence of another option for the foreign firm seeking to build a position in the Japanese economy. This was the possibility of acquiring a substantial equity position in, or majority control of, an existing Japanese company. Acquisition has long been the preferred mode of entry into a highly developed market. Entry into a developed market is, by definition, costly. Such a market is large, highly competitive, and has high costs of staffing, promotion, and distribution. Acquisition of a successful company in such a market can provide in a single stroke product line, facilities, staffing, distribution, and government and community relations.

American companies seeking to expand their position in Western Europe against the possibility of a more closed European Economic Community in the 1950s and 1960s depended heavily on acquisition of European firms as the mode of entry investment. In recent years, as European firms have sought to expand their U.S. positions, acquisition of successful U.S. companies has been the favored route of entry.

Not only does acquisition immediately provide the necessary staff and facilities, it can also provide an immediate positive cash flow. Entry by building a new business in any event is costly, with the probability of a negative cash flow for a number of years while the business is being built. These costs are a direct deduction from current earnings, a further discouragement for a profit-center manager whose compensation often depends on the level of current earnings. An acquisition is a capital cost, with no necessary impact on current earnings. Indeed, with some success in negotiations, the current earnings position may be improved. Given all this, it is no surprise that acquisition is the favored route.

Acquisition in Japan is especially attractive. Through acquisition of a successful company, the most serious problems of entry to the Japanese market can be quickly resolved. In a country in which labor and management cannot readily be recruited, acquisition would provide management and labor force already in place. Japan's distribution system is known to be complex and difficult to penetrate; acquisition would bring with it channels and position. In a country where land is very expensive and sites for facilities difficult to obtain, acquisition would provide immediate physical facilities. As Japan poses real market entry barriers, acquisitions of a thriving Japanese company is the answer to all of them.

A constraint on acquisition in Japan is the relatively high price of Japanese company shares, with the average price-earnings ratio more than twice that of the shares of U.S. companies. The asset position of most Japanese companies is considerably understated, however, principally from the fact that land and investments are still carried on the balance sheet at cost, or near cost, when their market values have appreciated many times over. Thus, a given amount of equity investment in a Japanese company could command a substantially greater asset position than the price might suggest. In general, acquisition would be a powerful and highly desirable entry mode into Japan.

Unfortunately for the would-be foreign investor, companies in Japan are generally not bought or sold, nor are individual businesses of Japanese companies bought or sold. An existing Japanese company can be acquired, by Japanese or foreign interests, provided only that all of the directors of the target company concur in the sale of the shares of the company. The problem is not one of government regulations or legal restrictions but involves the nature of the Japanese company, which differs significantly from the Western pattern.

The essence of the Japanese company is the people who compose it. The company personnel, including directors, who are themselves life-time employees and executives of the company, are very much a part of the company. This has two consequences in terms of acquisition. One is that buying or selling a business in Japan has about it the suggestion of buying or selling people. There is a sense of social irresponsibility and even immorality about it. The other is that the personnel of the company have a very real control over corporate decisions. They are to a considerable degree the owners of the Japanese company. To the extent that sale of the company is a threat to the company's personnel, sale of the company becomes difficult.

It is no surprise, then, to find that mergers and acquisitions in Japan are far less frequent than in Western economies. Mergers that do take place tend to occur between companies that are already related in ownership, banking relationships, and business relations. Outright acquisitions are few. Like Japan's distribution system, and Japan's language, this pattern was not designed to frustrate foreigners, but it works well in doing so.

Despite all this, the pattern is beginning to change. There has been a steady increase in mergers and acquisitions in the postwar period, even though the level remains low relative to other economies (see table 9–2). Moreover, events in the past few years suggest that as the economy matures and as its financial systems become more sophisticated, there is likely to be a considerable increase in acquisitions, making them a more customary part of business practice. For example, Kyocera, the fast-growing ceramics and electronics company, recently acquired Yashica, a troubled camera maker, and Minebea, a diversified bearings maker, acquired an audio equipment subsidiary of Sony.

It is relevant that Kyocera and Minebea are outside the Japanese business establishment, both being companies given to unusual and nontraditional moves. It is also relevant, however, that these acquisitions occasioned no special outcry or surprise. Because acquisitions often make good business sense, one can only expect them to increase in incidence in Japan, and steadily.

But there are some patterns of acquisition that are unlikely to be seen in Japan for a long time. Takeover bids opposed by management are not possible, from the requirement that sitting directors must all approve sale of the company. In any event, it would be a rash and foolish investor who would undertake a hostile takeover in an economy in which staff cannot easily either be discharged or replaced.

Acquisition is also most unlikely to occur in Japan in order to enrich the company's current shareholders. Acquisitions will take place if and when they are seen to be strengthening the company and thereby improving the prospects of the employees. It is not the interests of the shareholders that will deter-

TABLE 9–2

Mergers and Complete Acquisitions in Japan
(Approximate)

	Total	Average per Year
After World War II to the Korean War	2,360	337
Korean War to 1970	8,100	507
1970 to 1980	10,210	1,021

Source: *Kosei Torihiki Iinkai Nenji Hokoku* (Annual Report of the Japan Fair Trade Commission) (Tokyo: Kosei Torihiki Kyokai, 1982), p. 305

mine whether the transaction takes place, but rather the interests of the employees of the company.

Finally, it will be a long time before highly successful companies in Japan are bought and sold. Acquisition will occur in industries that are in trouble, like cameras and audio equipment, where certain companies are under pressure for survival. The acquired company will have problems for which presumably the acquirer, by virtue of technology, distribution power, cash, or some combination of these assets, can provide solutions.

All of these issues are critical to the foreign company seeking to invest in Japan because over recent years it appears that acquisition of significant share positions in Japanese companies is possible, and available, as a strategic option to foreign investors. Early indications of this occurred in the early 1970s, notably when General Motors acquired 34 percent of the shares of Isuzu. General Motors was actively seeking to establish a position in Japan within the limits imposed by U.S. antitrust law. Isuzu was in trouble, a major truck and bus producer that had had a very costly failure in passenger car production. For GM, the share acquisition provided an instant supply of needed light-duty trucks. For Isuzu, GM's equity infusion was preferable to the alternative of being swallowed up by the Nissan group.

Not all of these share acquisitions were successful in turning around a troubled Japanese company. Firestone withdrew from its minority equity holding in Ohtsu Tire, and Owens Illinois was unable to improve the situation of Nippon Electric Glass. Nonetheless, a pattern began to appear where foreign companies were able to acquire a share position in Japanese firms that were usually in some trouble, where the foreign firms could—presumably through technology and overseas distribution channels—provide relief to the Japanese company.

But in all of these cases, the foreign investor was far from exerting control over the Japanese company. General Motors was careful to avoid preempting executive positions or decision-making power in Isuzu. Textron, a conglomerate, remained a passive investor in Max, an office equipment producer, without even posting a representative in Japan. These investments sometimes had the potential for integration into the foreign investor's worldwide system, but little direct integration actually took place.

But now that pattern is developing. The change was signaled by the 1982 acquisition of a 43 percent share position in Osaka Oxygen by BOC, a world leader in industrial gases that was without a significant position in Japan. Osaka Oxygen is the third-ranking industrial gas producer in Japan, but its sales and earnings were flat as the traditional markets for industrial gas, like the steel industry, matured. The shift was toward more exotic gases, like argon, sold to the electronics industry, where BOC's technology could help Osaka Oxygen make the transition.

The breakthrough event in this acquisition trend occurred in 1983, as Merck, the U.S. pharmaceutical company, acquired a majority equity position in Banyu Pharmaceuticals. This was the first case in Japanese industrial history where a company listed on the first section of the Tokyo Stock Exchange—that is, limited to Japan's top companies—was majority acquired by a foreign company. Merck topped this unprecedented move by simultaneously acquiring a majority interest in Torii Pharmaceuticals, an established but troubled company trading over the counter. When these two acquisitions are integrated with Merck's existing joint venture with Banyu, Nippon Merck Banyu, Merck will become a major power in Japan's pharmaceutical industry, the second largest in the world, and one that is fast becoming a major source of new pharmaceutical products.

It is of special interest that the Japanese government posed no obstacles to these acquisitions. The chairman of BOC took occasion in his 1982 annual report to thank the Ministry of Finance and MITI for their advice in carrying out the Osaka Oxygen transaction.[4] In the case of Merck, despite a complex financial arrangement, the Ministry of Finance raised no objections to the acquisition, and it was promptly approved both by that ministry and the Ministry of Health and Welfare, as was the Torii acquisition.

Nor was there any notable reaction to the BOC or Merck moves from the press or industry. Once the negotiations had been completed to the satisfaction of both parties, the fact that

4. Sir Leslie Smith, *The BOC Group Annual Report 1982* (London, England), p. 9.

foreigners were buying Japanese firms did not occasion any special outcry. This is interesting both because the pharmaceutical industry is sensitive politically, and because in the industrial gas industry foreign investors now, in three of the six producers in Japan, hold substantial or controlling share positions. No doubt a considerable number of acquisitions of major Japanese companies by foreigners would raise political problems, but none resulted from these acquisitions.

These acquisitions have all of the characteristics noted earlier regarding acquisition in Japan in general. The industries involved are going through difficult transitions—a technological one in industrial gas and a shakeout period in pharmaceuticals as prices come down and marginal producers are squeezed. The companies acquired are not the leaders in their industry. Management, and other personnel in the company, can see real problems ahead for the company. The foreign acquirer provides a possible solution that will strengthen and prolong the life of the company. From the acquirer's point of view, these are not the ideal candidates for acquisition—they have real problems that will require real effort and resources to deal with.

Furthermore, the acquisitions did not benefit the shareholders of these companies. Of course, to the extent that the company becomes healthier, existing shareholders will benefit. But the shares acquired were not acquired at a premium price; they were made available to the acquirer at or below the then market price. These were not takeover bids, nor did they make management or shareholders wealthy.

The Merck example raises additional questions. Does the acquirer need a majority shareholding position to control the acquired company? Does the acquirer in fact want to hold a majority share position, given the requirement to consolidate the purchased company onto his own balance sheet? American firms in particular have a propensity to define control as the holding of a majority of shares. But clearly control can be exercised in many ways without necessarily meeting that narrow definition of control. Moreover, the Japanese companies that have been acquired are not outstanding performers. Had they been, they would not have been candidates for acquisition. Their financial performance is less than outstanding, with considerable debt in most cases, and low levels of profitability. The result is that if and as they are consolidated in the financial statements of the acquirer there is likely to be considerable dilution of the acquirer's position. Indeed, the chairman of Merck warned of dilution in his annual report announcing the Banyu acquisition. The foreign company needs to think its way through these questions as it considers the acquisition option.

Whatever the specific circumstances of a given transaction, the foreign company seeking to build a major position in Japan has an additional option available now that was not available earlier, the acquisition of a significant position in an existing Japanese company. This is not to say that Japanese companies are suddenly up for sale, but the option is now available as one of several investment alternatives, and needs to be explored before final decisions are made regarding mode of entry to and investment in Japan.

In analyzing the mode of entry to the Japanese market, it is important to bear in mind that the needed capability for market penetration may be that of distribution and sales rather than that of local manufacture. Japan is and will increasingly be a very large and critically important market. But for many products— non-ferrous metals, petrochemicals, pulp and paper products, light electrical products such as radios, and basic textile products—Japan is no longer a cost-effective production site. That site may be North America, or South Korea, or Southeast Asia. For labor-intensive, or energy- and material-intensive products, it is unlikely that establishing production in Japan will be cost competitive. Thus, whatever the mode of entry—acquisition, joint venture, or green-field investment in a newly built, wholly owned facility—production in Japan may not be advisable.

For such products, what is needed in Japan is expense investment in distribution facilities and sales capability in support of off-shore production. DuPont has established an important position in the Japanese market in specialty chemicals through carefully building a sales force and distribution system, sourcing products from cost-effective, world-scale facilities in North America. Weyerhaeuser has long since realized the critical importance of the Japanese market for its products, and has made the necessary expense investments in building an importing and sales operation. Unfortunately for the U.S. trade balance with Japan, this kind of expense investment is often the most difficult form of investment to justify to skeptical or ill-informed managements sitting in review of investment proposals.

The Strategic Requirement

Whether it is a capital investment in bricks and mortar, or an expense investment in salaries and merchandising, it is quite clear that the controlling issue regarding foreign investment in Japan is the understanding and conviction on the part of top management of the U.S. or European company that the key competitors are the kaisha, and that the competitive arena is Japan itself. Japan has been protected from foreign investment by Japanese government regulation, but another, considerable part of the protection from foreign investment has been the ignorance, indifference, or failure of nerve of the foreign companies that might have built positions in Japan.

Those companies that have a full appreciation of Japan's importance, and a conviction that they will do what is required to build a major position in Japan, have done so. Nestlé, IBM, and NCR took their prewar positions to major strengths in the postwar period; ITT, GE, and Siemens did not. The difference was not Japanese government regulations. Coca Cola and AMP took full advantage of the yen company route; most companies did not. The difference was not from Japanese obstacles. Texas Instruments drove its way into a major position in Japan; Motorola, Fairchild, RCA, and Zenith did not. The Japanese government and Japanese discrimination does not account for the difference. Merck and BOC spent years working to the position they now have; others could have done so too.

The case of Eastman Kodak is especially instructive, and from an American point of view, especially painful. Eastman Kodak has long been one of America's premier companies, dominant in its markets, highly profitable, a world technological leader. It is precisely companies like Eastman Kodak that must meet competitive threats successfully if the U.S. economy is to continue to prosper.

In the playing out of the competitive game in photographic film and equipment, the end game turns out to be similar to that in a number of industries. Eastman Kodak now has one significant competitor in the world, the Japanese Fuji Photo Film. Fuji is now as profitable as Eastman Kodak, much faster growing, fully competitive in conventional photographic film and equipment technology, and leading Eastman Kodak in the electronically driven technologies that seem likely soon to make conventional imaging products obsolete.

The urgent prospect that one of America's leading companies might be outpaced by a once-insignificant Japanese company is the result of Eastman Kodak's delay in responding to Fuji's competitive challenge. Although Eastman Kodak has been in business in Japan for more than sixty-five years, it does not yet have manufacturing or research and development facilities in Japan. Nor does it have control over its sales in Japan. It continues to sell through an agent, maintaining a liaison office with no direct sales force or sales management, and only indirect influence on pricing and promotion.

The key to any successful business strategy is influencing the behavior and plans of one's competitor. A few years ago, by aggressive investment and marketing, Kodak might well have been able to stop Fuji while Fuji was still relatively weak. Kodak can no longer stop Fuji, but it might be able to deflect Fuji's energies, exercise some control over Fuji's cash flow, and bring its still considerable strengths to bear against this key competitor.

In one sense, what has happened to Kodak does not matter; companies come and go. In another sense, the Kodak case matters very much indeed for it is a microcosm of the failures of U.S. and European companies to deal with the competitive threat that Japan's kaisha pose. If the Western best do not respond, what then of Western economies as a whole?

Happily, some of the Western best have responded, aggressively and effectively. Their managements have appreciated the importance of the competition from Japan, and the opportunity in Japan. They have fully realized the need to fight the competitive battle on Japanese territory, taking the battle to the competitor. These companies have accepted the need to play by Japanese rules: short-term returns are likely to be lower, dividend payouts need to be deferred, Japanese performance perimeters need to be accepted, and a long-term view of the competitive process is required.

There are recent indications that the required appreciation of the strategic importance of competing in Japan is becoming more widespread. In this, too, Kodak is an an example because in late 1984 it moved senior management into residence in Japan and in 1985 began a program of more aggressive marketing there, of capital investment through purchase of equity in a Japanese company, and of sourcing product from Japanese makers for sale in Japan, as well as in Western markets. This reversal of policy indicates what can and must be done if competitive balance is to be restored in dealing with the kaisha.

In the authors' consulting experience, in order to focus corporate attention and resources on the competitive issues and market opportunities that Japan poses, it is often necessary to effect a major organizational change. Japan operations for most companies are a part of a regional organization, or are fragmented among several product organizations. As a result, it is difficult to bring to bear the full interest and concerns of the organization in dealing with Japanese issues. However, business in Japan is more than a subset of off-shore, Asian business.

It has proved useful for several major companies to isolate corporate attention on Japan by making Japan operations organizationally separate, which report directly to the chief executive officer. This need not, and organizationally should not, be a permanent reporting pattern. When put in effect for a period of, say, two years, however, it raises the importance of the company's Japan efforts to their appropriate level, forces corporate attention to the issues and opportunities of its Japan position, and helps ensure that sufficient resources of people and capital are available to put an effective strategy for Japan in place. After this is accomplished, the Japan operations can revert to a second-level reporting relationship.

Competing in Japan is not easy. It is hard, but necessary. A Japan strategy is required, and is difficult to put in place in most conventional corporate structures. Still, the obstacles to success are not inherent in the situation in Japan, but are largely in the minds and behaviors of U.S. and European companies. Patience, determination, and skill in investing in Japan do provide a high final payout, in profits and in world strategic position.

10

MULTINATIONAL *KAISHA*

AND CO-PROSPERITY

_____

WITH the focus of attention on Japan's kaisha as competitors in export markets, their increasing importance and influence as investors abroad is often overlooked. Over the next two decades, it is likely that the most significant impact of the kaisha on the world, and the most severe challenge to their own management and organization, will be their effort to become global companies with major, Japanese-owned operations throughout the world. From exporters with supporting overseas investments, they are becoming multinational companies.

Given the dynamism of the economies of East and Southeast Asia, and the mutually supportive interaction of these economies with that of Japan, a true co-prosperity sphere bids fair to develop. As a source of capital, technology, and market, as well as the provider of the pattern for development planning, Japan's economy is both model and engine for other rapidly growing economies of Asia. And in turn, Japan's economy moves to higher levels of output and technology through the Asian interaction. Should relations with the developed economies of the West not progress well over the coming decades, Japan may well have an Asian option to its current U.S.-focused policies.

242

The Move to Direct Investment Abroad

While the Asian option is not officially discussed in Japan, the shift of the economy from pure export of goods toward direct investment is clear. In the Japanese government's Economic Planning Agency's discussion of Japan's economy in the year 2000, internationalization was seen as a major theme of the coming decades. In terms of direct investment:

> In a long-term view of the future of the economy, it is inevitable that Japan will take the route from being a major trading power to being a major power in direct investment. There are a number of forces at work, including the relatively rapid increase in international standing of Japanese companies in terms of financial, technological and management strength, and the difficulty of acceptance of trade from a single point for those major export items in which Japan has established a leading position. The increase in real incomes from Japan's relatively high rate of economic growth (a rise in wage and service prices), the possibility of a sustained increase in the yen exchange rate, and the relative increase in production costs in Japan, will be the forces making for overseas direct investment henceforth.[1]

The strong factors working to cause Japanese companies to invest abroad are increasing in strength. The exchange rate alone is one. A rising yen exchange rate makes export goods from Japan more expensive in other currencies. At the same time, a higher yen value makes the purchase of foreign assets relatively less expensive. No doubt the traditional propensity of Japanese firms to invest at home and export abroad was in part the result of an undervalued currency. But now, as the exchange rate pattern changes, the behavior of firms can be expected to change.

The Economic Planning Agency noted that increasing wage rates in Japan will also work to encourage investment abroad. Average Japanese wage rates are now at or near the level of

1. Keizai Kikakucho Hen (Economic Planning Agency), *2000 Nen no Nihon—Sekai Keizai, Takyoku Antei e no Dohyo* (Japan in the Year 2000—Guideposts to the World Economy, Multipolar Stability) (Tokyo: Okurasho 1982), p. 69.

wages in other developed countries, including those in many areas of the United States, but these can be balanced by increased productivity—through automation, for example. The wage rate factor is a mixed one, given differences in quality and discipline of work forces. High levels of factor costs other than wages are likely to increase foreign investment by Japanese firms.

Here the shifts in the industrial structure of Japan need to be kept in mind. It was clear by the late 1960s that raw material processing industries would come under pressure to reduce production in Japan. The choice was either to source semi-finished or finished product from off-shore, or move off-shore to control the sourcing by investing in facilities in foreign countries. This shift in structure away from on-shore processing was likely for a variety of reasons: pressures from material-supplying countries to add value to the materials in the source country before their export; costs in Japan from very stringent pollution control requirements; and energy and land cost disadvantages in Japan. The probability of this industrial structure change became an inevitability as energy prices exploded in the 1970s.

The Strategic Dilemma

The need to move raw material processing industries off-shore raises difficult strategic issues for Japanese companies. With no domestic sources of raw materials for most products, they are highly vulnerable to interruption in supply. This vulnerability increases as more of the value added is transferred abroad. Furthermore, Japan is at the end of a long supply line, and has had the experience in the past of arbitrary curtailment of supply from abroad—most recently, U.S. soybeans and Mideast crude oil.

In the aluminum industry, high electricity costs are ravaging Japan's once large bauxite smelting industry. Off-shore supply of ingot is the only economic solution. The industry's response has been striking. Japanese companies now have substantial interests in smelting operations in Canada, the United States, Venezuela, Brazil, Australia, and Indonesia. In the United States, Alumax, owned jointly by Mitsui and Nippon Steel with AMAX, is now the fourth largest U.S. aluminum producer, and with the acquisition of Howmet from Pechiney is well up in the Fortune 500 list of largest U.S. manufacturers. Nippon Asahan Aluminum in Indonesia, with Sumitomo Chemical as the organizer, has the Indonesian government as 25 percent equity participant and is one of the largest overseas investments ever undertaken by Japanese interests.

The strategic dilemma of increasing dependence on potentially unreliable foreign suppliers is being met in the aluminum industry, and no doubt will be managed in other industries by diversifying sources. Any single source might pose a problem at a given time, but many sources are not likely to present problems simultaneously.

The Need and Ability to Invest Abroad

Fortunately, the pressures of cost and supply that drive foreign investment are occurring as Japan's companies have the capital resources to become a major foreign investor. Japan's economy is now a major exporter of capital to the world, with net capital outflows of $50 billion annually at current rates of flow. The extent of change in this regard can be appreciated by noting that in the early 1960s Japan borrowed heavily from the World Bank to build its famous "Bullet Train." Only twenty years later, Japan is the second largest shareholder in and provider of funds to that same World Bank.

More important, because investment is by companies rather than by governments, Japan's once heavily leveraged companies have greatly strengthened their financial positions in recent years. Japan's leading companies are now, as the Economic Planning Agency report noted, very strong financially.[2] For some, their principal strategic decision concerns the question of

2. Keizai Kikakucho Hen, *2000 Nen no Nihon*, p. 9.

how best to invest rapidly accumulating financial assets. Foreign investment is clearly an important option.

For the kaisha, foreign investment is feasible in terms of funding, and is influenced by changing cost positions. But it is also influenced by more immediate market concerns. For a great many kaisha, Japan's general trading companies have provided an efficient and relatively low cost channel into foreign markets. It is not surprising to find that in the Japanese magazine *Toyo Keizai*'s ranking of the largest foreign investors, six of the top ten companies are general trading companies with Marubeni, Mitsubishi Shoji, and Mitsui Bussan ranking first, second, and fourth respectively.[3] It was the general trading companies that first built the logistical and sales channels for exports, and which organized and took equity positions in early overseas investments.

However, as a foreign market expands, the Japanese exporter needs to provide the kind of sales engineering and service for the sale of sophisticated products that the general trading company is not staffed for. The exporter needs to gain control of pricing and marketing to build a permanent place in the market. The trading company, as distributor, has less interest in that kind of marketing investment. Finally the exporter needs to gain control of the value added in marketing and of the marketing margins to finance these investments. Thus, Japanese manufacturers move past the trading company and begin to make direct marketing investments themselves.

This tends to leave the general trading company dealing in low-margin commodities. It is this process that has put the general trading companies under severe growth and profit pressure in recent years. But from the point of view of the exporter, the process is an inevitable one. As the change to direct control of marketing takes place, the stage is set for direct investment in overseas manufacturing as the market expands, or as protectionist sentiments rise in foreign markets' reactions to Japan's export success. Thus, in addition to cost pressures and financial capability, the dynamic of competitive success abroad leads in turn to direct overseas investment, first in marketing and subse-

3. *Kaigai Shinshutsu Kigyo Soran* (Directory of Companies' Overseas Advances) (Tokyo: Toyo Keizai Shinpo Sha, 1984), p. 12

TABLE 10–1

Foreign Direct Investment

	Cumulative Total Investment (Billions of $)		Annual Increase 1977–82 (%)	Change in Total 1981–82 (Billions of $)
	1977	1982		
United States	149.8	221.3	8	−5.0
United Kingdom	45.0	79.6	12	−1.5
West Germany	26.8	39.5	8	2.3
Japan	11.9	29.0	20	4.5
France	22.9	24.8	2	−0.7

SOURCE: Adapted from *1981 Kaigai Shijo Hakusho* (1981 Overseas Markets White Paper) (Tokyo: Nihon Boeki Shinkokai, 1981), p.4 and *1984 Kaigai Shijo Hakusho* (Tokyo: Nihon Boeki Shinkokai, 1984), p. 3

quently in fully integrated off-shore development, manufacturing, and marketing facilities.

Japan as a Capital Source to the World

In terms of direct investment, Japan's position is changing rapidly. The role of U.S. companies as direct investors abroad is declining, with West German and Japanese companies taking up much of the slack (see table 10–1). The rate of increase of Japanese investment has been especially rapid as Japan moves toward becoming second to the United States in foreign direct investment. One Japanese estimate suggested that from 1980 to 1990 Japanese direct overseas investment would increase from some $36 billion to nearly $160 billion, or more than four times in ten years. Over half of the total is expected to be about equally divided between North America and Asia as host areas.[4]

Should this emphasis on the United States and Asia materialize as this huge investment flow takes place, it will largely represent a continuation of past trends. From 1950 to 1983,

4. *NRI Yosoku Shiryo* (NRI Projection Material) (Tokyo: Nomura Sogo Kenkyusho, 1983), p. 42.

Asia and the United States have been the major sites for Japanese investment (see table 10–2). Interestingly, more direct investment has been made in Central and South America by Japanese firms than in Western Europe. These four areas account for over 80 percent of total direct investment. In terms of amounts of investment by country, Japan's direct investments are quite concentrated: United States, 26 percent; Indonesia, 14 percent; Brazil, 7 percent; Australia, 5 percent; and the United Kingdom, 4 percent; make up 56 percent of the total. Obviously, the nature of investment objectives in such very different economies must differ greatly.

Another dimension of difference is clear when numbers, rather than amounts of investment are examined. In terms of number of separate investments, the United States again leads with 34 percent of total cases of investment. The United States is followed in terms of numbers of investments by Hong Kong, 7 percent; Singapore, 5 percent; Taiwan, 4 percent; and Brazil, 4 percent. The concentration is again considerable with these five countries accounting for 54 percent of the total cases of investment, but the pattern is different with the East Asian economies, which have a great many investments, though

TABLE 10–2

Japan's Direct Foreign Investment: 1950–1983

	Foreign Investment (Millions of $)	Total Investment (%)	Number of Investments	Total Number of Investments (%)
Asia	14,552	27.4	9,344	32.2
United States	13,970	26.3	9,995	34.4
Central and South America	8,852	16.7	3,427	11.8
Western Europe	6,146	11.6	3,023	10.4
Oceania	3,370	6.3	1,478	5.1
Africa	2,507	4.7	923	3.2
Mideast	2,479	4.7	274	0.9
Canada	1,225	2.3	599	2.0
Total	53,131	100.0	29,063	100.0

SOURCE: Ministry of Finance, *Zaisei Kinyu Tokei Geppo, Taigai Minkan Toshi Tokushu,* (Financial Statistics Monthly, Special Issue on Private Foreign Investment) (Tokyo: Okurasho, 1983), pp. 31–33.

smaller in amount, and thus have a different investment objective.[5]

Foreign Investment Objectives of the Kaisha

Differences in objectives and patterns of investments can best be seen by examining the flow of Japanese funds into the major host areas by type of business activity. In table 10–3, four categories of business are listed, along with the flow of funds into each of the six major and analytically useful host areas. The largest amount of Japanese manufacturing direct foreign investments has gone to East and Southeast Asia, followed by the United States, Brazil, and Mexico taken together. Direct investments in mining have been overwhelmingly in Southeast Asia (mainly Indonesia) and Australia. The category of commerce includes all of those activities related to trading. More than three-quarters of purely commercial investments have been in Europe and the United States, and nearly the same proportion of investments have been in such areas as banking, insurance, and other financial activities.

The overall pattern then is as follows: the United States is the leading host to Japanese direct foreign investment, both in total amount of investment and in number of cases. The major thrust of Japanese investment has been into U.S. commerce and finance, in support of export marketing, with less emphasis on manufacturing investment. There has been little manufacturing investment flow from Japan into Western Europe; what there has been went mainly into the United Kingdom. Europe has been the focus for a good deal of Japanese investment in commerce and finance, but these investments, like

5. These and the other data in this discussion of direct foreign investments are drawn from publications of the Ministry of Finance, primarily from *Zaisei Kinyu Tokei Geppo, Taigai Minkan Toshi Tokushu,* (Tokyo: Okurasho, 1983), except where otherwise noted. These data are based on approvals by the Ministry of investment applications. Some investment amounts may have differed from the applied amount. In any event, retained earnings or local funding are not reflected in these data. These are, however, the only detailed data available, and are reliable in terms of general levels and general trends.

TABLE 10–3

Patterns of Japanese Foreign Investments: 1980–1983

	Total Japanese Investments (%)	Manufacturing (%)	Mining (%)	Commerce (%)	Finance (%)
United States	21	23	4	60	38
Western Europe	12	7	8	17	34
Asia*	9	15	——	6	7
Southeast Asia†	18	19	51	1	3
Brazil and Mexico	9	16	7	4	9
Australia	5	4	12	4	2
Other	21	16	18	8	7
Total	100	100	100	100	100

*South Korea, Taiwan, Hong Kong, and Singapore.
†Indonesia, Malaysia, the Philippines, and Thailand.
SOURCE: Ministry of Finance, Zaisei Kinyu Tokei Geppo, pp. 59–63.

similar ones in the United States, have been in support of export marketing.

The newly industrializing countries (NICs) of Asia have been the major site for Japanese foreign manufacturing investments in terms of numbers of cases, though the total capital amounts have been small. For the most part, these investments went into such labor-intensive sectors as textiles and light assembly. Brazil and Mexico have also been important sites for investments, with manufacturing being the focus of Japanese investments in those two countries.

Even with this general review, it is clear that an examination of the kaisha as they move investments out of Japan must be done in terms of the objectives of the move. Two geographic areas are of critical importance—the United States, and East and Southeast Asia. Furthermore, it appears that Japanese investments in the United States have been mainly technology- and market-driven, while their investments into East and Southeast Asia have been driven by wage costs and by the need to secure sources of raw materials.

The weighting of Japanese investments in the United States toward finance and commerce is likely to continue for some time. The acquisition by the Fuji Bank of part of the Walter

Heller organization and by the Mitsubishi Bank of the Bank of California are examples of continuing investment interest in the financial sector. The United States is not an attractive site for most of the raw material-related industries when compared with less-developed and lower-cost locations such as Indonesia, Australia, and Brazil. However, low electrical costs explain the Alumax aluminum-manufacturing operation, and favorable wood fiber costs account for ventures like the Jujo Paper-Weyerhaeuser newsprint venture. United States food supply availability and low cost has attracted investment as well, a Kikkoman soy sauce venture in Wisconsin being one example. However, relative to other sources for raw materials, the U.S. role will be minor.

It is the manufacturing sector that is the increasing focus of Japanese investment in the United States, now that market positions have been established and distribution and finance infrastructures put in place. In their annual survey of Japanese manufacturing investment in the United States, the Japan Economic Institute reported:

> At the end of 1983, Japanese corporate investors held controlling interests in 309 U.S. manufacturing companies, including nine firms scheduled to go onstream later this year. While small and medium-sized operations dot the list, some Japanese production subsidiaries qualify as big businesses. . . . An integrated aluminum manufacturer, Alumax, has 91 plants and fabricating warehouses in 29 states and more than 13,000 people on its payroll. Other big ventures include the two Japanese-owned automotive assembly plants in the United States: Honda of America Manufacturing, Inc., . . . with a work force approaching 2,000 employees, and Nissan Motor Manufacturing Corporation U.S.A., which has hired close to 2,000 workers at its Tennessee compact truck plant. . . . Sony Corp. of America employs 1,600 workers at its San Diego, California color television plant, while 1,500 people turn out cassette tapes at Sony Magnetic Products Inc.'s Alabama factory. Sanyo Manufacturing Corp., which has 2,000 employees on the payroll of its Arkansas plant, produces color televisions and microwave ovens. The same two product lines are manufactured as well by the 1,350 production workers at Matsushita Industrial Co.'s facility in the Chicago, Illinois sub-

urbs. Rounding out the list of big investments is Kyocera International, Inc., which employs 1,700 people at three plants in San Diego that make ceramic packages for integrated circuits and electronic components. The 309 U.S. manufacturing companies in which Japanese investors owned a majority stake at year-end 1983 had 479 plants in operation or under construction at that time.[6]

While these facts somewhat understate the situation, as much Japanese investment still takes the route of minority or joint interest rather than controlled operations, they reflect some broad trends. It is reasonable to conclude that the main spur to Japanese investment in manufacturing in the United States is rising U.S. protectionism. There are business advantages to direct investment—better customer contact, tighter control over distribution, reduced transport and tariff costs, and reduced exchange rate exposure. But, manufacture in the United States poses some real dilemmas for the successful Japanese producer. With scale facilities in Japan, scale advantage is dissipated with dispersed manufacture. With established reliable and cost-effective parts supplier relations in Japan, problems in delivery and quality result when dependent on U.S. suppliers. With commitments to a highly reliable labor force in Japan, there exist real concerns about the quality and cost of U.S. factory labor, especially in those U.S. industries where labor has achieved monopoly wage rate levels. In terms of product cost and product quality, manufacture in the U.S. poses real risks. Production focused within Japan is probably the desirable option, given free choice, for most Japanese producers.

Protectionism has tipped the scales. When the United States imposed import quotas on consumer electronics, all of the major Japanese producers moved to set up U.S. assembly operations. (Sony had long pursued a separate strategy as a result of its relatively weak market position in Japan, and was already established abroad.) The Japanese auto industry followed a similar pattern, responding to U.S. import controls by establishing U.S. operations. A major motive in recent electron-

6. Susan MacKnight, "Japan's Expanding U.S. Manufacturing Presence: 1983 Update," *Japan Economic Institute Report,* no. 15A (13 April 1984):3.

ics investments is to forestall protectionism as the U.S. industry pushes for import restrictions. These responses to protectionism have a multiplying effect since the move of the assemblers into the United States tends to pull the parts suppliers in as direct investors in their wake. The Japan Economic Institute reports that "at least 17 Japanese-affiliated component manufacturers are in operation or have plants under construction [in the automotive field]."[7]

Much of this Japanese investment has been reluctant. It is not at all clear, for example, that Toyota, with highly concentrated and very efficient production at its Nagoya facilities, welcomes or benefits from U.S. manufacture. The U.S. and Japanese governments' cartel concerning U.S. market share imposed in 1980, of which Toyota was a principal beneficiary, provided extraordinary profits to Toyota as the low-cost producer with a guaranteed leading import share. It is continuing protectionist pressures that force Toyota to invest in U.S. manufacture, not Toyota's economic need or preference.

On the other hand, U.S. protectionism results in very high prices for its steel and autos. These attract investment into the United States by those Japanese companies who have a limited position in the Japanese market. Honda, a good example, had a position in Japan that was constrained by its late entry into the industry in the mid-1960s, when it had to confront large competitors with strong domestic distribution positions like Toyota and Nissan. High U.S. price levels made it possible for Honda to do an end run around the domestic distribution problem by opening manufacturing facilities in the U.S. market in the early 1980s. This was in large part a repeat of the strategy pursued earlier in consumer electronics by Sony as it sought relief from Matsushita's dominant position in the Japanese market. Similarly, investments in the U.S. steel industry have been made by Nippon Kokan and Kawasaki Steel, rather than by Nippon Steel or Sumitomo Metals, which are respectively the largest and most profitable in their domestic production base.

The U.S. political reaction to these investments in the United States by the Japanese companies who are escaping do-

---

7. Ibid., p. 4.

mestic market pressures is positive. The view is that they are providing jobs to U.S. workers. This is true, but overlooks the fact that these new and modern Japanese-owned facilities will displace less efficient U.S. producers, with subsequent job loss in U.S. corporate employment. Thus, the perverse result of protectionism in auto and steel is to reward the leading Japanese producers that maintain profitable export positions and at the same time protectionism makes it possible for the secondary Japanese producers to prosper through investment in the protected, and thus high-priced, U.S. market. The loser in the process is the original set of U.S. competitors, who are being attacked on two fronts: by exports from off-shore and by investors on-shore.

When Will the Kaisha Buy Foreign Companies?

Japanese investment in U.S. manufacturing has another special feature. This is the Japanese tendency either to establish new and wholly owned facilities, or to take a minority or joint venture position in established operations. There are exceptions to this pattern—Matsushita's acquisition of Motorola's Quasar television division, or Sanyo's acquisition of Warwick. But the Nippon Kokan purchase of 50 percent of National Steel, the GM-Toyota joint venture, and the Nissan establishment of a "green-field" plant in Tennessee are more typical Japanese approaches to entry.

The Japanese entry approach of using joint ventures or green-field operations is in marked contrast to the preferred approach of U.S. and European companies as they venture abroad. American companies in the 1950s and 1960s made direct investments in Western Europe in numbers sufficient to earn the description "the American challenge." American firms sought direct positions in Western Europe for many of the reasons that Japanese firms now invest directly in the United States, including the threat of protectionism raised by the Treaty of Rome and formation of the European Economic Community. In the majority of cases, however, and certainly in most of the successful cases, entry was through acquisition of a competent European company as a base for further expansion. Indeed, Charles de Gaulle accused the Americans of buying Europe, and doing so with European money in the bargain, because of the common American practice of borrowing from European financial institutions to fund the acquisitions.

In the 1970s and 1980s there has been a similar approach to direct investment in the United States by Western European firms seeking positions, especially in the higher technology sectors of the U.S. economy. Acquisition, done with adequate planning and care, is by a good margin the most rapid and effective entry to a developed economy, providing as it does staffing, facilities, product, and distribution channels all at once. Moreover, entry costs through acquisition can be capitalized rather than being funded out of current earnings, thus leaving unaffected the performance measures of the executives concerned.

Unfortunately for the kaisha, the climate regarding acquisition in their home economy predicate that their managements have little or no experience with it. This has made them timid when considering the possibility of acquisition in a Western economy. The lack of understanding and experience with acquisition presents a formidable handicap to rapid and large-scale entry to U.S. manufacturing. It means that the direct investment requires a reduction of current earnings, and further means that the investment can be expected to pose a negative cash flow for those years required to get the new venture fully underway. Finally, all the problems of recruiting and training staff, of establishing distribution, and of building supplier, customer, and community relations must be dealt with on the basis of little or no direct experience.

There are some indications that attitudes and practices regarding acquisition are beginning to change in Japan. Certainly the logic of acquisition as a mode of entry to a highly developed and highly competitive market is powerful. A shift toward acquisition strategies would probably make for a sharp increase in the amount of Japanese direct manufacturing investment into the United States and Western Europe. This may well be a significant development in investment strategies of Japanese firms in the next few years.

Japanese direct investment in the United States is still too limited in scale, and too recent, to attempt conclusions as to its relative success. There is no reason to assume that Japanese management will suffer any special organizational handicaps in managing the process or in managing the ventures, given experience. But there is one area that seems likely to pose problems, and that is the issue of personnel—the recruiting, motivating, and integrating into the company of foreign personnel, especially at the management level.

It is evident from the experience of all companies, whatever their national ownership, that a key to successful foreign operations is staffing with able local managers. Indeed, for foreign companies operating in Japan, the biggest single barrier to success is the difficulty of recruiting highly qualified Japanese. This problem stems from special patterns of employment in Japan, with employees typically recruited directly from school into a very tightly integrated corporate culture, and employed for their entire career.

Just as this employment system creates major difficulties for foreign companies seeking to do business in Japan, so the Japanese company operating abroad encounters the mirror image of the problem. Even assuming that the Japanese company is able to recruit successfully—an easier task abroad, by far, than in Japan—there remains the considerable problem of motivating and retaining highly qualified personnel. For example, when asked when their company might first have a foreigner as senior manager or president—in ten or fifty or one hundred years—a Japanese business audience responds with disbelieving stares. The very thought is bizarre. That is a measure of the distance Japanese companies must traverse in dealing with the problem of executive selection and promotion abroad.

There is a similar problem at the shop floor level. Does the foreign work force of the Japanese company have the same assurance of permanent employment as the domestic Japanese work force? If it does not have such assurance, which seems likely if competitive position abroad is to be gained, then are foreign employees relegated to second-class status in the total Japanese company work force? Will that be acceptable? Conversely, will foreign employees, including management personnel, accept the concept of permanent employment? Are they likely to be as responsive to the concept as Japanese employees?

The questions of personnel management posed for the Japanese company as it moves abroad are difficult ones, and there is little indication that they have worked out answers as yet. Rather, there is puzzled concern over foreign executive mobility, and over the hazards of investing in training men and women who are prone to switching employers. And there is little taste for engaging in negotiations with trade union leaders who, rather than being company employees, represent wide constituencies, are inclined toward confrontation as a negotiating mode, and often place the union's interests ahead of concern for the health of the company.

In short, there can be no question of the trends in Japanese direct foreign investment and multinational movement. Japanese companies will become major direct investors in an increasing range of U.S. industries, and their positions in these industries will then expand considerably. The process will not be an easy one—problems regarding mode of entry, and especially regarding personnel practices, remain to be resolved.

There is still another issue that may dampen the rate at which investment takes place. This is the question of political reactions, both in Japan and in the United States. On the whole, U.S. host communities have encouraged and welcomed Japanese investment. However, when that investment becomes overly concentrated, as it did in Hawaii in the 1970–1973 period, with a large number of Japanese investments in hotels and real estate, rather sharp negative political reactions can occur. It is not clear as to how Americans might react to a large number of acquisitions of U.S. companies by the kaisha. Given the current climate of "Japan-bashing," there might be strong negative reactions, rather like the U.S. reaction to the earlier threat—but not in fact realized—of Arab buy-outs of U.S. land and companies.

The political question is not confined to U.S. reactions. Even at the current level of investment abroad, there have been negative reactions in Japan. Concern has been expressed regarding export of jobs through overseas investment in the face of a rise in unemployment at home, a protest familiar to Americans who have heard similar complaints about U.S. investment abroad. Further, it is already argued in the Japanese press that investment overseas is a drain on total Japanese investment to the disadvantage of the development of the domestic economy. Again, it is too early to assess the potential of these political reactions, but it can not be assumed that Japanese investments abroad will be welcomed either at home or in the host country. In any event, negative reactions to Japanese direct investment abroad within and outside Japan have as yet had no effect on the rapid growth of that investment. The strategic implications of the investment are clear.

Asia as the Focus of Manufacturing Investment

Investment by the kaisha in North America and Europe is driven first by the need to provide financial and distribution support to exports into those large and developed markets, and second by the need to respond to protectionism in both North America and Europe against Japanese imports to those markets. But Japanese investment in overseas manufacturing is a different matter. Leaving aside the responses of the auto, steel, and consumer electronics industries to increasing trade barriers, when the kaisha choose to invest abroad in manufacturing without negative forces at work their choice of location is overwhelmingly Asia. Americans tend to think of the United States as important in terms of off-shore manufacturing by Japanese companies, recalling the investments of Sony, Matsushita, and Sanyo in consumer electronics; Nissan, Honda, and Toyota in autos; and Nippon Kokan and Kawasaki in steel. These are highly visible investments, and represent an increasing trend toward investment overseas in markets that are being increasingly protected.

But the critical fact is that nearly 60 percent of Japan's foreign manufacturing investments are in Asia. On a total of 2,000 manufacturing subsidiaries abroad, MITI reported nearly 60 percent in Asia.[8] According to this survey, these overseas manufacturing subsidiaries of Japanese companies employ a

8. *Waga Kuni no Kaigai Jigyo Katsudo* (Overseas Enterprise Activities of Our Country's Companies) (Tokyo: Toyo Hoki Shuppan K.K., 1984).

total of about 700,000 persons. Of this substantial off-shore manufacturing labor force, 59 percent is in Asia, and 16 percent in Latin America, while only 10 percent are in North America and 5 percent in Europe. Further, less than one percent of this large overseas labor force in Asia are Japanese, while 3 percent of the North American manufacturing labor force are Japanese nationals. No less important is that Asian investment is profitable, while Japanese investment in North America is not, yet. The MITI survey reports total profits from manufacturing in Asia of 51 billion yen against total losses in manufacturing in North America in 1983 of 21 billion yen.

The pattern is clear. Japanese overseas investment is increasing rapidly. In manufacturing, the overwhelming thrust of the investment is into Asia, where Japanese firms are becoming substantial employers, and where the investments are proving to be profitable. These Asian investments are not all small. In *Toyo Keizai*'s listing of the 50 largest Japan-related manufacturing companies abroad in terms of sales, 19 are in Asia, 13 in the United States, 11 in Latin America, 2 each in Western Europe, Canada, and Australia, and 1 in the Middle East.[9]

This high level of Japanese corporate investment in East and Southeast Asia is both a partial cause and partial result of the extraordinary changes taking place throughout the region. Japan has been the critical factor during the entire process of the movement of the region to independence then economic success. It was the defeat of the Russian fleet at the Straits of Tsushima by the Japanese under Admiral Togo that marked the end of the tide of Western military imperialism in Asia and electrified Asians with the realization that Western imperial supremacy might end.

Japan became the training site for many leaders of Asia's independence movements, beginning with its support of the revolutionary Chinese leader Sun Yat-sen. Japan's advances in the Second World War, however intentioned, marked the end of colonial dominance in the region. Finally, Japan's rapid move to industrial leadership demonstrated for the first time in history that a non-Western culture and society could reach and even surpass Western levels of output and income.

9. *Kaigai Shinsutsu Kigyo Soran*, p. 12.

259

Japanese industrial policy explicitly calls for transfering to developing Asia those industries that are no longer appropriate for Japan's level of technology and labor cost. Thus, the former vice-minister of MITI, Y. Ojimi, stating Japan's industrial policy in 1970, said:

> Japan will need to supplement its own resources directly and indirectly through trade and production activities abroad, utilizing foreign labor, land and natural resources. This will demand a shift in Japan's industrial structure toward areas of higher productivity of labor, land and other resources. At the same time even greater emphasis will need to be placed on developing exports with a high technical and value-added content. . . .
>
> Industrialization in developing countries will stimulate competitive relations in the markets of advanced nations in products with a low degree of processing. As a result the confrontation between trade protectionism and free trade will become more intense.
>
> The solution to this problem is to be found, according to economic logic, in progressively giving away industries to other countries, much as a big brother gives his out-grown clothes to his younger brother. In this way a country's own industries become more sophisticated.[10]

An example of the actual working out of this broad policy is that in 1970 Japan had an enormously favorable balance on footwear trade, importing less than 3 billion yen in footwear and exporting nearly 50 billion yen. Footwear is not an appropriate industry for a nation that aspires to very high standards of living—the industry is labor-intensive with low technology, suitable for developing rather than developed countries. During the 1970s, footwear imports into Japan increased 30 percent per year, while exports declined 17 percent annually. The result at the end of the decade was a 31 billion yen trade deficit in footwear, with imports in 1980 totaling over 40 billion yen and exports from Japan less than 8 billion yen. Moreover, in 1970, more than two-thirds of Japan's very limited imports

10. Yoshihisa Ojimi, Vice Minister, MITI, speech delivered to the OECD Industrial Committee, Tokyo, 24 June 1970, p. 24. Translated and published in 1971 by Boston Consulting Group, Tokyo, Japan.

of footwear came from Western Europe and the United States. In 1980, over half of Japan's very large imports of footwear came from Taiwan and South Korea, with the Western suppliers providing only one-third of the country's greatly increased import demand.

The result of this interaction and the move off-shore of footwear supply to Japan, is mutually beneficial. Japan provides the market in support of the development of an industry in Taiwan and Korea that is appropriate for their stage of development. In the process these countries can buy increasingly sophisticated goods from Japan as a result of the improvement in their own economic position. In addition, their exports to Japan put pressure on an industry that it is in Japan's economic interest to divest. Japan's resources of capital and labor are better devoted to high-technology, high value-added sectors if its economy is to continue to grow.

An example of the other side of this interaction can be seen from the fact that over this same period of the 1970s, Asia's "gang of four"—South Korea, Taiwan, Hong Kong, and Singapore—became the major markets for rapidly expanding Japanese exports of integrated circuits. While Japan's integrated circuit exports nearly doubled annually over the decade, these four economies accounted for only one-third of the total in the early 1970s, but took more than two-thirds by the end of the decade. Machine tools provide a similar case of this process. The trade and investment interaction between developing Asia and Japan works to the advantage of both parties as Korea and Taiwan became larger machine tool markets for Japanese products than France and Germany.

These four NICs of East Asia are a special group within the East Asian area: each has a government dedicated to economic development, with economic policy in the hands of exceptionally well-trained specialists. Each has a largely homogenous population, well educated and disciplined, as suggested by the Confucian value system that dominates each culture. In each, birthrates are falling and are now low, with population growth under control. Each has, with the exception of Hong Kong, drawn on Japan's economy as a model in its economic planning and development.

As seen in table 10–4, it is these four economies that have been in the running in the economic race, each with sustained growth rates that more than doubled real output within a decade, and more than quadrupled it in less than twenty years. Not surprisingly, the economic growth, political stability, and supply of high-quality, relatively inexpensive labor has attracted a great deal of Japanese investment. Japan provides the technology and capital, as well as the market, that helps to make the continued rapid growth of these economies possible. Other markets, and other investors, have been very important to these countries and will continue to be so, but it is interaction with Japan that has made them remarkable.

Four other Asian countries that comprise another subset of economies and societies in their characteristics and in their interaction with Japan are Indonesia, Malaysia, the Philippines, and Thailand. Each is quite different in important ways from the Asian NICs. These Southeast Asian countries have heterogeneous populations, with notable differences in language and culture and resultant problems in national integration and identity. Each continues to have a problem of high birth rates that threaten to swamp economic growth. Each, with the exception of the Philippines, has relatively high levels of illiteracy and a shortage of trained leaders available to government and indus-

TABLE 10–4

Asian Real Annual GDP Growth Rates
1960–1983

	1960–1970 (%)	1970–1983 (%)
Korea	8.6	8.7
Taiwan	9.6	8.6
Hong Kong	10.0	9.5
Singapore	8.8	8.5
Malaysia	6.5	7.6
Indonesia	3.9	7.5
Thailand	8.4	7.0
Philippines	5.1	5.6
People's Republic of China	5.2	5.6

SOURCE: Adapted from The World Bank, *World Development Report 1984* (New York: Oxford University Press, 1984), pp. 220–21; Asian Development Bank, *Key Indication of Developing Member Countries of ADB* (Manila: Asian Development Bank, 1984), p.7

try. The focus on economic development as the principal thrust of policy has been less clear for these countries, though a change is occurring as leadership is more available and as social problems are dealt with. Here too, unhappily, the Philippines is an exception as its leadership remains unchanged and social and political problems worsen.

Another basic difference is in terms of raw materials. The NICs are, like Japan, resource-poor and driven to the manufacture of imported materials as the only escape from poverty. The four Southeast Asian countries are relatively rich in natural resources, and consequently agriculture, forestry, and mining are dominant in their economies rather than manufacture.

Yet, as the numbers in Table 10–4 suggest, these countries too are beginning to break out of the trap of their historical poverty. While the Philippines lags, growth rates in this area are now also at the decade-doubling rate. The once-small economic base of these countries is becoming substantial. More important, gross capital investment, like that of the Asian NICs, is now at high levels. Even Indonesia now invests well over 20 percent of its gross national product annually, a level of GNP investment higher than the United States or the United Kingdom, and at the level of France and West Germany. Yet, Indonesia's gross investment rate is lowest of all these countries. That is to say, all of the countries of East and Southeast Asia now have a savings and investment rate that will go far to ensure that their growth will continue well into the future.

As discussed earlier in this chapter, these countries of Southeast Asia have been host to nearly 20 percent of total Japanese foreign investment, largely in manufacturing. This overall figure disguises a striking phenomenon—the level of Japanese investment in Indonesia. Note Indonesia's large population, now more than 150 million persons and expected to reach 200 million by the turn of the century. Note further Indonesia's massive raw material position, including, but not limited to crude oil and natural gas. Note also that the economic performance of Indonesia is now impressive. In view of all this, note finally that a full 14 percent of all of Japan's direct investment abroad since 1950 has been in Indonesia, more than the Japanese investment in all of Western Europe.

The Japanese focus on Indonesia as an investment site has been taking place at the same time that U.S. companies have been withdrawing from Indonesia, most recently Goodyear and Weyerhaeuser. The large sums invested by Japanese companies in Indonesia are a result in part of the large capital requirements for the development of energy and raw material sources, notably the Asahan hydropower and aluminum project and the liquid natural gas investments in Sumatra, rather than investment in the Indonesian market as such.

A scan of Japanese companies in Indonesia with more than 1,000 employees turns up such familiar names as Toyota in autos, Bridgestone in tires, Asahi Glass, Ajinomoto in processed food, Yoshida Kogyo in fasteners, and Kanebo and Teijin in natural and synthetic textiles. The Japanese position in Indonesia is by no means limited to exploitation of raw material sources. It is a large and growing direct position in the Indonesian economy, an economy that must be seen as potentially one of the world's most important.

The Asian Option

The position of the kaisha in East and Southeast Asia is not only encouraged by the industrial policy of the Japanese government but is reinforced by the government's actions. This is notable when the flows of Japanese aid funds are examined. There is a current fashion to denigrate Japan's efforts in development assistance, so it might first be noted that Japan now provides a somewhat greater amount of net flow of official development assistance than does the United States, relative to gross national product. The 1983 figure for Japan was 0.33 percent of GNP, 0.24 percent for the United States. Neither proportion reflects any great credit for either country, but Japan's aid programs can no longer be described as niggardly, at least by Americans. (The proportion for West Germany was 0.49 percent.)[11]

11. Rutherford M. Poats, *Development Cooperation: 1983 Review* (Paris: Organization for Economic Cooperation and Development, 1983), p. 82.

Both the United States and Japan provide about one-third of their total official development assistance (ODA) through multilateral agencies. It is the distribution of the remaining two-thirds that is of special interest in terms of policies. Japan provides nearly half—47 percent—of its total ODA that does not go through multilateral agencies to East and Southeast Asia. The comparable figure for the United States is only 7 percent, and less than 5 percent for West Germany. Japanese aid is extremely focused. A further quarter of Japan's ODA of this type goes to the countries of South Asia. Thus, nearly 75 percent of Japan's ODA not channeled through multilateral agencies flows to Asian economies. The comparable figure for the United States is just under 20 percent, and about 25 percent for West Germany. Forty percent of the U.S. total is provided to Israel and Egypt.

There is much talk of the "Pacific Rim" and of the "Pacific Basin," reflecting a growing appreciation of the economic dynamism and fast-growing importance of the area. Norman Macrae of *The Economist* captured something of this view in his remark that while the period from 1775 to 1875 might be seen as a British century, and 1875 to 1975 as an American century, the century following 1975 might well become the Pacific century.[12] Certainly the center of world manufacturing is shifting from a point somewhere in the mid-Atlantic to a point nearer the Western coast of the Pacific. The U.S. now trades more across the Pacific than across the Atlantic, still another measure of the changes taking place.

Much has been made of the attitudes of other Asian peoples toward Japan and the Japanese as an obstacle to the development pattern that is underway. There undoubtedly have been and are anti-Japanese attitudes and feelings, though no doubt these have been exaggerated in the Western telling of them. In any event, Japan's value to these countries as a source of capital and technology, and as a market, goes far to overcoming antipathies. Even the mutual antipathy of the Koreans and Japanese is yielding to economic realities.

The ending of an era of suspicion and antagonism has been

---

12. Norman Macrae, "Pacific Century, 1975–2075?" *The Economist,* 4 January 1975, p. 15.

marked by Malaysia's "Look East" policy. More than many, Malaysians had reason to remember the behavior of the Japanese during the Second World War. In a 1982 speech setting forth Malaysia's industrial policy, the Deputy Prime Minister Datoh Musa Hitam stated:

> Even before Merdeka, achieved 25 years ago, and until very recently, Malaysia has been modelling herself on the pattern of the West, principally of Britain. . . . As we grow and mature as a nation, and as we develop an awareness of our place under the sun, the Western model begins to come under critical review and to lose its dominance in our thinking.
>
> Over the years we have had the opportunity to compare the performances of different nations and their relevance to Malaysia. If we are going to learn and benefit as in fact we are doing now, we should learn from people who are the best in the field. That is the philosophy behind the "Look East" policy now in force. In particular, we try to find out what contributed to the remarkable Japanese recovery after devastating defeat in the Second World War. They may have lost the war, but they have won for themselves a place in the world of today.
>
> Presently Malaysian work ethics are somewhat without basis of direction, and if at all, are closer to those of the West. The Japanese work ethic constitutes one of the most important factors in contributing to Japan's breathtaking recovery and progress. If we can adopt or adapt those same ethics, we in Malaysia may be able to improve our performance economically as well as in other fields.[13]

The mutual involvement of the economies of East and Southeast Asia with Japan's can be seen in terms of overall trade figures as well as in terms of investment. The area may be as large an export market for Japan as is the United States. Of greater significance, over the 1970s the U.S. position as supplier to Japan has declined steadily from more than 25 percent of Japan's imports to under 20 percent. The pattern for East and Southeast Asia is the reverse, as a quarter of Japan's imports are now from that area. Imports are critical to Japan, and it is in that

13. Deputy Prime Minister Y.A.B. Datoh Musa Hitam, "Japanese Management and Malaysian Industrialization." Speech delivered to UMW Seminar, 28 October 1982, Syah Alam, Malaysia.

sector especially that East and Southeast Asia are displacing the United States.

A review of the emerging patterns of economic and business interaction between Japan and Asia must take account of the role or potential of mainland China. Japan continues to be China's major trading partner, despite the swings over the years in the policies of the People's Republic. Like other countries, there is interest in Japan in ventures in China, coupled with hesitation over Chinese laws and regulations, the adequacy of Chinese labor and infrastructure, and, more basically, concern over continued Chinese political stability and economic rationality.

Japanese businesses are slowly moving toward joint venture and other arrangements in the PRC. Ventures have been established by Hitachi in color television and elevators, Sanyo in television assembly, Honda and Yamaha in small motorcycles, Isuzu, Daihatsu, and Nissan Diesel in trucks and vans, and Fanuc in factory automation equipment. The list is lengthening, albeit slowly, with most ventures still cautiously modest in scale. A good deal of technology sale to China has occurred, but this too with caution, in part for fear of a boomerang effect in the future.

Similarly, Japanese government economic relations with China remain cautious. Grants and loans began in 1980, and in the four years through 1983 totaled only 17 billion yen. Loans increased more rapidly, partly owing to PRC policies accepting of foreign loans, and totaled 300 billion yen by the end of 1983, with Export-Import Bank loans also reaching that approximate level.

But the great moves in Asia's development have already taken place and are likely to progress whether or not the People's Republic of China succeeds in achieving its economic goals. However, the extent to which the PRC is successful in maintaining political stability, a rational economic policy, and sustained economic growth, will be reflected in the progress of the area as a whole. Yet the prospects of this extra stimulus to the area from Chinese success remain problematic.

The term "co-prosperity sphere" resurrects memories of Japanese military aggression and drive for dominance in the Pacific. Yet paradoxically, Japan's defeat in World War II and its economic success since have turned an ugly propaganda phrase into a real and positive process. Over the past two decades, Japan and the developing countries of East and Southeast Asia have emerged as the most rapidly growing and successful of the regions of the world. Japan, in a quite different fashion than the militarists meant, but in a fashion hoped for by more thoughtful Japanese, has become a model and, more important, an engine for the economic progress of these nations.

A close economic relationship between Japan and the countries of East Asia can be of great advantage to the West. A prosperous East Asia protects the strategic flank of the United States and provides markets of great opportunity and potential. But to the extent that Japan is excluded from Western councils, and Japanese goods and the goods of the rest of Asia are denied access to the markets of the West, a closer relationship with East Asia may become an increasingly attractive alternative, thereby diminishing the influence of the West on Japan and on the region.

American views often assume that Japan has no alternative but to continue in its commitments to the Western alliance and to the United States. From the Japanese point of view, the Western commitment is now the favored course of policy. But there is a point at which Japan may find it cannot, or chooses not to accede to U.S. demands and will seek an alternative. East Asia, especially if it comes to include a resurgent mainland China, may provide that alternative.

The countries under discussion, including Japan, comprise a total population of some 450 million. Many are only a generation past colonial status. Yet they have on the whole maintained a remarkable stability given their new position as independent nations. Their development, together with the historically unprecedented economic success of Japan, is setting in motion a massive shift in the economic configuration of the world. Japan's kaisha will be a principal instrument of and beneficiary from that change.

11

THE FUTURE OF

THE *KAISHA*

THE success of the Japanese economy, and the continuing strength of the kaisha in world trade competition, has led to numerous analytical efforts to identify the causes of this economic achievement. Increasingly, attention has focused on Japanese management methods as a major factor in the continuing, effective performance of the economy and its companies. The role of Japanese management methods has been important, but their contribution to the success of the economy needs to be kept in proper proportion.

At their best, the kaisha are indeed well managed, and deserve study. The Japanese system of management is an important part of the total pattern of Japan's economic success. The best of the kaisha are creative, flexible, and powerful competitors. However, it is also true that at their worst, many of the kaisha are slow to react, with underutilized assets, poorly rewarded employees and shareholders, aging facilities, and undistinguished management. It is the best of the kaisha that comprise the competitive threat to Western companies. But the range of competence amongst Japan's companies should not be overlooked.

It is important too to keep some perspective on the role of

management methods and competence in the performance of the economy. The kaisha are products of Japan's economy, and their effectiveness is largely controlled by the effectiveness of the economy as a whole. The causes of Japan's postwar economic success are many. They include:

- The long national development effort that provided an effective infrastructure, notably in terms of education
- A domestic market that is generally free and competitive, with a pricing mechanism that functions well to allocate resources
- A high savings rate, and a well-developed financial system, providing ample and low-cost funds for industrial investment
- A stable government that is relatively competent and relatively small, and is supportive of the private sector
- A superb labor force, in terms of numbers, education and discipline, that is moderately priced
- Rapid increases in domestic demand that provide the basis for the kaisha to establish world competitive scale and cost positions
- Access to world technology at reasonable price
- A world environment for most of the postwar period of expanding trade with adequate and generally low-cost supplies of raw materials and energy
- Alliance with the United States, thus obtaining reasonable strategic security and access to the U.S. market

Different analysts will assign various weights to these factors to help explain the economic success of Japan, and would probably add factors to this list. A full explanation of and agreement on causes is not yet in sight.

For this book's analysis of the kaisha, however, the point is clear. One can go very far in explaining the success of the economy without recourse to management methods as a major cause. No doubt effective management of private companies is an important factor in Japan's economic success, and belongs on the list. But it is only one factor, and the success of Japan's companies can be explained by the economy's success more readily than attempting to explain the success of the economy in terms of management competence. Japan's companies are the beneficiaries of a convergence of a number of highly favorable environmental factors that go far to explain their corporate behaviors, and their successes.

The Future of the Kaisha

All of this is not meant to denigrate the effectiveness of Japanese management methods. It is meant rather to try to put the issue in some perspective. Many factors have caused Japan's great economic success. The cause is not simply Japanese management, which often is undistinguished or even incompetent. Furthermore, however effective Japanese management methods may be, economic forces can be overriding and result in company failure. In addition, because Western companies compete only with Japan's winners, and know little or nothing of Japan's losers, it is all too easy to exaggerate Japanese managerial competence. Finally, even in Japan, Japanese companies are not always the winners in the competitive game.

Nonetheless, in all too many critical industries, Japanese companies are gaining market share at the expense of Western competitors. The greatest of the manufacturing companies of Europe and the United States are under pressure—General Motors, Eastman Kodak, Caterpillar, Philips, and Siemens are all facing competitive threats. It takes no great stretch of imagination to see this list extending to banking, insurance, and other services in the near future. The kaisha are setting the standard of competition: in cost position, in product quality, in technology, in manufacturing methods and costs, and in investment rates. Their methods of management deserve the closest attention.

What Is "Japanese" about the Kaisha?

This book was written in an effort to identify and explain the sources of competitive strength of the kaisha. The question inevitably arises as to what can be learned that might be applied usefully to the management of non-Japanese companies. What can be transferred from the Japanese experience to the West, to the competitive advantage of Western companies?

The answer depends very much on the analytic approach used in studying the Japanese firm—whether they are studied primarily as social organizations or as economic organizations. Many analyses begin from the perspective of Japan's differences from other nations. The emphasis of these studies is on the unique history, culture, and organization of Japanese society. The management methods of the kaisha are seen as the unique products of a unique society. It follows from this view that efforts to transplant Japanese management methods into a different cultural milieu are bound to fail.

This is a view not to be dismissed lightly. Japanese history and culture are unique, as indeed are the histories and cultures of all of the world's peoples. These leave special imprints on the nature of economic organizations, as they do on all other social organizations. It seems likely that the patterns of adversarial interaction that are imbedded in the common law of Great Britain and the United States helped give rise to the adversarial interactions between government and business, and between unions and management, that are characteristic of these two societies. The contrast with the tradition of mediation and compromise of much of East Asia is obvious.

There is little question of the existence of disparities between Japan and the West regarding group values contrasted with individualism. These no doubt help bring about different patterns of careers and different degrees of willingness to identify with the company as an organization. Patterns of reward and recognition are likely to differ also as a result of these broad differences in values, with the Western focus on individual performance and output.

One conclusion then is that when the kaisha are looked at as social organizations there is likely to be an emphasis on their uniqueness and on the difficulties of transferring methods from Japanese social organizations to social organizations in other cultures with different histories. But the analysis need not and should not stop at this point. The fact is that Japan's kaisha are economic organizations as well as social organizations, and nothing in Japan's dash for affluence has allowed its economy to repeal the basic laws of economics, or change the basis and nature of economic competition.

When the kaisha are analyzed as economic organizations, the questions of lessons to be learned and transferability of methods receive quite different answers. There is a great deal to be learned, and much that can be transferred. The kaisha as competitors are not products of "the mysterious East," but are economic organizations responding rationally to opportunities and problems. In the process, the best of the kaisha have developed approaches to dealing with competitive problems that can be used to advantage in any competitive system.

The approach Japanese manufacturing firms are taking to increasing productivity and reducing costs in the manufacture of a wide range of products is a good example of developments that Western firms are able to, and urgently need to, adopt. It took Toyota some twenty years to develop its manufacturing system. It is possible that the system could only have been developed in the context of Japanese labor-management relations, building on a competent and dedicated labor force. Yet, the system is not Japan-specific—it is the result of applying rigorous economics and engineering to the factory system to optimize the volume, quality, and variety of output.

At present, the Japanese approach to manufacturing is yielding cost advantages in the range of 30 percent over Western competitors. The advantage is unbearable, competitively, and will destroy important Western firms if they fail to respond. The response of Western firms should not be constrained by culture. There is nothing in their system of manufacturing that is peculiar to Japan, or to Japanese companies. It can be adopted abroad, as the example of Omark Industries well illustrates. A medium-sized Portland, Oregon, company, and the world's leading producer of saw chain, Omark perceived the competitive advantages of Japanese manufacturing methods and pioneered their introduction into U.S. factories. The system can be considered a Japanese invention, but like most inventions, can be adopted elsewhere if adequate study and efforts are made. A failure to adopt the Japanese flexible manufacturing system is likely to ensure competitive failure of Western companies in many industries.

Just as there are important lessons to be learned in the area of manufacturing methods, so too many Western firms can study Japanese financial methods for a competitive advantage. It is not news to Western firms that dividend policy powerfully affects the firm's ability to fund growth at relatively low costs of capital. A number of fast-growing U.S. companies pay little or no dividends. Japanese levels of dividend payments are possible in the

West without unduly damaging share price levels. The mystery is why so few Western companies take advantage of that fact, when so many Japanese companies do.

Complaints by Western firms that their boards of directors and shareholders will not tolerate higher levels of earnings retention, and that thereby the Western firm is at a disadvantage against its Japanese competitor are simply not credible. If a change is needed, present shareholders should be warned so that widows and orphans in search of dividend income can be given the opportunity to change their portfolios. The market as a whole, however, is quite likely to prefer growth and capital gains to dividends, and is likely to welcome a coherent and determined growth strategy based on earnings reinvestment. Western complaints of Japanese advantage are misplaced; the Japanese lesson needs the attention.

It is similar with debt levels. The cost and growth advantages of debt are familiar, and indeed it is because they are well known that Japanese firms are attacked for unfairly using high levels of leverage in asset acquisition. Yet, the same Western companies that complain are using levels of debt well below those commonly available to Western companies. If even these levels are below those available to the Japanese competitor, perhaps the Western competitor needs to reexamine its banking relations, and move to a greater degree of bank dependence and involvement in its affairs so as to achieve higher levels of borrowings. Japanese financial practices provide a powerful competitive advantage, but it is an advantage available to Western firms as well.

There is plenty for Western firms to learn from the kaisha in the area of employment practices as well as in finance and in manufacturing. It is probably the case that the specifics of Japanese compensation and career patterns will not lend themselves readily to adoption in the West. But study of the kaisha brings into sharp focus areas of practice, and patterns of practice, that Western companies might emulate. The first is variable compensation. Compensation contingent on organization performance is widely practiced in the service sector in the United States, in law and consulting offices especially. A first, faltering step has even been taken in Detroit in recent contract settle-

ments. The example of the kaisha illustrates how much further
this practice can be taken to the advantage of the Western
company.

Truly contingent compensation, shared proportionately
equally throughout the organization, is a necessary step for
moving the Western company toward a system that might begin
to match the kaisha in the degree to which the interests of the
employees are linked to the interests and well being of the total
organization. Deliberate efforts to encourage the formation of
enterprise unions and to establish unions sympathetic to the
goals of the enterprise, are other practices of the kaisha that
might be emulated by Western companies.

A precondition to this linking of fortunes of the employee
and the company is establishing a Western equivalent to the
pattern of job security enjoyed by employees of large Japanese
companies. From the perspective of the kaisha, the grudging,
halfhearted, and limping moves of U.S. companies toward providing greater job security are self-destructive. Such a reluctant
approach to providing job security risks incurring the cost of
employment guarantees without reaping the benefits of enhanced morale and company identification.

The companies of the West need to rethink their rationale
for being in operation. The kaisha are dramatic testimony to the
power of an organization that does in fact consider and treat its
workers as its "most important asset." The kaisha's strength
argues that Western firms must give substance to what to them
has become an empty phrase.

In terms of technology, the lesson to be learned from the
kaisha is clear. While there is little that a company in the West
can do to improve the level of education or output of engineers
in its society, it can improve its position through consistent and
sustained hiring policies and increased opportunities for its engineering staff. More important, there is a great deal the Western company can do to ensure that it is searching the world, and
Japan in particular, for new products and processes. The kaisha
have been beneficiaries of a massive transfer of technology, a
transfer made possible by constant assessment of potential
world sources of technology.

Japan is now generally recognized as a major source of new

technology in many of its industries. Yet very few foreign firms possess the capability of searching for and acquiring the results of Japan's research efforts. Few foreign firms are prepared even to acknowledge the value of acquired technology. Most technology evaluation is in the hands of technicians with a "not-invented-here" bias, rather than business executives who are seeking competitive opportunities. The lesson from the kaisha is that these attitudes are costly and inefficient, that technological arrogance is an expensive luxury, and technological complacency is an unwarranted weakness.

The single overriding characteristic of the kaisha is their unrelenting focus on competitive position. They constantly search for growth, driven by the economics of relatively high fixed costs and the dynamics of their system of labor relations. The result is a preoccupation with market share and competitive position in contrast to the Western firm's return on investment objective. Leading market share will provide high margins in time, which in turn makes possible investment in still another growth area, and still another drive for leading share. The Western firm's preoccupation with current earnings and current stock price poses no problem when dealing with competitors with the same objectives. A preoccupation with current profits can be a devastating weakness when competing with a market share-preoccupied competitor. That competitor takes a leading share, and in time the profit position reverses.

Consistent with their corporate objective of increasing market share, the kaisha do their planning in competitive system terms, with a focus on relative competitive position and prospects. This is in contrast to the planning of a great many Western firms, whose plans are often prepared and implemented as though the firm operated in isolation. The single greatest weakness in most U.S. corporate planning is the absence of the "what if" question in their competitive analysis. That is, little or no attention is paid to competitive reactions to changes in capacity, distribution methods, pricing, and the like, or to the possibility that competitors may see very different patterns and opportunities in different parts of the business. This is an omission that the kaisha are most unlikely to make, as they work in competitive system terms.

One highly visible consequence is that the kaisha are positioned in the home markets of Western competitors who are not positioned in the home market of their Japanese competitors. Such positioning has a real price, in terms of current earnings. However, it has a very high earnings payout, in terms of long-term competitive position. Too many Western competitors have ceded the emerging "high ground" that fast-growing Asia is to the kaisha.

Perhaps, then, the single most important lesson to be learned from the study of the kaisha is in terms of corporate objectives and corporate planning. For a great many products and companies, the competitive arena has become the world market. World share is the measure of corporate stability and success. The kaisha's preoccupation with competitive position has equipped them well for planning for and dealing with worldwide competition.

Where Are the Kaisha Going?

The precise future of the kaisha cannot be predicted with any confidence. But there are trends already visible that will impact the kaisha. An examination of the forces underlying these trends allows some speculation about the directions the kaisha are likely to move in in the coming years.

First, the best of the kaisha are truly formidable competitors, moving to leading positions in many of the world's businesses and industries. They possess a competitive orientation in approaches to manufacturing, financial policies, technological efforts, and personnel systems that goes far to ensure that they will continue to compete effectively. Furthermore, their continued effectiveness will be greatly supported by the Japanese economy, which continues to outperform the other major economies of the world in terms of real growth.

This continued growth of the economy requires a continued shift in the mix of industries in Japan. The main thrust of Japanese technological efforts is in the three sectors of microelectronics, new materials, and biotechnology. While the results of the latter two are still largely problematic, there can be no question of Japanese progress in microelectronics. In 1983,

MITI reported that for the first time, electrical and electronic product shipments made up the largest proportion of total shipments by Japanese manufacturers. Total shipments were up about 2.5 percent, and electric products accounted for 70 percent of the increase, surpassing transportation machinery for the first time in history. Nearly one-third of total industrial shipments in Japan were electrical goods.[1]

Some of the implications of this massive thrust into electronics are startling. One projection holds that by the turn of the decade, annual investment in semiconductors will total $20 billion at current exchange rates. The current level of investment is about $2.5 billion. Semiconductor manufacture alone is creating some twenty to thirty thousand jobs per year, while displacing workers through the effects of electronic products on the production system. T. Sekimoto, president of NEC, offers the startling prediction that by the end of the century more than 5 million Japanese workers will be employed in software related jobs.[2] That is equivalent to nearly 10 percent of Japan's entire labor force today. Far from lessening employment, the thrust of the kaisha into microelectronics has, as industrial revolutions always have, created employment.

The results of the move to microelectronics seems very likely to parallel Japan's past. Just as Japan's textile companies lost pride of place as industrial leaders to steel and shipbuilding companies, and these in turn lost to the auto companies, so Toyota, now Japan's largest company in terms of total sales, will by current trends lose its leadership position by the turn of the decade to Hitachi and Matsushita, leaders in the electronics industry. At current growth rates, the Hitachi group of companies will pass the Toyota group in total sales by 1989. In contrast, Nippon Steel, only a few years ago Japan's largest company, is now in seventh place, dropping rapidly as the economy shifts forward to still higher levels of value-added outputs.

Such a continual dynamic economy means that some of the kaisha will come under severe pressure as others prosper. The

1. Research and Statistics Department, Minister's Secretariat, MITI, *Industrial Statistics Monthly* 37, no. 3 (March 1984): 17.

2. T. Sekimoto, "2000 Nen e no Kigyo Senyaku" (Corporate Strategy in the Year 2000), *Nikkei Sangyo Shimbun*, 16 January 1985, p. 20.

flexibility of the kaisha should not be underestimated, however. For example, in the shift forward to new technologies, Nikon came under pressure as the growth of the camera industry slowed. From 1980, Nikon moved aggressively, based on its optics technology, into the role of supplier of manufacturing equipment to the electronics industry. By 1984, Nikon had transformed itself from a company with an unrivaled reputation in cameras and lenses to a company that has become predominantly a supplier of electronics equipment.

Nikon appears to be making the transition successfully. Not all of the kaisha will. As Japan's sewing machine industry moved offshore, Brother moved into such new technologies as electronic printers and had great success—Riccar chose hotels and leisure businesses and went bankrupt. In part from the difficulty of acquiring companies as a technique for rapid entry into new fields, many of the kaisha will have real difficulties in escaping from dying industries. There will be dying industries over the next years, as there have been throughout the past. There will be kaisha that will fail in the transition, as there have been in the past. The Japanese economy will continue to present a mixed corporate picture of stunning successes and abject failures, as it does today.

The issue here is not one of high drama, as for example whether Japanese companies succeed or fail in the fifth-generation computer shoot-out. Nor is the issue that of whether one country or another "wins" the technology race. These kinds of dramatic confrontations are interesting ways to consider future developments. But the fact is that the kaisha are moving rapidly and massively into microelectronics, and will become major factors in related developments, whatever the outcome of a particular product development effort. They are in competition, and will remain in the competition.

The pattern likely to develop is that the kaisha will become the innovators. Japan will be a major source of technology to the world over the coming years. In the process, the kaisha are likely to begin to move from their current role as leaders in production technology to an increasing role as designers of systems, as sources of product design, and as sources of new products. This shift implies a drifting from Japan of the manufacture of conventional components, sub-assemblies, and products to siting their manufacture elsewhere in Asia, including the People's Republic of China, and in such economies as Brazil and Mexico.

The current conventional view is that the United States is the innovator, with Japan having exceptional strength in mass manufacture as Japanese firms adopt and improve on U.S. designs and products. The change will be toward higher levels of innovation by Japan. Current and probable future levels of research and development expenditure make this likely, as does the rapid advance of Japanese companies in the frontier technologies. The conventional wisdom needs to be reexamined, as the kaisha move forward to higher levels of value of output and become sources of invention.

This shift toward an emphasis on design, systems formulations, and new products in Japan, with manufacture shifting off shore, will be accelerated by the inevitable expansion of the service sector. As incomes continue to increase, the level of product demand in the economy is enriched and deepened. This means in part that certain kaisha will become competitors in the service sector on a worldwide basis. McDonald's has had a huge success in Japan as Japan's service sector has been growing rapidly. An interesting parlor game can be developed around the question of which Japanese company, providing which service, will be the Japanese equivalent of McDonald's. There will almost certainly be one.

Yet the expansion of the service sector brings with it a reduction of the manufacturing sector, and further pressure on the manufacturing kaisha to readjust to changing demand. Japan too will have its regions and industries that are left behind in the move to higher income levels and to higher technologies. This has been the case until now with textiles and the problem will recur in other industries.

There may be relief to Japan's conventional manufacturing sector from the move already widespread to flexible manufacturing. As was noted, this approach to manufacturing appears to be the logical and perhaps necessary precursor to fully automated production. With low-cost funds for investment, and with a tendency to high rates of capital investment, it is possible that the conventional manufacturing sector may survive in Japan through the rapid and widespread introduction of automation. Japanese industry leads the world in production and utilization of robots and numerically controlled machine tools. Unmanned factories are already in operation for specialized applications. It is quite possible that the kaisha will be able to extend the life cycle of their industries though heavy capital investment and high levels of flexible automation.

Japan's steel industry is a current example of this phenomenon. By heavy investment in continuous casting, for example, and in the substitution of coal for oil in the steel-making process, the industry has succeeded in remaining competitive. This same pattern of investment in automation may allow conventional manufacturing to remain on shore in Japan longer than would otherwise be expected. Steel is interesting too as a case where the industry is under pressure in part because its transfer of technology to developing countries, notably to South Korea, has accelerated the growth of competitive pressures. This mistake in strategy, the so-called "boomerang effect," has not gone unnoticed by other industries which will be less ready to transfer technology abroad.

One view of the future of the kaisha, then, would be of a heavy emphasis on design, on systems technology, and on new products, while maintaining manufacturing competitiveness through investment-intensive moves to factory automation. This pattern of a people-centered focus on innovation and machinery-centered focus on manufacture is consistent with and may be driven by changes in the work force of the kaisha.

In the near future the kaisha must deal with some difficult problems in terms of labor force, heretofore one of its principal assets. The Japanese population is aging, more rapidly than has been the case in any other nation's history. By the turn of the century, Japan will have a population age distribution much like that of Sweden and West Germany today, with more than 15 percent of the total population 65 years of age and over. This means that the average age of the labor force is rising. One symptom is the increase in retirement age; only a few years ago it was fifty-five for most workers, now it is fifty-eight with Ministry of Labor plans to extend the retirement age to 65 years.

These factors work against the competitive capacity of the

Japanese company, especially in manufacture, all else being equal. The kaisha face a problem of an increasingly inflexible labor force, of steadily increasing average cost, with increasing competition for new entrants to the labor force. Clearly, one solution to this set of problems, as well as to the problem of the drift of manufacturing to lower wage rate economies, is the rapid shift to highly automated—but flexibly automated— manufacturing facilities. This prevents "rusting," and maintains competitive cost levels. The work force is dedicated to service and maintenance of the plant and to research, development, design, and planning. The kaisha becomes the design center, manufacturing locally where automation is efficient, and sub- contracting off-shore manufacture if labor rates determine it.

It is a curious fact that the kaisha remain almost without exception national, rather than multinational, companies. Their great export successes have been built on domestically concen- trated manufacture with only limited investments in support of export sales. This is now changing, and the change will acceler- ate. The move by the kaisha to off-shore manufacture and mar- keting is without question a major development over the next years. This move will be driven not only, nor even mainly, by the search for lower cost sources of product. It will be driven at least as much by the need to maintain and build position in overseas markets.

The Japanese economy as a whole is becoming a major exporter of capital to the world. Indeed, with the shift of the United States to the position of a net debtor, Japan is a principal capital source, with high savings rates and a considerable sur- plus on its current account. This shift of the economy to the role of a capital exporter coincides with the requirement that the kaisha establish substantial positions for both manufacturing and marketing in off-shore economies.

The leader of the semiconductor industry in Japan provides an example of this move. With six semiconductor plants over- seas (as of late 1984) NEC has plans to increase the number steadily, at an average capital cost per plant of some $150 mil- lion. It expects to achieve semiconductor sales of nearly $10 billion by 1989, and expects that 20 percent of that total will be from manufacturing facilities outside Japan. This overseas investment program is quite explicitly driven by concern over trade frictions and trade barriers, and by a conscious effort to overcome those problems by direct participation in NEC's market economies.

NEC is at the forefront of this move in its industry, but the investments of Honda, Nissan, and Toyota in the United States in autos, of Nippon Kokan and Kawasaki Steel in U.S. steel facilities, and a long series of similar moves in the last few years make it clear that the kaisha are moving to become multinational.

This must surely be the greatest challenge to Japanese management over the coming years. It is hardly surprising that Toyota, Japan's largest and in many ways most successful company, has been notably reluctant to undertake major investments abroad. It is by all reckoning a good deal easier for Toyota to manage its complex of factories in Nagoya, Japan, often called "Toyota City," than for Toyota to manage a multinational organization with major investments scattered across the world.

A case can be made that the kaisha have a special problem in multinational management. Many of their strengths arise out of special aspects of Japanese society and culture, as has been noted. These very strengths turn to disadvantage as the kaisha must try to deal with personnel, legal structures, and social customs as participants in other societies. It is one thing to ship goods for sale; it is quite another to be a member of another society. Just as foreign companies find dealing with Japanese society a formidable learning task, so Japanese companies confront the mirror image of the problem as they set up integrated businesses abroad.

Indications of the kinds of problems that will be encountered are already apparent. Two major trading companies, Sumitomo Trading and C. Itoh, have had legal problems from their failure to appreciate the subtleties of U.S. affirmative action legislation. American staff members of Japanese companies are reported to be disaffected by the fact that they are layered over with Japanese expatriates, and that all basic decisions are made by the head office in Japan with which they have no communication. These are not problems unique to Japanese companies abroad: indeed, they are familiar to anyone who remembers the early history of the efforts of U.S. firms to become multinational.

But the kaisha have some special handicaps in the effort to become international. First, they are based in a notably homogeneous society, with little experience of differences in religion, race, and culture. Second, the kaisha are notably integrated institutions. How does one integrate a non-Japanese speaking foreigner, who is some thousands of miles from the company's main facilities, into the culture of Hitachi or Toyota or Nippon Kokan? Trial efforts at extended residence in Japan have been made—with the looming risk that after all of the investment, the foreign employee will leave to work elsewhere. It is not clear that any Japanese company has yet developed a system to deal with these problems of personnel selection, training, and motivation as the kaisha move to be multinational.

One major company, NEC, appears to have taken a rather different and significant approach to the problem. Quite simply, NEC leaves personnel matters in the hands of local, non-Japanese personnel, and is quite prepared to tolerate substantial differences in personnel practices from one overseas subsidiary to another. This seems a sound approach, if the economics of the organization are more powerful than the social aspects in competition.

But this approach does not address a basic question that will be hard for the kaisha to answer. To succeed abroad, a good deal of management authority needs to be given to local management. But as local managements come to comprise an important part of the total kaisha, they need a voice in corporate affairs. Question to senior Japanese managers: When will foreigners begin to take positions in the top management of the parent Japanese companies? Typical answer: "No one in Japan is prepared to consider the question as yet." That inability to consider foreigners in the management of Japanese companies is a measure of the magnitude of the problem of the kaisha becoming multinational.

The personnel issue is but one, though perhaps the most dramatic, of the problems facing the kaisha as they move abroad. Financial management becomes far more complex, logistical systems are not simply matters of orders and delivery but multidimensional, and research programs at multilocations pose intricate planning and control problems. The kaisha will invest heavily abroad; they will become truly multinational. They will learn to deal with the problems that multinational organization raises. But the process will be a difficult and costly one, even more than it has proved to be for European and U.S. firms. In the world context, many of the kaisha's strengths are based on organizational policies that present very real potential disadvantages in the future.

The issue of East Asia, and the position of the kaisha in that region, is a dimension of internationalization that deserves special note. In Japan, one often hears the view that the Japanese, and by extension the kaisha, have some special advantage in Asia from being Asian, thereby sharing a world view and intimacy. There is very little, apart from hubris, to support this view. The kaisha have no special advantage in East Asia, and indeed in some areas are at a real disadvantage from history and prejudice, as in Korea.

Nonetheless, the kaisha are physically *in* Asia. They have the advantage of proximity—of ready geographical access, of transport cost advantage, and of established lines of communication. It seems certain that East Asia will play a greater part in world industrial affairs in the coming years, with the entire area, including Japan, comprising the world's factory. With Japan's changing role, the area will become not only factory but designer as well. Just as Japan will benefit greatly from the rapid economic advance of the rest of East Asia, so the kaisha are likely to be the beneficiaries in terms of market access and product sourcing in this rapidly growing area of the world.

There is real, and warranted, concern that increased protectionism against Japanese goods will prove to be a major obstacle to further kaisha growth and market share increase. However, the trends noted in chapter 10 will go far to ameliorate protectionist moves by the United States and Western Europe. Just as the center of trade gravity for the United States has shifted from the Atlantic to the Pacific, so Japan's trade pattern is changing with rapid Asian economic growth.

Furthermore, an increasing number of Japan's direct exports will be in products in which there are few competitors abroad. Video cassette recorders and facsimile machines are current examples of major Japanese export items where Japanese companies are virtually the only suppliers. The exports of these innovative products impact trade balances heavily, but do not impact specific employment in Western markets. The political consequences of their export are therefore much diminished. As Japanese firms increasingly provide innovative products and services, the cry of "export of unemployment" will be less and less frequent.

In addition, as conventional parts and sub-assemblies are produced elsewhere in Asia and Latin America, the exports of these products becomes a third-country issue, rather than Japan specific. Japanese firms, like NEC, are investing abroad in an effort to forestall protectionism. In view of all this, and a shift toward more Japanese activity in such invisible sectors as insurance and banking, it is quite possible that the current period of trade friction represents a peaking of the problem, with a gradual lessening of trade tensions over the rest of the decade a real possibility.

In summary, the kaisha will be moving to major positions as innovators, as systems designers, and as central contractors in a multinational system of manufacture and distribution. Their domestic manufacture will become notably automated as the domestic labor force slows in growth and continues to increase in wage and qualification levels. There will be massive investments in overseas locations, both to secure lower cost manufacturing sources, to secure market positions, and to forestall protectionism. The process of becoming multinational will be difficult and costly, but will take place. The thrust will be into the newer, high-technology sectors of new materials, microelectronics, and biotechnology, all of which offer Japan relief from its dependence on imported raw materials and energy, as these sectors are less energy- and material-intensive. In the process, the current levels of trade tensions are likely to lessen, in part as the kaisha move into sectors in which they have not to date been major factors, such as services, banking, insurance, and the like.

Dramatic changes in the internal structure of the kaisha

appear unlikely. There will likely be an increase in merger and acquisition activity, as indeed there has already been on a small scale. There will continue to be cases where companies in trouble find affiliation with a more successful company to their advantage, and where the affliation offers improved prospects to the kaisha's labor force of continued job security. The "money game" acquisition activities of the West, with asset stripping and forced, massive reductions in employment, are unlikely to become an issue with the kaisha.

In terms of financial management, the best of the kaisha are now (and more will be) well financed by Western standards. The steady strengthening of balance sheets will continue, except in those industries where the growth rates are so high as to require continued heavy use of debt. That is to say, aggressive financial policies will continue to characterize those kaisha with major growth opportunities.

Manufacturing practices will continue to advance rapidly, driven by high rates of capital investment, the pressure for high-quality output, and increasing problems of labor supply and cost. The move from flexible manufacturing systems to automated flexible manufacturing systems will continue, unencumbered by labor force resistance to these changes. There is no foreseeable diminution in the drive of the kaisha toward ever higher levels of productivity of capital and labor. Perhaps more important in terms of improved productivity, the availability of office automation equipment capable of handling the Japanese language will facilitate significant productivity improvements in the white-collar sectors of the kaisha.

Research expenditures will continue to increase rapidly. The implementation of research outputs will be greatly facilitated by the ability of the large Japanese company to overcome the hazards of size by setting up numbers of affiliates and subsidiaries. The danger for the kaisha is that corporate bureaucracy and corporate overhead will smother initiatives and prevent aggressive development of new ideas and products. The kaisha's approach to this problem is illustrated by Fujitsu, which in 1984 had a total of thirty-seven software subsidiaries, ten established in 1984. Fujitsu's handling of its important developments in numerical controls, and the in-company entrepreneur who built that position is also instructive. It spun the activity out into what has become the remarkably successful company called Fanuc, under the unique management of S. Inaba. The large corporation need not be the burying ground for entrepreneurship; the kaisha appear to have developed an effective organizational solution.

Japan's kaisha are survivors. They have survived the most rapid and far-reaching changes in economic history, the move of the Japanese economy to world levels of output and competitiveness. As survivors, they are at their best highly competent and highly competitive. They are setting the standard of world competition, and their high morale is the deserved result.

But perhaps the kaisha's success and confidence will be their weakness—with confidence can come an arrogance toward the products and methods of others, rather than receptivity. The Japanese may convince themselves of their moral and intellectual superiority, as the West once convinced itself of the same things, and consequently lose sight of the economic fundamentals that account for their success. As this happens, these kaisha open the possibility of reversal of their fortunes. The confidence of the companies of the West has surely been one source of their current difficulties. Also, as the kaisha move abroad, seeing the world as market, they will encounter increasing levels of political risks. Their insular histories and methods do not prepare them well for dealing intensively and directly in that riskier world. Nevertheless, it would be reckless to once again underestimate the prospects of the kaisha.

A SELECTED

BIBLIOGRAPHY

Management in Japan

The literature in English on Japanese management is considerable and expanding rapidly, but it is of uneven quality. The following list includes some of the useful works published in recent years.

HISTORY

Fruin, W. Mark. *Kikkoman: Company, Clan, and Community.* Cambridge: Harvard University Press, 1983.

Hirschmeier, Johannes, and Tsunehito Yui. *The Development of Japanese Business.* London: George Allen & Unwin, 1981.

MANAGEMENT, GENERAL

Clark, R.C. *The Japanese Company.* New Haven: Yale University Press, 1979.

INDUSTRIAL RELATIONS

Cole, R.E. *Work, Mobility and Participation.* Berkeley, Calif.: University of California Press, 1979.

Shirai, Taishiro, ed. *Contemporary Industrial Relations in Japan.* Madison, Wis.: University of Wisconsin Press, 1983.

MANUFACTURING

Hall, Robert. *Zero Inventories.* Homewood, Ill.: Dow Jones-Irwin, 1983

Shingo, Shigeo. *Study of Toyota Production System from an Industrial Engineering Viewpoint.* Tokyo: Japan Management Association, 1981.

FINANCE

No work is currently available on corporate financial management, but note the following:

Bronte, Stephen. *Japanese Finance: Markets and Institutions.* London: Euromoney Publications, 1982.

Prindl, Andreas R. *Japanese Finance.* New York: John Wiley & Sons, 1981.

MARKETING

No work of substance on marketing management is currently available, but for general interest note the following:

Fields, George. *From Bonsai to Levi's.* New York: Macmillan, 1983.

Yoshihara, Kunio. *Sogo Shosha.* Tokyo: Oxford University Press, 1982.

RESEARCH AND DEVELOPMENT

Little work is currently available on the management of R&D, but the following touch on the subject:

Kikuchi, Makoto. *Japanese Electronics.* Tokyo: Simul Press, 1983.

Lynn, Leonard H. *How Japan Innovates.* Boulder, Colo.: Westview Press, 1982.

JAPANESE MULTINATIONALS

Ogawa, Terutomo. *Multinationalism, Japanese Style.* Princeton, N.J.: Princeton University Press, 1982.

BUSINESS-GOVERNMENT RELATIONS

Johnson, Chalmers. *MITI and the Japanese Miracle.* Stanford, Calif.: Stanford University Press, 1982.

Lincoln, Edward J. *Japan's Industrial Policies.* Washington, D.C.: Japan Economic Institute of America, 1984.

INDEX

Absentee rates, 182

Accelerated depreciation, 141

Acquisitions: difficulties of, 202, 232–35, 237; entry costs of, 255; future increase in, 287; inability to restructure through, 78–79; by *kaisha*, of foreign companies, 254–55; as option to enter Japanese economy, 231–39

Adaptation of Western products, 54–55

Advantage, competitive, 67–90; changing sources of, 89–90; cost, 60, 64, 68–69, 75–78, 273; exploitation of, 10–14; flexibility as, 117–18; focused manufacturing as, 79–89; low wages as, 10, 11, 60, 68, 70–72; productivity as, 60–64, 68–69, 75; scale as, 72–79; technology-based, 12–13; *see also* Financing

Aerospace industry, 64, 177

Affiliates, 189–91, 287

After-tax interest rate, 157

After-tax return on equity, 149, 150

Aging of population, 40–41, 203–4, 210, 211–12, 281–82

Agriculture: policy for, 31; research in, 138

Aid programs, 264–68

Air conditioning industry: product line variety in, 135

Ajinomoto, 219, 226, 264

Allied Manufacturers Association, 67

Alumax, 245, 251

Aluminum industry, 24–25, 78, 244–45

AMAX Inc., 245

Amerada Hess, 155

American Chamber of Commerce, study by, in Japan, 215

American Motors Corporation, 88

AMP Inc., 218, 219, 239

Analytic approaches to *kaisha*, 271–77

Antitrust law, 23, 139–40

Apple Computer, 8

Art forms, 145

Asahan, 264

Asahi beer company, 159

Asahi Chemical, 229

Asahi Dow, 229

Asahi Glass, 264

Asia, Japanese investment in: development of, 242; growth rate and, 262, 263; imports from, 266–67; independence movements and, 259; manufacturing, 258–64; official development assistance to, 264–68;